AUTOMATIC FISCAL POLICIES TO COMBAT RECESSIONS

AUTOMATIC FISCAL POLICIES TO COMBAT RECESSIONS

LAURENCE S. SEIDMAN

M.E.Sharpe
Armonk, New York
London, England

Library of Congress Cataloging-in-Publication Data

Seidman, Laurence S.
  Automatic fiscal policies to combat recessions / by Laurence S. Seidman.
    p. cm.
  Includes bibliographical references and index.
  ISBN 0-7656-1110-4 (hc : alk. paper) ISBN 0-7656-1111-2 (pbk. : alk. paper)
    1. Fiscal policy—United States. 2. Income tax—United States. 3. Taxation—
United States. I. Title.

HJ257.2 .S44 2003
339.5′2′0973—dc21   2002036587

Printed in the United States of America

The paper used in this publication meets the minimum requirements of
American National Standard for Information Sciences
Permanence of Paper for Printed Library Materials,
ANSI Z 39.48-1984.

BM (c)   10   9   8   7   6   5   4   3   2   1
BM (p)   10   9   8   7   6   5   4   3   2   1

For my parents,

Eleanor and Irving Seidman

Contents

Acknowledgments

I am indebted to the many authors of the articles and books that are cited or quoted in this book, and to my coresearcher in macroeconomics, Ken Lewis.

Introduction

In the three decades following the publication of John Maynard Keynes's *General Theory of Employment, Interest, and Money* in 1936, countercyclical fiscal policy achieved a gradual ascendancy within the economics profession and in the practical realm of economic policy. By the 1960s, it was widely agreed that fiscal policy should be used to counter fluctuations in the economy. In particular, to combat a recession, taxes should be cut, cash transfer payments increased, and government purchases of goods and services increased.

But the final three decades of the twentieth century witnessed the decline and fall of countercyclical fiscal policy both in theory and in practice. The majority of economists concluded that monetary policy alone should be used to stabilize the economy, and a minority argued that the government should not use either monetary or fiscal policy to try to combat a recession. Whereas Congress enacted a major fiscal stimulus package to counter the 1975 recession, it did not even consider a serious fiscal stimulus package in the 1991 recession.

The recession of 2001 prompted a revival of countercyclical fiscal policy in practice. The second half of the 1990s was a time of economic prosperity and fiscal discipline. By the year 2000, the large federal budget deficits of the 1980s and early 1990s were gone. Not only was the federal budget balanced, but large surpluses were forecast, not only in Social Security, but in the rest of the budget. When recession hit the economy in 2001, Congress and the president moved quickly to enact a fiscal stimulus—a tax rebate of $600 per family—to combat the recession.

Many economists were caught by surprise. For the three preceding decades, Keynesian countercyclical fiscal policy had been either ignored or criticized by many economists. Suddenly, in mid 2001, Congress and the president revived countercyclical fiscal policy in practice. After enacting the $600 rebate in June (the U.S. Treasury mailed out the $600 checks to families in July, August, and September), Congress tried in the fall of 2001 to craft another fiscal stimulus as the recession deepened. Unfortunately, partisanship returned as Republicans and Democrats each tried to fashion a stimulus that promoted their long-term agendas, and 2001 ended without the passage of a second fiscal stimulus. Nevertheless, the prompt $600 tax rebate, and the attempt to pass a second fiscal stimulus, shows that countercyclical fiscal policy is once again being taken seriously in the political arena. It is time for economists to revisit countercyclical fiscal policy, and to work seriously on designing fiscal policies to combat recession.

But does monetary policy need help combating a recession? In the 2001 U.S. recession, the Federal Reserve cut the federal funds rate from 6.5 percent to 1.75 percent. The dominant view that countercyclical monetary policy can handle most recessions may be correct. Nevertheless, the Japanese recession of the 1990s suggests that it would be worthwhile taking out a prudent insurance policy: the strengthening of automatic countercyclical fiscal policy. Most economists are justifiably skeptical that Congress can always be counted on to implement *discretionary* countercyclical fiscal policy in a timely and effective manner. At the same time, most economists nevertheless believe that *automatic* fiscal stabilizers are useful. In this book, I offer new automatic fiscal policies that can complement current automatic stabilizers and countercyclical monetary policy.

In the 1950s, two decades after the publication of Keynes's *General Theory,* A.W. Phillips (1954) published a pathbreaking paper on automatic stabilization policy taking his inspiration from the engineering literature. In his important book on public finance, Richard Musgrave (1959) argued that serious consideration should be given to enacting what he called "formula flexibility," the automatic variation of tax rates or cash transfers in response to a decline in output to help stabilize the macroeconomy. Automatic fiscal policies based on Phillips's and Musgrave's work were analyzed by Pack (1968) and Duggal (1975), each using a different Keynesian macroeconometric model, and by Seidman (1975). Keynes's *General Theory* emphasized that economic stability would be promoted if economic agents—households and business managers—expected stable output. In that Keynesian era, it was taken for granted that agents' expectations about output were important, and expectations of stable output would be strengthened by the knowledge that fiscal stimulus would automatically be triggered in an economic downturn (Baily 1978).

The 1970s, however, witnessed the launching of a classical counterrevolution in macroeconomics (Lucas and Sargent 1978), and work on the design and testing of automatic fiscal policy in Keynesian macroeconometric models virtually ceased. I share Blinder's view of this counterrevolution expressed in his "Keynes after Lucas" lecture:

> *The Forgotten Agenda.* Despite some important new ideas, the New Classical Economics (NCE) counterrevolution does not seem to me to mark a

major step forward from the Keynesian tradition it supplanted. The attempted revival of market clearing was quixotic, in the worst sense of the word. . . . The wholesale adoption of rational expectations was dubious. . . . To my mind, that does not add up to a major improvement over the macroeconomics of 1972. Does that mean we had it all right in 1972? Hardly. . . . I begin with a brief mention of an obvious flaw. Vintage 1972 macroeconomics—whether it was Keynesian or monetarist—was all about demand fluctuations, a term then thought to be synonymous with economic fluctuations. The 1970s and 1980s destroyed this narrow-minded focus forever. We now know that Marshall's celebrated scissors also comes in a giant economy size. Economic fluctuations can, and sometimes do, emanate from the supply side—from oil shocks, food shocks, and the like. Much theoretical and empirical work has been done on supply shocks in the last dozen years. . . . This work will have a lasting and salutary effect on macroeconomics. . . .

In conclusion, by the early 1950s, the Keynesian revolution was consolidated. The next 20 years or so were a productive time in which Keynesian ideas were developed further, modified in places, and given empirical content. . . . Much, but not all, of that development stopped in the 1970s as macroeconomics turned introspective and nihilistic. Some of the fundamental questions raised were good ones (why should expectations be adaptive), others were not (does the labor market really clear every period). But they did stop a constructive research agenda dead in its tracks. Some will say that was necessary, for the 1972 consensus was leading us astray. I am less convinced. . . . I cannot help thinking that macroeconomics would be better off today if Lucas's valid questions about how expectations were handled in theoretical and empirical models had redirected the Keynesian research agenda rather than derailed it. It may now be time to get the train back on the tracks. (Blinder 1989 108–111)

In this book, I simply pick up where the early studies of automatic fiscal policy left off, as though a Keynesian Rip Van Winkle had slept through the past two and a half decades and missed the new classical counterrevolution. In chapter 11, I discuss the classical counterrevolution and argue that it has been a false path for macroeconomics. In my view, a Keynesian Rip Van Winkle is perhaps better prepared to pursue a practical and fruitful macroeconomic policy agenda today than someone who was forced to stay awake throughout the new classical counterrevolution.

In chapter 2, I evaluate an automatic tax rebate (cash transfer) of specific magnitude triggered by a decline in the output of the economy of particular magnitude. Recent empirical studies reviewed in chapter 6 provide strong evidence that there is sufficient short-run response of consumption to temporary changes in disposable income due to transfers or income tax cuts to make such a policy sufficiently effective; in that chapter, I explain why one consumer survey (Shapiro and Slemrod 2001) that at first glance appears to run counter to the other studies has serious problems. In chapter 3, I evaluate an automatic cut in a consumption tax (such as a retail sales tax or value added tax) of specific magnitude triggered by a decline of particular magnitude in the output of the economy. The special feature of a temporary consumption tax cut is that it provides an incentive for consumers to spend while the cut is in effect. The same incentive can be delivered by a temporary consumer durable tax credit that is analogous to the investment tax credit. The fiscal policies analyzed in chapters 2 and 3 have been previously proposed by other economists and Lewis and Seidman (2003). I view both kinds of automatic fiscal policies as complementary to each other, to current automatic stabilizers, and to countercyclical monetary policy.

But how do these automatic fiscal policies differ from current automatic stabilizers? Current automatic stabilizers are unintended by-products of setting the tax/transfer system to meet other objectives such as the ratio of tax revenue to GDP, the degree of progressivity of the tax system, and the level of unemployment benefits. Hence the magnitude of their stabilizing impact is held hostage to other objectives. By contrast, the automatic fiscal policies considered in chapters 2 and 3 are designed with the sole objective of combating recession, with magnitudes set solely for that purpose.

Why an automatic policy? Discretionary fiscal policy often takes too long to move through the legislative process. It should be noted that this is not always the case. In the 1975 recession, from the time Republicans shifted their top priority from inflation to recession (January 1975), thereby joining the Democrats, it took just three months for a tax cut stimulus package to be enacted, and tax rebate checks to households were sent out in the next three months. In the 2001 recession, Congress and the president enacted tax legislation in June, and tax rebate checks were mailed to households in the next three months. But even these two cases illustrate the importance of making the policy automatic. In 1975, an automatic policy would have sent checks out beginning in January, rather than April. In 2001, action occurred in June because tax legislation that was aimed at long-run objectives, not recession, had been introduced at the beginning of 2001 by President George W. Bush as a fulfillment of his campaign promise to reduce the tax burden. As the economic slowdown became evident in mid 2001, it was easy for Congress to tack on a tax rebate at the last minute to a comprehensive tax bill that had been debated for a half year. In the fall of 2001, with the recession deepening, Republicans and Democrats deadlocked over the best way to further stimulate the economy. Experience therefore suggests that it is important to make countercyclical fiscal policy automatic. The automatic policy can always be overridden by discretionary action by Congress and the president. The automatic policy is simply a default position: If Congress fails to take discretionary action, stimulus is promptly triggered by the decline in the economy.

In chapter 2, I consider an automatic tax rebate, and in chapter 3, an automatic consumption tax cut. I focus on these two policies because they have the potential to maintain consumption evenly across all sectors of the economy, keeping workers in the private sector jobs they held prior to the recession, thereby minimizing dislocation. By contrast, government purchases of goods and services—for example, public works projects—are more likely to require a shift of workers from their current jobs to public works jobs and, therefore, to involve greater dislocation. On the other hand, public works projects may have a role to play in countering a severe or prolonged recession. One of the tasks of the fiscal policy advisory board proposed in chapter 5 is to recommend to Congress the set of fiscal policies that, in its judgment, is most effective in combating recessions.

An Automatic Tax Rebate

The automatic tax rebate (cash transfer) to households that I consider in chapter 2 was once called "formula flexibility" to distinguish it from built-in automatic stabilizers. In his book on public finance, Musgrave devotes a section to "formula flexibility":

> *Formula Flexibility*
> Formula flexibility refers to an arrangement whereby changes in tax rates and/or expenditure levels are legislated in advance, to go into effect if and when specified changes in income occur. For instance, it might be legislated that income tax rates be reduced or public expenditures raised by x percent if income falls by y percent. (Musgrave 1959, 512)

The automatic tax rebate aims solely at stimulating demand when the economy is in recession. The policy is asymmetric: It does not attempt to restrain demand when demand is excessive. That task is left to monetary policy. I offer an asymmetric policy because Congress may be more willing to preenact fiscal stimulus than to preenact fiscal restraint. Although the policy is automatically triggered by the state of the economy, Congress must preenact the automatic policy—it must be willing to vote for a bill that would trigger a cash transfer according to the state of the economy. It may be more willing to vote to trigger a tax rebate to counter recession than to vote to trigger a tax increase to counter inflation. For example, the 1968 tax surcharge to counter inflation took much longer to enact than the 1975 tax rebate to counter recession.

The "tax rebate" would be implemented by either sending U.S. Treasury checks that "rebate" some of the preceding year's tax, or simply providing a specific cash transfer to each household regardless of the preceding year's tax (for example, $600 per family, $300 per single person), or by cutting withholding and tax due on the next income tax return. I will use the phrase "tax rebate" to cover any of these options.

The automatic tax rebate triggers a cash transfer to households whenever real GDP is at least X percent below "normal real GDP" (the real GDP that would have occurred if there had been a normal unemployment rate) in the preceding quarter, and the amount of the transfer is proportional to this "excess-output gap" (the gap below the threshold X percent).

Note that the rebate is triggered by actual data from the economy—the GDP gap in the preceding quarter as reported by the U.S. Commerce Department. A more ambitious approach would be to trigger the rebate according to an "official" forecast of next quarter's GDP gap. This approach would attempt to stay ahead of the economy rather than lag behind. This approach, however, would require a willingness by Congress to trigger funds based on a forecast. In chapters 2 and 3, I assume that Congress does not have sufficient confidence in a forecast to enact an automatic fiscal policy that utilizes a forecast instead of actual data. In chapter 5, however, in my description of the tasks of my proposed fiscal policy advisory board, I consider how a forecast might be used if Congress proves willing to use one for automatic fiscal policy.

The Automatic Tax Rebate versus Current Automatic Stabilizers

How does this automatic tax rebate differ from our current automatic stabilizers? Current automatic stabilizers are not designed with the aim of providing the optimal demand stimulus to a slumping economy. For example, consider a society debating whether government spending should be 20 percent or 40 percent of GDP, and therefore whether its income tax rate should be 20 percent or 40 percent. The decision, as it should be, is motivated by the debate over the proper size of government, the merits of particular government programs, and so on. The consequence for macroeconomic stability is an accident. With a 20 percent income tax, if national income drops $100 billion, tax revenue automatically drops only

$20 billion, so disposable income drops $80 billion. With a 40 percent income tax, tax revenue automatically drops $40 billion, so disposable income drops only $60 billion. The society with the larger government spending (40 percent of GDP instead of 20 percent) by accident has a stronger automatic stabilizer. But there is no reason why the society should consider macroeconomic stability when it debates the appropriate size of government and the merit of particular programs.

The automatic tax rebate breaks the link. Consider the society that chooses government spending to be 20 percent of GDP and adopts a 20 percent income tax. Now suppose it also adopts the automatic tax rebate: Whenever GDP drops $100 billion below its "natural" (trend) value, automatically the treasury mails checks to households totaling $20 billion. As a consequence, despite the 20 percent income tax rate, households' disposable income will fall only $60 billion, just as if its government spending and income tax were 40 percent of GDP. Thus, the automatic tax rebate focuses on stabilization only. It takes as given the current automatic stabilizers that were an unintended by-product of accomplishing other goals, and supplements them to get the desired macroeconomic stimulus.

Similarly, consider a society choosing between a proportional income tax and a progressive income tax. Under the proportional tax, everyone pays 20 percent on all income. Under the progressive tax, the first $X of a person's income is exempt from tax, but above the exemption, additional income is taxed at a 40 percent rate. Once again, if GDP drops $100 billion below its "natural" (trend) value, tax revenue will automatically drop only $20 billion with the proportional tax, but $40 billion with the progressive tax. But suppose society prefers the proportional tax to the progressive tax. With the automatic tax rebate, the treasury can offset the smaller macroeconomic effect. Whenever GDP drops $100 billion below its "natural" (trend) value, automatically the treasury mails checks to households totaling $20 billion. As a consequence, despite the 20 percent income tax rate, households' disposable income will fall only $60 billion, just as though the top bracket income tax were 40 percent.

To summarize: current automatic stabilizers are accidental by-products of addressing other important societal objectives: the ratio of government spending to GDP, the degree of progressivity of the tax system, and the level of unemployment benefits. The automatic tax rebate focuses solely on trying to achieve the optimal degree of stimulus to aggregate demand in an economic downturn. It takes as given the current automatic stabilizers enacted for other reasons, and then supplements them to get the desired macroeconomic stimulus.

It must be emphasized that Congress would be free at any time to override its automatic tax rebate with discretionary action. The automatic tax rebate is a default position: it occurs only if Congress fails to enact a discretionary change. Thus, the question is simply: What should happen if Congress fails to take discretionary action? Currently, tax rates stay fixed and there are no rebates. Under the proposed automatic tax rebate, a tax rebate would be triggered automatically according to the output gap. The relationship between the magnitude of the rebate and the magnitude of the output gap would be preenacted by Congress. Thus, under this proposal, Congress does not delegate any authority over fiscal policy, and fully retains the ability to adjust fiscal policy through discretionary action. Moreover, it is Congress that approves in advance all aspects of the automatic tax rebate. The automatic action is a default position in the event Congress does not take discretionary action.

An Automatic Temporary Consumption Tax Cut

In "Japan Needs to Stimulate Spending," an editorial page article in the *Wall Street Journal*, Martin Feldstein recommends that Japan enact a temporary consumption tax cut (along with other measures) to counter its prolonged recession:

> The [Japanese] government could also temporarily suspend the value added tax, which is currently 5%, and announce that the tax will return at a 10% rate in the middle of 2003. Consumers would have a strong incentive to spend now, especially on consumer durables, because of the resulting 10% price rise that will occur in 2003. (Feldstein 2001)

Just as a one-week sale at a department store encourages consumers to buy this week, Feldstein's proposal should encourage consumers to spend before the consumption tax cut is terminated. One concern about Feldstein's proposal is that the government would be committed to a termination date. Suppose the economy has not recovered by that date? It might be better to automatically trigger both the beginning and end of the temporary tax cut according to the gap between target GDP and actual GDP. I consider this proposal more fully in chapter 3.

In a *New York Times* op ed article, "The Economic Stimulus We Need," Alan Blinder describes a way for the U.S. Congress to implement a temporary consumption tax cut to counter the U.S. recession, despite the fact that the U.S. federal government does not currently have a retail sales tax or a value added tax:

Let Congress offer to reimburse the tax receipts lost by any state that agrees to cut its sales taxes over the next 12 months (up to some limit). Since almost every state levies a sales tax, this plan should be well received by both Republican and Democratic governors and legislatures throughout the country. A sales tax cut aims its medicine squarely at boosting consumer spending, which is the highest priority right now. (Blinder 2001)

Feldstein and Blinder are not the first to recommend a temporary consumption tax cut to combat recession. Decades ago, Branson (1973) and Madigliani and Steindel (1977), proposed a temporary incentive for consumer spending. Recently, Lewis and Seidman (2003) noted that the same incentive can be delivered by a temporary consumer durable tax credit which is analogous to the investment tax credit. I will consider a temporary inventive for consumer spending in chapter 3.

Fiscal Discipline in a Normal Economy

This book will concentrate on reviving the use of automatic fiscal policy for the short-run goal of combating a recession: countercyclical fiscal policy. It is important, however, to consider how short-run and long-run fiscal policy should relate. Here is my recommendation, described further in chapter 4.

Social Security and Medicare should be treated separately from the rest of the federal budget. The two social insurance programs should run surpluses every year and accumulate large funds to prepare for the retirement of the numerous baby boomers (Seidman 1999, 2000).

For the rest of the federal budget, I propose (Seidman 1998, chap. 5) that Congress enact a statute entitled NUBAR—a "normal unemployment balanced budget rule." NUBAR states that Congress shall enact a *planned* budget for the coming fiscal year that technicians *estimate* will be balanced *if* the unemployment rate is normal (the average of the preceding decade). If Congress adheres to NUBAR, and the technicians are accurate, then if the economy has a boom with a below-normal unemployment rate, the budget (excluding Social Security and Medicare) will run a surplus that can pay down the national debt. If the economy has a recession and an above-normal unemployment rate, however, the budget (excluding Social Security and Medicare) will be in deficit. Part of the deficit will be due to the automatic stabilizers—the automatic fall in tax revenue and increase in transfers for unemployment insurance benefits; and part will be due to the new automatic fiscal policy. Of course, in a severe recession that overwhelms both monetary policy and the automatic fiscal policy, Congress should take discretionary action and suspend adherence to NUBAR in order to provide even greater stimulus through even larger transfers, tax cuts, and increases in government purchases.

Maintaining fiscal discipline when the economy is normal enables the use of an automatic fiscal policy to combat recession. By running surpluses in Social Security and Medicare, and by adhering to NUBAR for the rest of the budget, fiscal discipline will be maintained, and the ratio of national debt to GDP will be kept low despite deficits that occur during recession due to the recession itself and the triggering of the automatic fiscal policy.

A Fiscal Policy Advisory Board

In chapter 5, I propose the establishment by Congress of a fiscal policy advisory board. Note the word "advisory." Its main tasks would be to recommend to Congress the design of automatic fiscal policies to combat recession and emergency fiscal policies in a severe recession. Congress would retain full control of all fiscal policies.

Would a new advisory board be worth establishing? Currently there is no institution that focuses exclusively and continuously on the design and operation of countercyclical fiscal policy. The House and Senate budget and tax committees are responsible for handling numerous other issues and objectives. Chapters 2 and 3 will demonstrate that designing the best possible set of automatic fiscal policies is a challenging task. Chapter 1 shows that preparation should also be made for emergency fiscal and monetary policies in the face of a severe recession.

The assignment of the fiscal policy advisory board would be to work continuously on monitoring the design of automatic fiscal policies and preparing emergency fiscal policies for a severe recession. Initially, the board would formulate a set of automatic fiscal policies and recommend their adoption first by the House and Senate tax and/or budget committees, and then by the entire House and Senate. Thereafter, the board would monitor and reevaluate these policies, and from time to time recommend design alterations to the relevant House and Senate committees.

The establishment of a new fiscal policy advisory board would have several other benefits. The public would learn that monetary policy is not the only tool for countering recession. The public would ask not only what the Fed is doing, but also what the fiscal policy advisory board is recommending to Congress. In a recession, the board would focus on the most effective measures for combating recession, and oppose partisan attempts to use the recession as an excuse for adopting tax or spending policies that are really sought for other reasons, but are poorly designed to combat the recession. If the current automatic fiscal policies, along with monetary policy, seem unable to overcome a deep or prolonged recession, the board would recommend emergency fiscal policies designed solely to counter the recession rather than promote partisan or other objectives. A final task of the fiscal policy advisory board would be to prescribe a rule such as NUBAR to maintain fiscal discipline in a normal economy, in order to assure that fiscal policy can be used to combat recession.

Organization of the Book

Part I consists of five chapters that set out my proposals for the conduct of countercyclical fiscal policy. Chapter 1 proposes a money-financed fiscal stimulus to combat a severe recession. Chapter 2 proposes an automatic transfer (tax rebate). Chapter 3 proposes an automatic consumption tax cut. Chapter 4 proposes NUBAR (normal unemployment balanced budget rule) to provide fiscal discipline in a normal economy, so that the strong fiscal position of the government enables it to run temporary deficits during a recession. Chapter 5 proposes the establishment of a fiscal policy advisory board.

Part II consists of four chapters that provide support and background for the proposals of Part I. Chapter 6 reviews recent empirical studies that support the case for the automatic tax rebate proposed in chapter 2. Chapter 7 describes the tax rebate implemented in the 1975 recession, and chapter 8, the tax rebate implemented during the 2001 recession. Chapter 9 reviews early studies of automatic fiscal policy.

Part III consists of three chapters that consider criticisms of countercyclical fiscal policy. Chapter 10 reviews several early criticisms of countercyclical fiscal policy. Chapter 11 discusses the new classical counterrevolution that began in the 1970s, and contends that it was a false path for macroeconomics. Finally, chapter 12 discusses the recent challenge to the view that fiscal policy played an important role in ending the Great Depression, and concludes that the challenge is unpersuasive.

The Rationale for the Substantial Quoting of Economists

In this book I make frequent use of quotes from economists. There are three reasons for this. First, one purpose of my book is to collect and organize, for the convenience of the reader, many important quotes from economists that bear on my subject. It would take a reader a long time to track down these quotes—it took me a long time. Second, although I paraphrase as well as quote, I believe that it is often more useful for the reader to see the actual quote. These economists have usually weighed their own words carefully. Let the reader read them without an intermediary. Third, I want to give credit where credit is due, and not give the false impression that another economist's ideas or words are my own. Despite the substantial quoting that I do in this book, I hope I have made some useful contributions of my own to this topic. I leave that for the reader to judge.

The Paucity of Reference to Particular Branches of Recent Macroeconomic Research

Although I quote and paraphrase from many recent macroeconomic articles (just check the references at the end of the book, or chapters such as 1 and 6), I make little reference to particular branches of macroeconomic research of the past two and a half decades. As I explained earlier in this chapter, I fully agree with Blinder that the new classical counterrevolution —which rests crucially on the unrealistic assumption of instantaneous labor market clearing—has been enormously counterproductive; I therefore relegate reference to this literature to chapter 11. I am in agreement with much of the "new" Keynesian literature, but most of it has focused on either providing microeconomic foundations for the Keynesian behavior of the macroeconomy or refuting new classical economics rather than on designing automatic fiscal policies to combat recessions, so there is not much to quote or paraphrase from this literature for this book. One purpose of this book is to encourage more macroeconomists to devote their skills and energies to the practical design of automatic countercyclical fiscal policies that would be helpful in the actual economy—an economy that exhibits Keynesian rather than classical behavior in the short run.

Part I

1
Fiscal Policy to Combat a Severe Recession

Suppose the economy falls into a severe, prolonged recession. What should be done?

A half century ago, most economists would have prescribed a combined expansion of both fiscal and monetary policy—a money-financed fiscal stimulus. In the past few decades, however, many economists have ignored fiscal policy and recommended sole reliance on a monetary expansion; some economists have contended that simply keeping the money supply from contracting would be sufficient. This chapter makes the case for implementing a money-financed fiscal stimulus to combat a severe, prolonged recession.

Krugman's Challenge

In an article titled, "It's Baaack: Japan's Slump and the Return of the Liquidity Trap," Paul Krugman (1998) asks whether monetary policy has the power to rescue a depressed economy when the interest rate is already near zero. John Maynard Keynes, observing the near-zero interest rates during 1930s, argued that monetary policy alone could not revive an economy mired in such a "liquidity trap." Krugman says that since World War II the liquidity trap has generally been unimportant because interest rates have stayed well above zero. He notes that most modern macroeconomists think that a liquidity trap "cannot happen, did not happen, and will not happen again" (1998, 138). He then says, "But it has happened, and to the world's second-largest economy." He points out that over the past few years, Japanese money market rates have been below 1 percent, yet the Japanese economy has remained depressed for a decade. Krugman warns that if this can happen to Japan, it can happen elsewhere.

Krugman is surely correct that policy makers should be ready to revive a depressed economy in which the interest rate is very low. He acknowledges that economists in the Keynesian tradition have prescribed a simple straightforward solution: expansionary fiscal policy. Expansionary fiscal policy means either a cut in taxes, or an increase in government cash transfer payments, or an increase in government purchases of goods and services. Tax cuts and cash transfers should raise consumer spending, stimulating production of consumer goods, and in turn inducing businesses to raise their investment spending in order to develop the capacity to produce these consumer goods. Government purchases stimulate the production of the goods that the government buys. All of this generates income that in turn further raises consumer spending.

But rather than simply recommend this straightforward solution, Krugman surprisingly chooses to investigate the problem in a "modern" macroeconomic model in which fiscal expansion does not work. A key element of this "modern" model is the unrealistic assumption of Robert Barro (1974) that people will *entirely* save any tax cut or cash transfer. Why would people, who usually spend most of their disposable income and save only a small portion, now save *all* of their additional disposable income and spend none of it? According to Barro, it is because the typical person would say to himself, "If the government leaves me with more cash today (either by cutting my tax or sending me a cash transfer), it will have to borrow more today and will therefore have to tax me more tomorrow to pay back its debt; so I better set aside all of the cash I get today so that I am ready to pay the tax tomorrow." Barro, however, has never provided any empirical evidence whatsoever that people (other than a few economists) actually think this way.

Krugman knows Barro's assumption is unrealistic, but he finds it intellectually challenging to figure out how to rescue a depressed economy in a liquidity trap without using fiscal policy. How can it be done? Krugman says by having the central bank announce it will bring about a steady inflation of 4 percent per year for a decade and a half. Why will this work? According to Krugman, the central bank's announcement will cause people to believe there will be 4 percent inflation, and this belief will cause them to borrow and spend. Thus, two things must happen for Krugman's plan to work: people must believe there will be 4 percent inflation, and this belief must induce them to borrow and spend more. Each can be questioned.

First, will the central bank's announcement actually raise the inflation rate that people in Japan expect? In the discussion following Krugman's presentation of his paper at the Brookings panel, several panel members were skeptical. Robert Gordon doubted that the Bank of Japan can easily change inflationary expectations because expectations depend largely on actual experience, and actual inflation will rise only when there is excess demand in the markets for goods and labor. I interpret Gordon's comment this way: There is no magic connection from a central bank's increase in high-powered money to a rise in the price of goods and services; only if the central bank's action actually raises people's demand for goods and services will it result in a rise in the price of goods and services. Hence, people are right to be skeptical about whether the central bank, with the nominal interest rate near zero, has the power to raise the price of goods and services. Alan Blinder noted that Krugman's policy would require the Bank of Japan to persuade people that the future was going to be fundamentally different from the past because Japan has had no inflation for most of the 1990s. Martin Baily said that it would be easy for Russia to be credible in announcing inflationary policy but hard for Japan.

Second, even if the announcement causes people in Japan to believe there will be 4 percent inflation, will this belief induce them to borrow and spend more? Many economists contend that people "should" borrow and spend more if they suddenly expect more inflation, because people "should" look at the "real" interest rate—defined as the nominal interest rate minus the expected inflation rate—not at the nominal interest rate per se, and a rise in expected inflation, by definition, reduces the real interest rate. Thus, many economists contend that a rise in expected inflation from 0 percent to 4 percent "should" do as much to stimulate borrowing and spending as a cut in the nominal interest rate from 4 percent to 0 percent. But will it? It is obvious to the ordinary person that a cut in a bank's interest rate from 4 percent to 0 percent makes it a better time to borrow. But it may not be obvious to the ordinary person that expected inflation is a good reason to borrow and spend more.

Krugman concedes that in the actual economy a fiscal policy would do some good and should therefore be utilized, but he worries about whether fiscal policy can be sufficiently expansionary in practice. He notes that to cure a severe recession a successful fiscal expansion might have to be large and continue for several years. He wonders whether the consequences in terms of government debt are acceptable, and whether any Japanese government would have the "political nerve" (1998, 178) to propose a fiscal package large enough for long enough to cure a stubborn recession.

Gordon's Reply

Krugman's concern about running up too much debt with an expansionary fiscal policy is directly addressed by Robert J. Gordon (2000). He compares Japan in the 1990s to the United States in the 1930s. Although Japan's slump has not been nearly as deep as the Great Depression, it also has lasted a decade. In both cases, interest rates have been very low. The Japanese short-term interest rate fell below 1 percent after 1995 and in 1996–99 was roughly constant at about 0.5 percent. In the United States the short-term interest rate fell below 1 percent after 1931 and in 1938–40 was less than 0.05 percent. Gordon says that if monetary policy is impotent because it cannot reduce the interest rate any further, a fiscal stimulus is required to end the slump. Gordon notes that the Japanese government appears hesitant to propose a large fiscal stimulus because the public debt in Japan, roughly 100 percent of GDP, is high among economically advanced countries.

But Gordon argues that this reluctance is mistaken, *provided* the fiscal stimulus is combined with a monetary expansion. He makes this crucial point that with a joint fiscal/monetary expansion there is no need for a further increase in the national debt *held by the public,* because to achieve its monetary expansion, the central bank can buy the government bonds issued as a result of the increased fiscal deficit. Gordon notes that Japan has not pursued this "obvious solution." Why not? The joint fiscal/monetary expansion requires the Bank of Japan to buy up the government bonds issued when the government spends more than it taxes, and this purchase of bonds by a central bank is sometimes called "monetizing the debt." Historically, excessive infusion of money into an economy has often led to high inflation, and apparently the Bank of Japan seems reluctant to do it.

Gordon explains his prescription in terms of the standard textbook IS/LM diagram shown in Figure 1.1. In that diagram, the interest rate is plotted vertically and output horizontally. The IS curve has a negative slope and the LM curve has a positive slope. The intersection of the IS and LM curves determines the interest rate and output of the economy. The IS curve embodies spending by consumers, businesses, and government. A fiscal stimulus (a tax cut or increase in government spending) shifts the IS curve to the right, thereby raising output (while raising the interest rate). The LM curve embodies monetary policy. A monetary stimulus (engineered by the Federal Reserve System through open market operations) shifts the LM curve to the right, thereby raising output (while lowering the interest rate). Now note a key point. As the monetary stimulus is raised further, the LM curve shifts further right, and the intersection with the IS curve occurs at a still lower and lower interest rate. When the intersection finally occurs at a zero interest rate, there is nothing more that monetary policy can do to raise output, because no matter how much money is injected into the banking system by the Federal Reserve, banks will not reduce their interest rate below zero; after all, what bank would lend $100 if the borrower agrees to repay only $99, implying an interest rate of –1 percent? Thus, the most monetary policy can do is raise output to point where the IS curve intersects the horizontal axis.

Figure 1.1 shows the problem for monetary policy in Japan in the 1990s

Figure 1.1 **IS/LM Diagram**

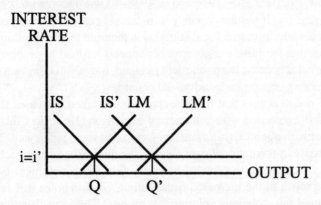

and the United States in the 1930s. In both cases, a stock market plunge, bank failures, and consequent pessimism caused consumers and businesses to reduce their spending so much that the IS curve shifted so far to the left that it intersected the LM curve at a very low interest rate and low level of output. The most monetary policy can do is nudge the interest rate to zero, resulting in only a slight increase in output. The fundamental problem is the position of the IS curve—it is too far to the left—and as long as it stays there, monetary policy will be powerless to cure the recession. The solution should be evident: shift the IS curve right to IS' with fiscal policy, and shift the LM curve right to LM' with monetary policy.

Gordon writes:

> If monetary policy is impotent because it cannot reduce the interest rate any further, a fiscal stimulus is required to end the slump and bring the output ratio [the ratio of actual output to "natural output"] back to its desired level of 100 percent. . . .
>
> The low level of the Japanese interest rate created a policy dilemma in Japan. Monetary policy could not push interest rates appreciably lower, yet fiscal policymakers felt constrained in achieving a large fiscal stimulus by the high existing level of the fiscal deficit in Japan and by the fact that the public debt in Japan had reached 100 percent of real GDP.
>
> However, the IS-LM model suggests a way out of the Japanese policy dilemma. As shown . . . , a *combined* monetary and fiscal policy stimulus that shifts the LM and IS curves rightward by the same amount can boost real GDP without any need for a decline in interest rates. (Gordon 2000, 137)

Recall, however, Krugman's concern that a large fiscal expansion, sustained for several years, will generate a huge national debt. Gordon responds directly to this concern:

Also, with such a combined policy there is no need for a further increase in the national debt held by the public, since to achieve its monetary expansion, the central bank can buy the government bonds issued as a result of the increased fiscal deficit. (Gordon 2000, 137)

Gordon laments the failure of the Japanese government to implement a sustained joint fiscal/monetary expansion. He asks:

Why did the Bank of Japan resist what seemed to be the obvious solution, which was that the Bank buy up the government bonds issued as a result of the fiscal stimulus? This solution, sometimes called "monetizing the debt," would be the real-world equivalent of shifting the LM curve rightward along with the IS curve, in contrast to the increased interest rates that would result if the IS curve were pushed rightward without a corresponding rightward LM movement. Bank of Japan policymakers retreated into the traditional fear of central bankers that monetizing the debt would undermine the Bank's independence and credibility, two goals that are embedded in the structure of beliefs of central bankers. In fact, as a result of rapid inflation after World War II, the Bank of Japan is legally banned from buying bonds directly from the government, although it is still able to purchase government bonds indirectly through financial markets.

The traditional reason for the historic reluctance of central bankers to monetize the debt and conduct a simultaneous monetary and fiscal expansion has been fear of inflation. Yet Japan's problem in the late 1990s was deflation, not inflation. In fact, Krugman's solution for the Japanese dilemma was that the Bank of Japan should buy up so much Japanese government debt that it would convince the public that there would be a steady inflation in the foreseeable future. Since spending decisions depend on the real interest rate (the actual interest rate minus the inflation rate), the combination of a zero actual interest rate and a positive inflation rate would imply a negative real interest rate, a situation that would stimulate private consumption and investment spending. Further, monetization of the debt would tend to depreciate the foreign exchange rate of the Japanese yen which . . . would stimulate Japanese net exports.

As the decade of the 1990s came to an end, a solution to the Japanese policy dilemma was not yet in sight. While the prescription of the IS-LM model in favor of a combined monetary-fiscal expansion seemed clear, implementing this policy recommendation was blocked by the reluctance of the Bank of Japan to give up its historic commitment to maintaining price stability. As Princeton economist Kenneth Rogoff concluded, "The real problem is that the Bank of Japan does not have the big picture right. It does not realize that a good conservative central bank should be willing to let the price level rise on a rainy day—and Japan is experiencing a typhoon." (Gordon 2000, 137–138)

A Money-Financed Fiscal Stimulus to Combat Recession

The aim, then, of a combined fiscal and monetary expansion is to restore aggregate demand to normal. Currently, Japan suffers from deficient demand, resulting in output below capacity and falling prices. The objective is to raise demand just enough so that output will be normal and prices stable (or rising slowly). Only if the fiscal/monetary stimulus is too large and causes excess demand will output strain capacity and prices rise rapidly. There is no magic link between a limited temporary monetizing of debt and inflation. Prices are determined by the supply and demand for goods. Demand for goods is either deficient, excessive, or just right. The right degree of monetization will cause demand for goods to be just right, restoring output to normal while prices remain reasonably stable.

Imagine that the treasury and central bank are actually consolidated into a single unit called "the government," the government budget is initially balanced, but the economy suffers from deficient demand. Then the government can inject a fiscal stimulus by either raising its spending or cutting taxes, thereby raising aggregate demand. But to spend more than it receives in taxes, the government must either borrow from the public (i.e., must sell government bonds to the public), or print money. Suppose the deficit is financed entirely by printing money. A particular money-financed fiscal stimulus raises demand by a specific amount. There is some particular magnitude for a money-financed fiscal stimulus that will raise demand to just the right level to restore normal output. With a consolidated government, a money-financed fiscal stimulus completely avoids any public debt problem because no debt is issued to the public.

Now suppose we restore the independence of the central bank from the treasury and prohibit the treasury from printing money so that the treasury must finance any deficit entirely by selling its bonds in the open market. The independent central bank then decides how much treasury debt to buy through open market operations. Suppose that the central bank decides to buy an amount of debt equal to the deficit. Then the monetary base increases by the amount of the deficit. If we conceptually consolidate the government, we see that "the government's" deficit is being entirely financed by "the government's" printing of money.

Further suppose that the central bank exempts the treasury from paying interest on the treasury debt it holds, and automatically renews its purchase of treasury debt whenever the debt comes due. Then the debt the central bank buys imposes no burden of either interest or principal on the treasury, in contrast to debt held by the public. In the United States, the Federal Reserve in fact returns almost all interest paid by the treasury to the treasury—in effect exempting the treasury from paying interest.

This suggests the following proposal (Seidman 2001): Official figures of "debt held by the public" should exclude debt held by the central bank. Currently, debt held by the "public" includes debt held by the central bank, so that the central bank is counted as part of the public. In the United States, roughly 10 percent of the "public debt" is held by the Federal Reserve. This inclusion means that a joint fiscal/monetary expansion to combat a deep recession raises the official public debt, and thereby appears to cause a public debt problem, even if the central bank accumulates all the new debt and the public accumulates none. In effect, Gordon makes this proposal in the above quote when he argues that with a combined fiscal/monetary expansion there would be no increase in the "national debt held by the public" because the central bank buys the treasury's bonds.

But what about inflation? Will a money-financed fiscal stimulus be inflationary? If money affects prices only through aggregate demand, then a money-financed fiscal stimulus of proper magnitude should not generate inflation because it raises demand only enough to restore output to normal. Some economists contend, however, that there is another way that a money-financed fiscal stimulus might generate some inflation. If workers believe that money-financed deficits cause inflation, and if they actually recognize that the fiscal stimulus is being financed by printing money, they may expect inflation, and therefore, they may hold out for higher wages, which would then result in higher costs and prices. However, there is no empirical evidence that workers actually think this way.

The institutional independence of the central bank from the treasury, and the prohibition on the treasury from issuing money to finance its deficits, helps prevent inflationary expectations. Historically, large budget deficits have indeed often led to inflation, even hyperinflation, when they have been money financed for a sustained period. In these historical episodes, the treasury and central bank were usually consolidated into a single unit so that "the government" simply printed money to finance its deficits. But with an independent central bank and a prohibition against printing money by the treasury, budget deficits need not lead to an excessive rise in aggregate demand. The impact on demand depends on the reaction of the central bank. If the central bank refuses to buy treasury debt, it can prevent excessive demand. If the bank earns a reputation, based on its actions, of preventing demand from becoming excessive and inflationary, then workers and managers are likely to continue to expect reasonable price stability despite budget deficits. Thus, the prohibition against printing money by the treasury, and the independence of the central bank, are important to the ability to use money-financed fiscal stimulus to combat a recession.

Milton Friedman's Helicopter Drop: A Money-Financed Fiscal Stimulus

In a famous passage, Milton Friedman colorfully describes an unconventional means of implementing a money-financed fiscal stimulus:

> Let us suppose now that one day a helicopter flies over this community and drops an additional $1,000 in bills from the sky, which is, of course, hastily collected by members of the community. Let us suppose further that everyone is convinced that this is a unique event which will never be repeated. To begin with, suppose further that each individual happens to pick up an amount of money equal to the amount he held before, so that each individual finds himself with twice the cash balances he had before. If every individual simply decided to hold on to the extra cash, nothing else would happen. . . . But this is not the way people would behave. . . . We know only that each individual will seek to reduce his cash balances at some rate. He will do so by trying to spend more than he receives. . . . It is easy to see what the final position will be. People's attempts to spend more than they receive will be frustrated, but in the process these attempts will bid up the nominal value of services. . . . It is much harder to say anything about the transition. To begin with, some producers may be slow to adjust their prices and may let themselves be induced to produce more for the market at the expense of non-market uses of resources. . . . (Friedman 1969, 4–6)

Friedman, however, does not describe his example as a money-financed fiscal stimulus. He entitles his section, "Effect of a Once-And-For-All Change in the Nominal Quantity of Money." The money is dropped on an economy that is fully employed and in multimarket equilibrium. Friedman contends that the change in the nominal quantity of money will have no permanent effect on the multimarket equilibrium. He never uses the phrase "cash transfer" or "fiscal policy" in his account, and gives the clear impression that he views his example, and article, as being entirely about monetary policy.

Friedman attributes admirable, courteous behavior to the citizenry as the huge volume of dollars, dropped by helicopters, fall onto the streets and public parks. But a safer, fairer, means of getting the dollars to citizens would be for the U.S. Treasury to mail each household a check. If this superior, though less colorful, method were utilized, it would be evident that government is indeed engaging in a fiscal policy—the payment of cash transfers to households—and that the transfers are money financed—implemented by the injection of an equal amount of new money into the economy. Households receiving checks would quite properly feel richer: each treasury check is a transfer, not a loan, so the household need never repay it. Some households will spend their transfer gradually over time, while others will spend most of it promptly, but there is no doubt they will eventually spend most of it. If the economy has unemployed resources for Keynesian reasons, these will be pulled into production by the increase in aggregate demand. Thus, without intending it, Friedman has provided a memorable example of a money-financed fiscal stimulus.

Bernanke's Prescription for Japan: Money-Financed Transfers

Ben Bernanke makes this same point in his analysis of Japan's stagnation:

> *Diagnosis: An Aggregate Demand Deficiency*
>
> Before discussing ways in which Japanese monetary policy could become more expansionary, I will briefly discuss the evidence for the view that a more expansionary monetary policy is needed. As already suggested, it cannot be denied that important structural problems, in the financial system and elsewhere, are constraining Japanese growth. But there is compelling evidence that the Japanese economy is suffering as well from an aggregate demand deficiency. If monetary policy could deliver increased nominal spending, some of the difficult structural problems Japan faces would no longer seem so difficult. (Bernanke 2000, 151)

He then reviews data on the Japanese economy in the 1990s to support his claim, citing slow output growth accompanied by price deflation. But then the question becomes: Can monetary policy do more?

> It is true that current monetary conditions in Japan limit the effectiveness of standard open-market operations in short-term Treasury debt. However, as I will argue in the remainder of this essay, monetary policy in Japan nevertheless retains considerable power to expand nominal aggregate demand and, consequently, to promote real economic recovery.

How to Get Out of a Liquidity Trap

> Contrary to the claims of at least some Japanese central bankers, monetary policy is far from impotent today in Japan. . . . (Bernanke 2000, 157)

He expresses support for Krugman's proposal to announce a positive inflation target, for "non-standard open market operations" that involves purchases of long-term financial assets such as corporate bonds and stocks, and for an effort to "achieve substantial currency depreciation through large open-market sales of yen." But he also offers the following proposal:

Money-Financed Transfers

> Suppose that the yen-depreciation strategy is tried but fails to raise aggregate demand and prices sufficiently, perhaps because at some point Japan's trading partners do object to further falls in the yen. An alternative strategy, which does not rely at all on trade diversion, is money-financed transfers to domestic households—the real-life equivalent of that hoary thought experiment, the "helicopter drop" of newly printed money. I think most economists would agree that a large enough helicopter drop must raise the price level. Suppose it did not, so that the price level remained unchanged. Then the real wealth of the population would grow without bound, as they are flooded with gifts of money from the government. . . . Surely at some point the public would attempt to convert its increased wealth into goods and services, spending that would increase aggregate demand and prices. Conversion of the public's money wealth into other assets would also be beneficial, if it raised the prices of other assets. . . .
>
> Of course, the Bank of Japan (BOJ) has no unilateral authority to rain money on the population. The policy being proposed—a money-financed tax cut—is a combination of fiscal and monetary measures. All this means is that some intra-governmental cooperation would be required. Indeed, the case for a tax cut now has already been made. . . . The willingness of the BOJ to purchase government securities equal to the cost of the tax cut would serve to reduce the net interest cost of the tax cut to government, which could not hurt the tax cut's chance of passage. By the way, I do not think that such cooperation would in any way compromise the BOJ's newly won independence, as some have suggested. In financing a tax cut, the BOJ would be taking voluntary action in pursuit of its legally mandated goal, the pursuit of price stability. Cooperation with the fiscal authorities in pursuit of a common goal is not the same as subservience. (Bernanke 2000, 162–163)

I fully agree with Bernanke's money-financed transfer. The objection I have with Bernanke's exposition is that he does not emphasize that his proposal involves *fiscal* expansion financed by monetary expansion—that it is a money-financed *fiscal* stimulus. He writes:

> Regarding the concern that not all these proposals are "pure" monetary policy, I will say only that I am not concerned here with fine semantic distinctions but rather with the fundamental issue of whether there exist feasible policies to stimulate nominal aggregate demand in Japan. As for the need for interagency cooperation or even possible legislative changes: In my view, in recent years BOJ officials have—to a far greater degree than is justified—hidden behind minor institutional or technical difficulties in order to avoid taking action. I will discuss some of these purported barriers to effective action as they arise, arguing that in many if not most cases they could be overcome, given the will to do so. (Bernanke 2000, 158)

But the issue here is not a "fine semantic distinction." The key point is that a transfer (or tax cut) is a fiscal policy that must be enacted by the legislature, not a monetary policy that can be implemented by the central bank. In my view, the role of economists should be to clarify exactly what the strategy entails: fiscal expansion enacted by the legislature, and monetary expansion implemented by the central bank. As I will review in chapters 10 and 11, countercyclical fiscal policy has been attacked by many prominent economists over the past few decades, and perhaps this is one reason Bernanke is reluctant to emphasize that a crucial component of his recommendation is a fiscal stimulus. But both economic understanding and the required legislative action are better promoted by emphasizing that a fiscal policy expansion is an essential component of the strategy, and that the legislature, not just the central bank, must take action if the strategy is to succeed.

Has Japan Tried Fiscal Stimulus? Posen's Answer

Recall that Gordon criticizes Japan for not attempting a substantial joint fiscal/monetary stimulus, and this criticism is implicit in Bernanke's call for Japan to attempt the same joint stimulus. But is it true that Japan has not tried aggressive fiscal expansion? Or has Japan tried aggressive fiscal expansion without success? In his book on the Japanese recession of the 1990s, Adam Posen (1998) provides a detailed analysis of Japanese fiscal policy. Following the bursting of the Japanese asset-price bubble at the beginning of the decade, the Japanese economy stagnated. A perception has arisen that the Japanese government aggressively pursued countercyclical fiscal policy to combat the recession, but that fiscal policy failed. Posen contends that this perception is incorrect. In a chapter titled, "Fiscal Policy Works When It Is Tried," he writes:

> The reality of Japanese fiscal policy in the 1990s is less mysterious and, ultimately, more disappointing. The actual amount injected into the economy by the Japanese government—through either public spending or tax reductions—was about a third of the total amount announced. This limited quantity of total fiscal stimulus was disbursed in insufficiently sized and inefficiently administered doses, with the exception of the 1995 stimulus package. That package did result in solid growth in 1996, demonstrating that fiscal policy does work when it is tried. As on earlier occasions in the 1990s, however, the positive response to fiscal stimulus was undercut by fiscal *contraction* in 1996 and 1997. On net, the Japanese fiscal stance in the 1990s was barely expansionary. (Posen 1998, 29–30)

Posen proposes a large fiscal stimulus of roughly 4 percent of GDP, primarily in the form of income tax cuts which stimulate demand across the board rather than in particular sectors. He concludes:

> The economic performance of Japan in the 1990s is the perfect illustration that discretionary counter-cyclical policy is appropriate under certain circumstances. In short, not only is the business cycle not dead in Japan, it has turned deadly. The usual reasons for avoiding discretionary fiscal policy clearly do not apply. The recession has gone on for so long that there is no danger that the lags of decision making and implementation will outlast the downturn. . . . The willingness to engage in discretionary fiscal policy in a clearly identifiable economic emergency must not be lost in the rush to meet arbitrary budget rules . . . any more than the driver who normally follows the speed limit must not forgo the possibility of accelerating well beyond 55 miles an hour in certain rare circumstances for safety's sake. (Posen 1998, 147–148)

In a recent paper on Japan's "Great Recession" of the 1990s, Kuttner and Posen write in their introduction:

> Our conclusions may be largely unsurprising to the core audience of this journal, but will likely come as something of a surprise to the more casual observers of the Japanese economic situation: despite the persistent stagnation, the Japanese economy has behaved much as the textbooks would have predicted. . . . Fiscal stimulus, whether in the form of tax cuts or

public works spending, is stimulative, though in Japan, tax cuts gave a bigger "bang for the yen" than public works spending. . . . In short, the basic lesson of Japan's Great Recession for policymakers is to trust what you learned in intermediate macroeconomics class: even under difficult economic circumstances, and even in institutional contexts far removed from the places in which they were developed, the stabilization policy framework of the mainstream textbooks still applies. (Kuttner and Posen 2001a, 4–5)

In their conclusion, they write:

Fiscal policy works pretty much the way Keynes suggested it does, with contractionary contractions and expansionary expansions, and even wasteful public spending having a clear multiplier (although disadvantageous in other ways). The structure and distribution of the tax burden do matter, however, and tax cuts targeted to the more liquidity constrained are likely to have larger effects. (Kuttner and Posen 2001a, 66)

They conclude:

This points to some policy guidance for Japan today, as well as for other large economies at risk of deepening recessions from a combination of asset price declines and external shocks. First and foremost, our results encourage a positive view of active counter-cyclical policy, particularly on the monetary side—the inflationary risks of quantitative easing appear to be non-existent precisely because near or at zero nominal short-term interest rates it is extremely difficult for the central bank to raise inflation expectations. Second, our analysis indicates that discretionary fiscal policy can get maximum bang-for-the-yen by increasing the average household's disposable income, and by recognizing that the budget deficit alone is not an adequate measure of fiscal stimulus. (Kuttner and Posen 2001a, 68)

But doesn't the substantial rise in Japan's ratio of government debt to GDP during the 1990s indicate that a large fiscal expansion was attempted over the decade? In another recent paper (2001b), Kuttner and Posen directly address this question:

The effectiveness of fiscal policy in Japan in the 1990s has been at least as controversial as the currently more public disputes over monetary policy. There has been open debate over the degree to which expansionary fiscal policy has even been tried, let alone whether it has been effective, along with widespread assertions about the degree of forward-looking behavior by Japanese savers. The highly visible and rapid more-than-doubling of Japanese public debt in less than a decade speaks for itself to a surprising number of observers: the fiscal deficit has grown sharply, yet the economy has continued to stagnate, so fiscal stabilization failed. No less an economist than Milton Friedman recently wrote, "[D]oes fiscal stimulus stimulate? Japan's experience in the '90s is dramatic evidence to the contrary. Japan resorted repeatedly to large doses of fiscal stimulus in the form of extra government spending. . . . The result: stagnation at best, depression at worst, for most of the past decade."

But it is easy to demonstrate from just charting publicly available data that the bulk of the increase in Japanese public debt is due to a plateau in tax revenue rather than to increased public expenditure or even discretionary tax cuts. This of course reflects the inverse cyclical relationship between output and tax revenue. If one applied a plausible tax elasticity of 1.25 to reasonable measures of the widening output gap (e.g., those estimated in Kuttner and Posen 2001a), the result would be a much-reduced estimate of the structural budget deficit. In fact, using the measure of potential based on a constant productivity trend growth rate of 2.5 percent a year all but eliminates the nonsocial security portion of the deficit. Moreover, as measured by the fiscal shocks derived from our estimates in this paper, fiscal policy has been generally contractionary since 1997. (Kuttner and Posen 2001b, 2)

Thus, the main reason for the run-up of government debt in Japan in the 1990s has been the recession itself, not expansionary fiscal policy. If a country becomes mired in recession for a decade, low tax revenue year after year results in continuous government borrowing and a huge run-up of debt.

Fiscal Discipline When the Economy is Normal

One final point should be made about the ability of a government to use aggressive fiscal policy to combat a recession. Any proposal for a large fiscal expansion always generates concern about government deficits and debt. If a government has kept "its fiscal house in order" so that its ratio of debt to GDP is low and has demonstrated the discipline to run balanced budgets and even surpluses when the economy is running normally, then that government will meet less resistance when it proposes running large deficits to combat a recession. As John Taylor (2000) notes, in the United States the large deficits and consequent rise in the debt/GDP ratio during the 1980s made it politically difficult for the government to enact a fiscal stimulus to combat the 1991 recession. The ratio of debt to GDP has figured prominently in the debate over whether and how much the Japanese government can use aggressive fiscal policy. Even though a money-financed fiscal stimulus would not increase the debt held by the public (excluding the central bank), large deficits per se will inevitably generate widespread concern. Moreover, many will no doubt count treasury debt held by the central bank when they evaluate the size of the debt/GDP ratio, even if such debt is officially excluded from "public debt" as I recommended above.

Thus, to create a political climate receptive to aggressive fiscal expansion in an economic emergency, a government should "reload its fiscal cannon" whenever the economy is running normally, balancing its budget and even running surpluses, thereby achieving a low debt/GDP ratio. An advocate of aggressive fiscal policy in a recession, rather than being indifferent to the deficits and debt in a normal economy, should be especially determined to keep the government's fiscal house in order when the economic sun is shining.

One way to do this is to separate Social Security and Medicare from the rest of the federal budget and run annual surpluses in these programs (Seidman 1999, 2000) to build up their trust funds in preparation for the retirement of the baby boomers. For the rest of the federal budget, Congress should enact a statute titled NUBAR—a normal unemployment balanced budget rule. NUBAR (Seidman 1998, chapter 5) states that Congress shall enact a *planned* budget for the coming fiscal year that technicians *estimate* will be balanced *if* the unemployment rate is normal (the average of the preceding decade). With NUBAR, if the economy has a normal unemployment rate, the budget (excluding Social Security and Medicare) will on average be roughly balanced, and the surpluses in these two programs will be used to pay down the national debt. If the economy has a boom with a below-normal unemployment rate, the budget (excluding Social Security and Medicare) will run a surplus that can further pay down the national debt. If the economy has a recession and an above normal unemployment rate, however, the budget (excluding Social Security and Medicare) will be in deficit. Part of the deficit will be due to the automatic stabilizers—the automatic fall in tax revenue and increase in transfers for unemployment insurance benefits; and part will be due to the new automatic fiscal policy. Of course, in a severe recession that overwhelms both monetary policy and the automatic fiscal policy, Congress should take discretionary action and suspend adherence to NUBAR in order to provide even greater stimulus through even larger transfers, tax cuts, and increases in government purchases.

Maintaining fiscal discipline when the economy is normal enables the use of countercyclical fiscal policy to combat recession. By running surpluses in Social Security and Medicare, and by adhering to NUBAR for the rest of the budget, fiscal discipline will be maintained, and the ratio of national debt to GDP will be kept low despite deficits that occur during recession due to the recession itself and to the countercyclical fiscal policy.

Countercyclical Fiscal Policy and Stabilizing Expectations

It is crucial that the public believe that the government is able and eager to use aggressive fiscal policy should a depression threaten. If the economy is hit with a shock that throws it into a recession, will households and business managers expect the economy to recover or will they expect the recession to deepen? If they expect the government to act aggressively and effectively to prevent depression, households and business managers will continue to spend, and this behavior will sustain aggregate demand, and in itself prevent depression. On the other hand, if they expect the government to be passive, they may cut their spending, thereby deepening the recession.

In the three decades following Keynes's *General Theory,* economists emphasized the importance of the public's expectations about output and employment. In the past three decades, economists have instead emphasized the public's expectations about inflation and often neglected the public's expectations about output and employment. Both expectations are important to the stability of the economy: private behavior will be stabilizing when the public expects the government to act aggressively to combat either inflation or recession.

As I will discuss in chapter 11, the classical counterrevolution of the mid-1970s, with its unrealistic but crucial assumption that the labor market always clears instantaneously, contended that a government commitment to countercyclical action was unnecessary and pointless. Its advocates appeared to imply that if economic agents were "rational," government countercyclical action was futile. But government action would be pointless only if there were instantaneous labor market clearing; rational expectations alone do not make government action pointless. In an important paper in the late 1970s entitled "Stabilization Policy and Private Economic Behavior," Martin N. Baily shows that if the economy has rational agents but also some wage and price stickiness—a central feature of Keynesian macroeconomics—the government's public commitment to pursue activist countercyclical policy is important for inducing stabilizing private sector behavior.

Post-Keynesian models often cite random shocks as the initiators of the business cycle, but stress the inability of the private economy to restore full employment in the short run. In this context it is more natural to think of the private sector welcoming the impact of policy and perhaps even reinforcing its effects. Since the view of the business cycle taken in this paper is in the post-Keynesian tradition, its conclusions, not surprisingly, differ from those of models with more classical assumptions. The rationality of expectations is the aspect of recent classical models that has received the most attention. But other assumptions are more crucial to the findings about policy, and they are much harder to accept. In particular, flexibility of prices is required in order that equilibrium be restored quickly after some disturbance. . . . The persistence of price and wage inflation through recessionary periods is a fact to which theory must adapt. (Baily 1978, 12)

Baily believes a public commitment by the government to activist countercyclical policies has a stabilizing effect similar to the commitment by government to guarantee bank deposits.

The Climate of Greater Stability

The Federal Deposit Insurance Corporation is a remarkable institution. Prior to its existence bank failures and runs on banks were very common. Since it came into being it has rarely had to pay out. Other things have not been equal, of course, but the fact that deposits are insured changes the behavior of depositors in a way that induces greater stability in the banking system. Fears of a run on the bank can become self-fulfilling as depositors scramble to withdraw funds. Even if an individual knows for a fact that a bank is basically sound, he is not being irrational to hurry to the teller's window for his money once the rush starts. The analogy to the existence of stabilization policy is not exact, but it has some validity. If everyone believes that major depression and runaway inflation can be controlled, these events become less likely. A recession will not induce the same panicky cutbacks in investment or employment; an inflation will not induce the same flight from money and financial assets. (Baily 1978, 13)

Thus, the public's confidence that the government is committed to countercyclical fiscal and monetary policy in itself helps stabilize the economy.

2

An Automatic Transfer

(Tax Rebate)

As explained in the introduction to this book, current automatic stabilizers are unintended by-products of setting the tax/transfer system to meet other objectives such as the ratio of tax revenue to GDP, the degree of progressivity of the tax system, and the level of unemployment benefits. They do help stabilize the economy (Cohen and Follette 2000; Auerbach and Feenberg 2000), but the magnitude of their stabilizing impact is held hostage to the other objectives. In this chapter I consider an automatic tax rebate (cash transfer), with a magnitude set solely to provide the proper degree of stimulus to combat a recession. In chapter 6, I review recent empirical studies that find a prompt and significant response of consumer spending to cash transfers (such as income tax refunds), and explain why one consumer survey (Shapiro and Slemrod 2001) that at first glance appears to run counter to the other studies has serious shortcomings.

The new automatic fiscal policy proposed in this chapter is analogous to, and complementary with, the "Taylor rules" that have been proposed for the Federal Reserve's conduct of monetary policy. The proposed automatic fiscal policy was once called "formula flexibility" to distinguish it from "built-in" automatic stabilizers. In his book on public finance, Musgrave devotes a section to "formula flexibility":

Formula Flexibility

While the power of built-in flexibility in the narrow sense of the term is limited, a much higher degree of potency may be secured by reliance on so-called formula flexibility. Formula flexibility refers to an arrangement whereby changes in tax rates and/or expenditure levels are legislated in advance, to go into effect if and when specified changes in income occur. For instance, it might be legislated that income tax rates be reduced or public expenditures raised by x percent if income falls by y percent. . . . If the formula flexibility thus provided is tailored properly to the structural relationships of the dynamic system to be stabilized, the remaining degree of instability might be reduced to narrow limits. Whether or not this can be done depends upon the structure of the instability that is to be dealt with. (Musgrave 1959, 512)

Pack explains formula flexibility this way:

> Formula flexibility is a fiscal action that activates a tax (or expenditure) change automatically when a certain pre-arranged signal of recession is observed. It differs from an automatic stabilizer in that the latter is built into the existing tax and transfer payment structure, while the former, when activated, changes the structure itself. . . . The objective of formula flexibility is to add another automatic, quick-acting, and quantitatively effective weapon to the counter-cyclical fiscal arsenal. Formula flexibility can be applied to expenditures as well as to tax changes. . . . Tax rates would be reduced (or rates of transfers increased) when some economic indicator forecasts a recession. The magnitude of the tax (transfer) change as well as precise details about when the change is to be activated would be embodied in prior legislation. Also, the conditions under which the rates would be restored to their previous levels . . . would be stipulated. Given such legislation, counter-cyclical action would not be subject to delays stemming from the need for legislative approval. (Pack 1968, 5–7)

The automatic transfer (tax rebate) would be preenacted: Congress would establish a schedule that relates the magnitude of the transfer to the magnitude of the output gap—the gap between actual output and "normal" output (the output that would have occurred if there had been a normal unemployment rate). Hence, the automatic policy would not require any legislative action such as voting by Congress at the time the position of the economy triggers it. It would be implemented either by sending U.S. Treasury checks that "rebate" some of the preceding year's tax, or simply provide a specific cash transfer to each household regardless of the preceding year's tax (for example, $600 per family, $300 per single person), or by cutting withholding and tax due on the next income tax return. I will use the phrase "tax rebate" to cover any of these options.

However, suppose the recession is induced by a supply shock, such as an increase in the world oil price in the mid 1970s, so that it is accompanied by a rise in inflation. Or suppose it is intentionally induced by tight monetary policy in order to subdue high inflation, as in the early 1980s. In these situations, there is a conflict: a tax rebate would counter the recession but worsen the inflation. Thus, in response to a recession, it seems sensible to automatically scale down the size of the tax rebate to the degree there is a simultaneous inflation problem. Thus, the automatic fiscal policy would respond to the output gap but the magnitude would be scaled down in proportion to the inflation gap (the gap between actual inflation and target inflation), just as John Taylor (1993, 2000) and others have recommended for monetary policy.

Under this approach, a tax rebate (cash transfer) would be automatically triggered by recent U.S. Commerce Department data according to a relatively simple rule. For example, if last quarter's actual real GDP is at least X percent below "normal" real GDP, then a tax rebate proportional to this "excess output-gap" (the gap below the threshold X percent) would be automatically triggered and implemented this quarter through the mailing of checks to households ("rebates") or a cut in income tax withholding by employers.

Although Phillips (1954), Pack (1968), and Duggal (1975) examined more complex automatic fiscal policies—their work will be reviewed in chapter 9—in this chapter I propose a simple, transparent automatic fiscal policy. The more complex fiscal policies may or may not outperform the simple one, but they would be harder for Congress or the public to understand. The automatic tax rebate in this chapter is simply proportional to the size of the excess output-gap in the preceding quarter. If last quarter actual real GDP is 5 percent less than normal real GDP and the threshold X percent is 2 percent, then a tax rebate will be triggered due to the excess output-gap of 3 percent.

Congress would preenact the automatic tax rebate of specified magnitude in response to the excess output-gap (with a scaling down if there is a substantial inflation gap). For example, if the excess output-gap were zero, and inflation were at its target, then there would be no stimulus. The tax rebate would be increased by a specified amount for each percentage point by which output is below the X percent threshold, except that the size of the rebate would be scaled down if inflation is currently well above its target.

The output (real GDP) gap depends, by its definition, on an estimate of normal real GDP. Congress would need to specify how normal real GDP is to be estimated by technicians in the Congressional Budget Office (CBO). One way to estimate normal real GDP would be to estimate what real GDP would be if the unemployment rate were "normal." The normal unemployment rate might be defined as the average unemployment rate over the preceding decade. Alternatively, it might be defined as the unemployment rate estimated to usually keep the inflation rate constant. A particular unemployment rate implies a particular level of employment in a given quarter. Combining this level of employment with the level of the capital stock (and assuming a normal capacity utilization rate), an aggregate production function can be used by CBO technicians to provide an estimate of normal real GDP.

It is important that the normal unemployment rate, and the aggregate production function, be subject to a prescribed periodic review by CBO technicians. Such periodic review would keep the official measure of the output gap up-to-date and relevant to the current economy.

The Formula for Automatically Triggering the Transfer (Rebate)

The formula for the *aggregate* cash transfer (total rebate dollars) R is

$$R/Y_n = a \, [Y\text{gap} - X]_{-1} \tag{2.1}$$

where R = the *new countercyclical* aggregate real transfer from the federal government to households,

Y_n = normal real GDP,

R/Y_n = the transfer ratio,

$Y\text{gap}$ = percent gap of real GDP below normal real GDP,

X = the percent threshold that must be exceeded before the transfer is triggered, and

a = the "power" coefficient.

Note that this quarter's transfer (rebate) depends on last quarter's $Y\text{gap}$ in excess of the threshold X, as indicated by the subscript -1 following $[Y\text{gap} - X]_{-1}$.

The cash transfer (rebate) per household equals R/N, where N is the number of households (for example, in 2001, $600 per household).

Congress must preenact the numerical values of X and a. Consider three pairs:

	X	a
Policy F1	2%	0.5
Policy F2	2%	1.5
Policy F3	0%	1.5

To illustrate, suppose last quarter's $Y\text{gap}$ was 4 percent (Y was 4 percent below Y_n). Then for each of the three policies, this quarter's transfer ratio R/Y_n would be:

$$a \, [Ygap \, -X]_{-1} \quad = \quad R/Y_n$$

Policy F1: $0.5\,[\,4\% \quad -2\%] \quad = \quad 1\%$

Policy F2: $1.5\,[\,4\% \quad -2\%] \quad = \quad 3\%$

Policy F3: $1.5\,[\,4\% \quad -0\%] \quad = \quad 6\%$

Note that policies F1 and F2 are "cautious" in that they have a threshold X of 2 percent; the transfer is triggered only if the $Ygap$ exceeds 2 percent. Also note that policies F2 and F3 are more "powerful" than F1 because a is 1.5 instead of 0.5.

If inflation is above a target set by Congress, however, then R/Y_n would be automatically scaled down. For example, in both the 1975 and 1982 recessions, inflation was well above target. In 1975 the recession was generated primarily by OPEC's sharp increase in the world oil price, which shifted up the aggregate supply curve in the United States, causing a simultaneous increase in price and fall in output. In 1982, the recession was generated by the Federal Reserve's high interest rates in its effort to bring down inflation. Thus, in both of those recessions, R/Y_n would be smaller than given by the formula above. By contrast, in the 2001 recession, with inflation low (roughly at target), there would have been no scaling down of the R/Y_n given by the formula.

If inflation is above target, the transfer (rebate) would equal only the percentage Z of the R/Y_n given by formula (2.1). The percentage Z would be computed from the following formula:

$$Z = [100\% - \beta(p_{-1} - p^*)], \qquad (2.2)$$

where $\beta > 0$.

Suppose last quarter's inflation rate p_{-1} is 7 percent, and Congress sets an inflation target p^* of 2 percent, and sets β equal to 8. Then $\beta(p_{-1} - p^*) = 8(7\% - 2\%) = 40$ percent, so the percentage Z equals 60 percent, so the transfer would equal 60 percent of the transfer given by formula (2.1).

Designing and Implementing the Tax Rebate

There have been two important tax rebates implemented in the United States to combat recession: the 1975 rebate, and the 2001 rebate. The 1975 rebate is discussed in detail in chapter 7, the 2001 rebate, in chapter 8. Here I provide a brief summary. The 1975 rebate was equal to 10 percent of the household's 1974 income tax up to a ceiling of $200, but was phased down to $100 for higher income households. The 2001 rebate was equal to $600 per married couple, and $300 per single individual, up to a maximum of the taxpayer's 2000 income tax. The 1975 rebate was enacted in March, and the U.S. Treasury mailed out checks in April, May, and June. The 2001 rebate was enacted in June, and the U.S. Treasury mailed out checks in July, August, and September.

An important issue in the design of the rebate is formula and coverage. In 1975, there was extensive debate in Congress over the formula. Some wanted 10 percent without limit, others wanted an equal dollar amount per household. The final formula represented a compromise. In 2001, there was quicker agreement on an equal dollar amount per household ($600 per married couple, $300 per single person), probably because the rebate was viewed as an advanced payment of the cut in the first-bracket tax rate of every household from 15 percent to 10 percent; the lower rate applied to the first $12,000 income for a married couple, so the tax cut was $600 (5 percent of $12,000) per married couple; and applied to the first $6,000 income of every single person, so the tax cut was $300 (5 percent of $6,000) per single person. The 2001 rebate, however, was limited to the taxpayer's 2000 income tax. For example, low-income workers who paid payroll tax but no income tax in 2000 did not receive a rebate. One reason given for this omission was that the U.S. Treasury would have needed more time to obtain the addresses of payroll taxpayers who did not pay income tax (although this could have been easily done by including recipients of the earned income tax credit).

Both the 1975 rebate and the 2001 rebate were enacted by Congress under the time pressure of responding quickly to a recession. My proposal is that an automatic tax rebate be preenacted, and then automatically triggered when GDP falls sufficiently below normal. Thus, the formula, coverage, and techniques of implementation would be debated and negotiated by members of Congress without the time pressure that constrained the 1975 and 2001 rebates. There would be time, for example, to have U.S. Treasury personnel provide advice on how to reach payroll taxpayers who had not paid any income tax, and on the pros and cons of using the tax withholding system (for income and/or payroll taxes) rather than mailing rebate checks. The preenacted rebate package could of course be amended from time to time. But at any moment, there would be a preenacted tax rebate in place with specific instructions for implementation, ready to be triggered by a sufficient decline in GDP below normal.

Objections and Responses

I will list four objections to the automatic rebate and briefly respond to each one.

Objection #1: Most of the rebate will be saved, not spent (permanent income hypothesis).

Response: Recent empirical studies that will be reviewed in detail in chapter 6 indicate substantial spending in response to tax refunds and rebates.

Objection #2: The 2001 $600 rebate didn't work.

Response: The jury is still out. Even the consumer survey (conducted in the fall of 2001) usually cited to support this view (Shapiro and Slemrod 2002) reported that 22 percent of consumers said they planned to "mostly increase spending" because of the rebate. Moreover, in chapter 6, I explain why more than 22 percent of rebate dollars were likely spent within a year:

1. The survey did not ask for the percent of rebate dollars consumers planned to spend.
2. The key question began with the phrase, "Thinking about your financial situation this year," which may have biased respondents toward answering "pay off debt."
3. The term "this year" may have been interpreted as before the end of the calender year 2001 rather than "within a year."

Objection #3: Japan tried fiscal stimulus in the 1990s and it didn't work.

Response: As shown by Posen (1998) and Kuttner and Posen (2001a, 2001b), fiscal policy worked when it was tried in Japan in 1995, but was undermined by fiscal contractions in 1996 and 1997. Most of the deficits and run-up of debt in Japan were due to the recession itself.

Objection #4: Wouldn't a temporary consumption tax cut be more effective?

Response: It might. It would give households an incentive to consume while the price is temporarily low. I consider this promising proposal in chapter 3. I recommend enacting both an automatic transfer (this chapter) and an automatic temporary consumption tax cut (next chapter). Also, Lewis and Seidman (2003) note that a temporary incentive for consumer spending can be delivered through a consumer durable tax credit analogous to an investment tax credit.

The Automatic Transfer (Rebate) versus Current Automatic Stabilizers

A numerical example illustrates the difference between current automatic stabilizers and the automatic tax rebate (Seidman 1987, 395–397). The important results from this example are presented in Table 2.1, and the text that follows explains these results.

Consider a simple Keynesian model of the macroeconomy in which producers set the output (Y) of the economy equal to the demand for consumer goods (C) by households plus the demand for investment goods (I) by business firms plus the demand for goods and services by government (G), so

$$Y = C + I + G.$$

Suppose demand for consumer goods (C) by households equals 80 percent of "disposable income"—income (Y) minus taxes (T) plus transfers (R)—so

$$C = 0.8(Y - T + R).$$

Initially, assume unrealistically that T is independent of Y. Suppose $I = 380$, $G = 300$, $R = 250$, and $T = 550$ (note that the budget happens to be balanced: the two components of government spending, purchases of goods and services G and transfers R, sum to 550). Then solving the two equations yields $Y = 2,200$ and $C = 1,520$.[1] If producers set output at 2,200—380 of investment goods, 300 of goods and services purchased by government, and 1,520 of consumer goods—then households receive an income of 2,200, pay 550 in taxes, and receive 250 in transfers, so that disposable income is 1,900, and therefore demand for consumer goods equals .8(1,900) = 1,520— exactly the amount supplied by producers.

Suppose demand for investment goods I falls from 380 to 300. With T independent of Y, solving the two equations yields $Y = 1,800$,[2] so that the fall in I of 80 results in a fall in Y of 400 (a multiplier of [400/80] = 5). This is reported in row 1 of Table 2.1. I falls 80, from 380 to 300; and C falls 320, from 1,520 to 1,200. Households receive an income of 1,800, pay 550 in taxes, and receive 250 in transfers, so that disposable income is 1,500, and therefore demand for consumer goods equals .8(1,500) = 1,200— exactly the amount supplied by producers.

Now suppose that society wants government spending ($G + R$) to be 25 percent of national income, and therefore establishes an income tax with a 25 percent rate, so we have a third equation:

$$T = 0.25Y.$$

Table 2.1

An Automatic Tax Rebate Reduces the Fall in Output
(the initial value of Y is 2,200)

	The value of Y after I falls by 80	The fall in Y after I falls by 80
1 $T = 550$, $R = 250$	$Y = 1,800$	400
2 $T = .25Y$, $R = 250$	$Y = 2,000$	200
3 $T = .25Y$, $R = 250 + .5(2,200 - Y)$	$Y = 2,100$	100
4 $T = .25Y$, $R = 250 + 1.5(2,200 - Y)$	$Y = 2,150$	50

If I is at its original value of 380, solving the three equations yields $Y = 2,200$,[3] just as before; T is 25 percent of 2,200 which equals 550. But now suppose I falls from 380 to 300. With $T = 0.25Y$, solving the three equations yields $Y = 2,000$,[4] so with this income tax, Y falls only 200 instead of 400; the multiplier is only 2.5 (200/80) instead of 5 (400/80). This is reported in row 2 of Table 2.1. Hence, the income tax is a built-in stabilizer. But notice that its stabilizing effect is an unintended by-product of its main objective: the desire of citizens to have government spending equal to 25 percent of national output. If the citizenry had wanted 15 percent instead of 25 percent, the stabilizing effect would have been weaker; if 35 percent, stronger. Thus, the strength of the stabilizer is an unintended by-product of its main objective.

By contrast, the sole objective of the automatic tax rebate is to stabilize the macroeconomy. It takes as given the other objectives of society such as a target ratio of government spending to GDP (for example, 15 percent, 25 percent, or 35 percent). The automatic "tax rebate" can take the form of the automatic triggering of an additional tax cut or an additional cash transfer. For convenience, I illustrate this here with an additional transfer.

As before, the regular ("base") transfer R_b is set at 250. But now an additional, special countercyclical transfer R_c is triggered if output Y is less than target output, 2,200:

$$R_c = a(2,200 - Y),$$

where the policy parameter a, which would be set by Congress, is positive. Hence, the combined transfer R, where $R = R_b + R_c$ is now governed by this equation:

$$R = 250 + a(2,200 - Y),$$

The key point is that Congress can set the policy parameter a with the sole purpose of trying to achieve, on average, the best stabilization result.

The choice of a numerical value for a is independent of choosing the normal ratio of government spending to national income (whether 15 percent, 25 percent, or 35 percent), or the degree of progressivity of the tax system, or the level of unemployment benefits.

For our initial example, suppose Congress sets $a = 0.5$ so $R = 250 + .5(2,200 - Y)$. Our system becomes:

$$Y = C + I + G$$
$$C = .8(Y - T + R),$$
$$T = .25Y$$
$$R = 250 + .5(2,200 - Y).$$

For the initial value of I equal to 380 (and G fixed at 300), once again $Y = 2,200$ is the equilibrium,[5] because if $Y = 2,200$, our automatic transfer is 0. Note that, coincidentally, the budget is balanced: $T = R + G = 550$. But now suppose I falls to 300. Solving the system now yields $Y = 2,100$.[6] Thus, the fall in Y has been cut from 200 (with the built-in stabilizer due to the 25 percent income tax), to 100 due to our automatic transfer with $a = 0.5$. This is reported in row 3 of Table 2.1. If Congress desires a still stronger response, it might set $a = 1.5$. In this case, with I at its initial value of 380, equilibrium Y would again be 2,200,[7] because if $Y = 2,200$ our automatic transfer is zero. But now suppose I falls to 300. Solving the system now yields $Y = 2,150$.[8] Thus, the fall in Y would be only 50. This is reported in row 4 of Table 2.1.

It must be emphasized that Congress would be free at any time to override its automatic tax rebate. The automatic transfer is a default position: it occurs only if Congress fails to enact a discretionary change. Thus, the question is simply: What should happen if Congress fails to take discretionary action? Currently, tax rates stay fixed and there are no rebates. Under the proposed automatic fiscal policy, tax rates and/or rebates would adjust automatically according to the output gap (scaled for the inflation gap). The exact adjustment would be preenacted by Congress. Thus, under this proposal, Congress does not delegate any authority over fiscal policy, and fully retains the ability to adjust fiscal policy through discretionary action. Moreover, it is Congress that approves in advance all aspects of the automatic adjustment of tax rates or transfers. The automatic adjustment is a default position in the event Congress does not take discretionary action.

Seidman and Lewis's Rebate Simulation Using the Fair Econometric Model

Kenneth Lewis and I (2002) use the 2001 version of Ray Fair's macroeconometric model, described in his book (Fair 1994), to simulate this automatic fiscal policy (Seidman and Lewis 2002). The Fair model is a mainstream traditional Keynesian model continuously updated, refined, and reestimated using quarterly data for the U.S. economy through 2001. In the introduction to his book describing his model, Fair gives a careful discussion of the relationship of his model to the classical counterrevolution and the Lucas critique (I discuss the Lucas critique in more detail in chapter 11):

> From Tinbergen's model building in the late 1930s through the 1960s, there was considerable interest in the construction of structural macroeconomic models. The dominant methodology of this period was what I will call the "Cowles Commission" approach. Structural econometric models were specified, estimated, and then analyzed and tested in various ways. One of the major macroeconometric efforts of the 1960s, building on the earlier work of Klein and Klein and Goldberger, was the Brookings model. . . . Two important events in the 1970s contributed to the decline in popularity. The first was the commercialization of macroeconometric models. . . . The second event was Lucas's critique, which argued that the models are not likely to be useful for policy purposes. . . . (Fair 1994, 1)

Later Fair comments on the Lucas critique:

> The logic of the Lucas critique is certainly correct, but the key question for empirical work is the quantitative importance of this critique. Even the best econometric model is only an approximation of how the economy works. Another potential source of coefficient change is the use of aggregate data. As the age and income distributions of the populations change, the coefficients in aggregate equations are likely to change, and this is a source of error in the estimated equations. This problem may be quantitatively much more important than the problem raised by Lucas. Put another way, the representative agent model that is used so much in macroeconomics has serious problems of its own, and these problems may swamp the problem of coefficients changing when policy rules change. . . . (Fair 1994, 13)

Fair concludes his introduction this way:

What follows is an application of the Cowles Commission approach. A structural macroeconomic model is specified, estimated, tested, and analyzed. (Fair 1994, 16)

Our policy aims solely at countering recession—stimulating demand when the economy is in recession, as a complement to monetary stimulus. The policy is asymmetric: it does not attempt to restrain demand when demand is excessive. That task is left to monetary policy.

The policy provides an automatic transfer whenever real GDP is at least X percent below "normal" real GDP (the threshold X percent is either zero or positive), and the amount of the transfer varies with the magnitude of this excess-GDP gap. Normal real GDP is the real GDP that would have occurred if the unemployment rate had been normal. The formula for automatically triggering the transfer (rebate) was given above in equation (2.1), and the scaling down of the transfer if inflation is above target was given above in equation (2.2).

As I will describe in chapter 9, Phillips (1954), Pack (1968), and Duggal (1975) investigated a more complex automatic fiscal policy with three components: proportional, derivative, and integral. Lewis and I did some preliminary testing with derivative and integral components, but found that the proportional component alone is satisfactory, simpler, and more transparent. Hence, we use only the proportional component in our automatic fiscal policy.

We test our automatic fiscal policy in the Fair U.S. quarterly model, estimated from 1952.1 through 2001.1. The model consists of 30 stochastic equations econometrically estimated by two-stage least squares, 101 identities, 131 endogenous variables, slightly over 100 exogenous variables, and many lagged endogenous variables. The model has six sectors: household, firm, financial, federal government, state and local government, and foreign. For monetary policy, the Fair model estimates an interest rate reaction function based on the historical behavior of the Federal Reserve. The estimated equation implies that the Fed generally engages in countercyclical monetary policy, lowering the interest rate (specifically, the three-month treasury bill rate, RS) in response to a rise in the unemployment rate (UR), and raising the interest rate in response to a rise in the inflation rate.

For our study of a countercyclical fiscal policy, implemented through automatic transfers to households, the key equations are the four household expenditure equations explaining consumption of services, nondurables, durables, and investment in residential housing. In all four, disposable income is a right-hand variable. Transfers enter the consumption equations through disposable income. Our policy introduces a new endogenous transfer from the federal government to households.

Under the tax act of 2001, a transfer of about $40 billion was paid by government to households in one quarter (July–September), 2001.3. Hence, at an annual rate, the transfer in that quarter was $160 billion. We therefore use a transfer of $160 billion and an initial quarter of 2001.3 in our multiplier simulations. The first quarter of our multiplier simulations is 2001.3. We do four multiplier experiments using the version of the Fair model estimated through 2001.2. In each experiment we raise nominal exogenous transfers (government to household), $TRGH_b$. The four experiments are:

1. Raise $TRGH_b$ by 160 for 1 quarter (2001.3), and then return it in the following quarter to its base value.
2. Raise $TRGH_b$ by 160 for 2 quarters (2001.3 and 2001.4), and then return it in the following quarter to its base value.
3. Raise $TRGH_b$ by 160 for 3 quarters (2001.3, 2001.4, and 2002.1), and then return it in the following quarter to its base value.
4. Raise $TRGH_b$ by 160 for 8 quarters (2001.3 through 2003.2).

The results are as follows: a transfer of $160 billion raises nominal GDP $36 billion above its base value in the first quarter, so the increase in nominal GDP is 23 percent of the transfer. If the transfer of $160 billion is sustained for two quarters, then nominal GDP is $81 billion above its base value in the second quarter, so the increase in nominal GDP is 51 percent of the transfer. If the transfer of $160 billion is sustained for three quarters, then nominal GDP is $123 billion above its base value in the third quarter, so the increase in nominal GDP is 77 percent of the transfer. If the transfer of $160 billion is sustained through eight quarters, then nominal GDP is $207 billion above its base value in the eighth quarter, so the increase in nominal GDP is 129 percent of the transfer.

A transfer of $160 billion is 1.55 percent of the base value of nominal GDP ($10,335) and 19.2 percent of the base value of transfers ($832 billion) in the first quarter of the simulation (2001.3). That transfer raises nominal GDP 0.35 percent above its base value in the first quarter. If that transfer is sustained for two quarters, then nominal GDP is 0.78 percent above its base value in the second quarter. If that transfer is sustained for three quarters, then nominal GDP is 1.17 percent above its base value in the third quarter. If that transfer is sustained through eight quarters, then nominal GDP is 1.86 percent above its base value in the eighth quarter.

The Fair model assumes that consumption reacts with a particular magnitude to a change in disposable income regardless of the source of the change in disposable income. The consumption equations econometrically estimate the coefficient of disposable income, and no attempt is made to estimate one coefficient for gross labor earnings, another for taxes, and another for transfers. How realistic is this assumption? Distinguish two situations. Under the first, gross labor earnings are growing normally, but a transfer jumps disposable income abruptly above its normal growth path. Under the second, gross labor earnings decline due to recession, but the transfer reduces the decline in disposable income, thereby keeping the growth path of disposable income closer to normal. In the first case, the transfer bumps disposable income above its normal growth path; here it seems plausible that consumers might raise consumption less than if gross labor earnings had risen. But in the second case, the transfer helps keep disposable income nearer to its normal growth path; here it seems plausible that consumers might continue normal spending in response to the transfer. The objective of our countercyclical transfer is to keep disposable income growing at its normal trend rate despite the recession. It therefore seems plausible that the Fair model might provide an accurate estimate of the impact on consumption of our countercyclical transfer that attempts to keep disposable income on its normal growth path.

We generate a severe recession beginning in 1986.1, a convenient period of relative macroeconomic tranquility with available historical data. The constant term is reduced by a fixed amount for eight quarters (1986.1–1987.4) in each of the following five behavioral equations: consumer expenditure for services, consumer expenditure for nondurables, consumer expenditure for durables, residential investment, and business capital stock (which thereby reduces nonresidential fixed investment). Following Fair's (2000a) analysis of a fall in the stock market, we reduce the constant term in the behavior equation for the capital gain (loss) on corporate stock in the first quarter (1986.1).

These changes generate a severe recession. We focus on three variables: the unemployment rate, the interest rate (the three-month treasury bill rate), and the deficit ratio (the ratio of the deficit, deflated by the the GDP deflator, to natural real GDP) beginning in 1986.1 under several alternative policy responses.

How severe would the recession be if there were no response from either monetary or fiscal policy? By this we mean that the Fed keeps the interest rate at its historical value in each quarter (instead of cutting the interest rate below its historical path as it usually would in response to a recession), and there is no fiscal policy other than the current automatic stabilizers due to the current tax and transfer system. We call this the shock simulation. The shock unemployment rate path is well above its historical path. The shock interest rate path coincides with the historical path because of our assumption of no monetary policy response. The shock deficit ratio path is above the historical path because the recession automatically reduces tax revenue.

Now suppose instead that the Fed responds as it usually does historically to changes in the unemployment rate and inflation rate. Recall that the
Fair model contains an econometrically estimated interest rate rule equation for the historical period indicating how monetary policy usually responds to these changes. It should be noted that the Fed's response to a
severe recession might differ somewhat from an equation estimated on data
with smaller changes in the unemployment rate. The simulation generated
by adherence to this interest rate rule equation we call the monetary policy
simulation (M). The M unemployment rate path is below the shock path but
still well above the historical path. The M interest rate path is well below
the shock path (which is the same as the historical path)—indeed, the interest rate hits the floor of zero for several quarters. The M deficit ratio path is
below the shock path because the recession is not as deep and the fall in tax
revenue is not as great; but the M deficit ratio path is still well above the
historical path.

What would happen if an automatic fiscal policy were in effect when the
recession occurs?

> We consider three automatic fiscal policies that respond to the level of
> the real GDP gap in the previous quarter. The first (F1) is both the most
> cautious and the least powerful policy; the third (F3) is both the least
> cautious and the most powerful. Under automatic fiscal policy 1 (F1), a
> transfer is triggered only when the percentage GDP gap exceeds 2.0%—
> hence, the policy is cautious—and the power coefficient a is only 0.5.
> Under fiscal policy 3 (F3), a transfer is triggered as soon as the GDP
> gap exceeds 0%—hence, the policy is not cautious—and the power co-
> efficient a is 1.5 so that the transfer equals one and a half times the GDP
> gap of the previous quarter. . . . We assume that the Fed adheres to its
> interest rate rule. Thus, the simulation generated by the Federal Re-
> serve monetary policy and an automatic fiscal policy we call the mon-
> etary/fiscal policy simulation and label it "M&F." (Seidman and Lewis
> 2002, 273)

We compare two alternative fiscal policies, 1 (the weakest policy) and 3
(the strongest policy), and label the monetary/fiscal policies $M\&F1$ and
$M\&F3$. The $M\&F1$ unemployment rate path is below the M unemployment
rate path (once the fiscal policy is implemented), and the $M\&F3$ path is
lower still. The $M\&F1$ interest rate path is above the M interest rate path,
and the $M\&F3$ interest rate path is higher still: although the Fed adheres to
the same interest rate *rule* (an equation that varies the interest rate according to the unemployment rate and the inflation rate), the $M\&F$ interest rate

paths are higher than the M interest rate because the automatic fiscal policy mitigates the recession and keeps the unemployment rate lower. The $M\&F1$ deficit ratio path is above the M deficit ratio path, and the $M\&F3$ deficit ratio path is higher still (through the tenth quarter).

It is interesting to focus on the eighth quarter of each simulation, roughly the trough of the recession. Under the shock, the "shortfall" in real GDP would be 12.7 percent—that is, real GDP would be 12.7 percent below its historical value, the unemployment rate (UR) would be 12.9 percent (compared with a historical value of 5.9 percent), and the interest rate (RS) would be at its historical value of 6.0 percent. The deficit ratio is 7.9 percent (compared to its historical value of 3.0 percent), and the debt ratio is 41.4 percent (compared to its historical value of 33.4 percent). It is important to emphasize that without our countercyclical fiscal policy, the recession itself causes deficits each quarter and therefore a significant increase in the debt ratio.

If monetary policy follows its historical estimated rule equation, it would react by cutting RS to 0.0 percent, and as a consequence the shortfall in real GDP would be reduced to 9.3 percent, and UR, to 11.1 percent. With the M policy, the deficit ratio is reduced to 6.5 percent (from 7.9 percent under the shock) for two reasons: the stronger economy is generating more tax revenue, and the lower interest rate is thereby reducing government spending for debt service. But even with monetary policy providing some help, the recession remains deep enough that the debt ratio still rises to 39.7 percent (compared to its historical value of 33.4 percent and to the 41.4 percent it would have reached if there had been no help from monetary policy).

With combined monetary and fiscal policy, the shortfall in GDP and UR would be reduced still further. We consider three alternative fiscal policies (F1, F2, and F3), where F2 is intermediate in strength between F1 and F3; F2 has the same threshold as F1 (2 percent) so it is as "cautious," but it has the same power coefficient a as F3 ($a = 1.5$) so it is as powerful as F3 once the threshold is surpassed. Together with monetary policy, the weakest fiscal policy ($M\&F1$) reduces the GDP shortfall to 6.4 percent (instead of to 9.3 percent with monetary policy alone) and the UR to 9.5 percent (instead of to 11.1 percent), requiring a cut in RS to 1.2 percent (instead of to 0.0 percent), whereas the strongest fiscal policy ($M\&F3$) reduces the GDP shortfall to 3.2 percent and the UR to 7.6 percent, requiring a cut in RS only to 3.9 percent.

However, the stronger the fiscal policy, the greater is the countercyclical transfer ratio R/Y_n—the ratio of the countercyclical real transfer to natural real GDP; the greater is the deficit ratio (D/Y_n); and the greater is the debt ratio (B/Y_n). In the eighth quarter the historical value of D/Y_n is 3.0

percent whereas under the shock D/Y_n would be 7.9 percent, and with monetary policy D/Y_n would be 6.5 percent; and the historical value of B/Y_n is 33.4 percent whereas under the shock B/Y_n would be 41.4 percent, and with monetary policy B/Y_n would be 39.7 percent. Under the weakest combined policy $M\&F1$, R/Y_n would be 2.4 percent, D/Y_n would be 8.5 percent, and B/Y_n would be 42.5 percent, whereas under the strongest combined policy $M\&F3$, R/Y_n would be 4.5 percent, D/Y_n would be 10.0 percent, and B/Y_n would be 46.8 percent. The deficit ratio under $M\&F1$ actually peaks in the fifth quarter (9.8 percent under $M\&F1$, and 13.4 percent under $M\&F3$).

Thus, strengthening the fiscal policy reduces the severity of the recession and reduces the required cut in the interest rate, but raises the deficit ratio and the debt ratio. For example, in the eighth quarter, relative to the shock path, $M\&F3$ reduces the unemployment rate 5.3 percentage points (from 12.9% to 7.6%), while raising the deficit ratio 2.1 percentage points (from 7.9% to 10.0%) and raising the debt ratio 5.4 percentage points (from 41.4% to 46.8%). This relatively small rise in the debt ratio is reassuring. By contrast, over the decade-long Japanese recession, the debt ratio rose from below 90% to well over 100%; much of the rise was due to the recession itself, and only part was due to discretionary fiscal stimulus. (Seidman and Lewis 2002, 275)

We also simulate the automatic fiscal policies in response to a false alarm of a severe recession, a supply shock, three U.S. historical recessions, and a severe recession that begins in 2001. In our conclusions, we write:

We generate a severe recession (beginning in 1986) and simulate the impact of our automatic fiscal policy using historical data for several years. We assume that the Federal Reserve adheres to a counter-cyclical monetary policy governed by the interest rate (Taylor) rule estimated on historical data in the Fair model. We find that the interest rate rule alone mitigates the severe recession only modestly, whereas our automatic fiscal policy (together with the interest rate rule) substantially reduces the severity of the recession while generating only a relatively small rise in the government debt/GDP ratio. We simulate a false alarm of a severe recession, and find that our automatic fiscal policy generates very little rise in inflation. In response to a supply shock due a sharp increase in import prices, our automatic fiscal policy moves less aggressively against the recession because of the concern for inflation, but our simulation shows that our policy still mitigates the recession with only a small rise in inflation. Simulating the policy in the 1975, 1982, and 1991 recessions, we find that the strongest version of our policy causes a significant reduction in the unemployment rate in all three recessions (while a weaker policy that is not activated unless the GDP gap exceeds 2% causes a somewhat smaller reduction in the unemployment rate in the 1975 and 1982 recessions, and is not activated in the milder 1991 recession). . . . We simulate a severe recession beginning in 2001 using a forecast for the next few years. Our automatic policy makes a substantial improvement in mitigating the recession while causing only a small increase in the government debt/GDP ratio. It should be noted that if the actual 2001 recession had turned into as deep a recession as the one we simulated, our policy would have generated much larger counter-cyclical transfer ratios than the income tax rebate recently enacted by Congress and implemented in 2001.3. (Seidman and Lewis 2002, 281)

Fair's "Fiscal Policy Rule for Stabilization"

Fair uses his model to simulate an automatic fiscal policy that utilizes the indirect business tax (IBT) rather than cash transfers:

The main idea of this paper is to propose a fiscal policy rule that would help monetary policy in its stabilization effort. A tax rate rule is proposed, where a particular tax rate or set of rates would be automatically adjusted each quarter as a function of the state of the economy. Congress would vote on the parameters of the tax rate rule as it was voting on the general budget plan, and the tax rate or set of rates would then become another automatic stabilizer. (Fair 1999, 2)

He selects as his instrument the indirect business tax (IBT), writing:

Consider, for example, the federal gasoline tax rate. If the short-run demand for gasoline is fairly price inelastic, a change in the after-tax price at the pump will have only a small effect on the number of gallons purchased. In this case a change in the gasoline tax rate is like a change in after-tax income. Another possibility would be a national sales tax if such a tax existed. If the sales tax were broad enough, a change in the sales tax rate would also be like a change in after-tax income. For the experiments below a constructed federal IBT rate based on data from the national income and product accounts is used for the tax rate rule. In practice a specific tax rate or rates, such as the gasoline tax rate, would have to be used, and this would be decided by the political process. (Fair 1999, 3)

Fair makes no attempt to capture the incentive effect on consumers to shift consumption to the recession period when the tax rate is temporarily low. His model incorporates only the income effect—the impact on after-tax income and hence consumption—resulting from changes in the IBT rate. Therefore, his study is reported here, not in chapter 3, because his IBT rate is simply another way of altering household disposable income, like the tax rebate.

Fair varies the IBT rate automatically with both the output gap and the inflation gap. He tests his automatic fiscal policy using stochastic simulation:

> Each trial for the stochastic simulation is a dynamic deterministic simulation for 1989:1–1994:4 using a particular draw of the error terms. . . . By using the estimated error terms for the draws, the trials are consistent with the historical experience: the estimated error terms are data determined. (Fair 1999, 11)

He draws this conclusion from his simulations:

> The proposed tax rate rule does help in stabilizing the economy, especially output. (Fair 1999, 21)

Notes

1. $Y = [.8(Y - 550 + 250)] + 380 + 300, Y = .8Y - 440 + 200 + 680, .2Y = 440$, so $Y = 2,200$.

2. $Y = [.8(Y - 550 + 250)] + 300 + 300, Y = .8Y - 440 + 200 + 600, .2Y = 360$, so $Y = 1,800$.

3. $Y = [.8(Y - .25Y + 250)] + 380 + 300, Y = .6Y + 200 + 680, .4Y = 880, Y = 2,200$.

4. $Y = [.8(Y - .25Y + 250)] + 300 + 300, Y = .6Y + 200 + 600, .4Y = 800, Y = 2,000$.

5. $Y = [.8(Y - .25Y + 250 + .5[2,200 - Y])] + 380 + 300, Y = .8(.25Y + 1,350) + 680, Y = .2Y + 1080 + 680, .8Y = 1,760, Y = 2,200$.

6. $Y = [.8(Y - .25Y + 250 + .5[2,200 - Y])] + 300 + 300, Y = .8(.25Y + 1,350) + 600, Y = .2Y + 1080 + 600, .8Y = 1,680, Y = 2,100$.

7. $Y = [.8(Y - .25Y + 250 + 1.5[2,200 - Y])] + 380 + 300, Y = .8(-.75Y + 3,550) + 680, Y = -.6Y + 2,840 + 680, 1.6Y = 3,520, Y = 2,200$.

8. $Y = [.8(Y - .25Y + 250 + 1.5[2,200 - Y])] + 300 + 300, Y = .8(-.75Y + 3,550) + 600, Y = -.6Y + 2,840 + 600, 1.6Y = 3,440, Y = 2,150$.

3

An Automatic Temporary
Consumption Tax Cut

Two recent articles by Martin Feldstein (2001) and Alan Blinder (2001) advocate a new approach to combating recession: a temporary cut in a consumption tax. Although they are not the first economists to recommend this approach, I will nevertheless begin with their articles.

Feldstein's Prescription for Japan's Recession

Martin Feldstein is skeptical, as I am, of the power of monetary policy alone to rescue Japan. But he is also skeptical, as I am not, of the power of traditional fiscal policy—income tax cuts, transfers, or government purchases, to combat a recession. Instead, Feldstein prescribes fiscal *incentives* to stimulate investment and consumption spending in "Japan Needs to Stimulate Spending," a *Wall Street Journal* editorial page article on July 16, 2001. Feldstein begins his article by explaining his skepticism of relying on monetary policy:

> Monetary policy is now the sole focus of Japanese attempts to breathe life into the economy. The short-term benchmark interest rate has been driven down to zero and the interest rate on long-term bonds is under 1.5%. The Ministry of Finance continues to urge the Bank of Japan to ease monetary policy even further. But additional reductions in interest rates are unlikely to stimulate borrowing and spending by firms that worry about surviving the economic and banking reforms, and by households that worry about unemployment and about the loss of government retirement benefits. (Feldstein 2001)

But what about Krugman's proposal for Japan, discussed in chapter 1, for setting an inflation target of 4 percent for a decade and a half, and then rapidly expanding the money supply through open market operations (central bank purchasing of government bonds) in an attempt to generate 4 percent inflation? In the past, Feldstein has advocated has zero inflation for the United States because he believes the interaction of inflation with the U.S. income tax system generates significant distortions and costs, so it is not surprising that he is reluctant to recommend a positive inflation target for Japan. But he is also skeptical about the feasibility of Krugman's prescription:

> Because prices are now falling in Japan, with the consumer price index down 1% from a year ago, consumers who wait to buy are rewarded with lower prices. The Bank of Japan is nevertheless wise to reject pressure to adopt a formal target of some positive inflation rate in order to encourage consumer spending, since there is nothing that the bank could plausibly do to bring about a significant rise in prices. (Feldstein 2001)

Even if the central bank, through open market purchases, adds reserves to the banking system, Feldstein contends that many banks will simply hold the reserves, rather than lend them out to finance economic activity. Historically, it has often been the case that, in recession, many banks will choose to maintain a relatively high ratio of reserves to deposits.

Some advocates of monetary expansion for Japan assert that it would stimulate the economy by depreciating the yen, thereby making Japan's exports cheaper. Feldstein writes:

> Even if the Bank of Japan could increase the money supply substantially by purchasing a large volume of long-term bonds, the primary effect would be to drive down the international exchange value of the yen. Since Japan already has an annual trade surplus of more than $100 billion, such a deliberate policy of making the yen even more competitive could damage relations with the U.S. and with other Asian countries. (Feldstein 2001)

Having rejected monetary stimulus, one might expect Feldstein to endorse traditional fiscal stimulus. But he doesn't:

> Japan has also pursued a traditional Keynesian fiscal approach to stimulating the economy by large budget deficits. This has succeeded only in creating an enormous government debt and in propping up inefficient local construction companies and their political patrons in Tokyo. The annual deficit of the central government now exceeds 7% of gross domestic product and the national debt is more than 100% of GDP. Servicing that debt and shrinking it relative to GDP is one of the major long-term challenges for the Japanese economy. Prime Minister Koizumi's

> promise to cut government borrowing in the coming fiscal year by about
> 10% is, however, another way in which the long-term reforms will be a
> short-term drag on the economy. (Feldstein 2001)

Feldstein clearly disagrees with Posen's (1998) account of fiscal policy
in Japan during the 1990s (discussed in chapter 1). But whether one agrees
with Posen or Feldstein's assessment of traditional fiscal policy, Feldstein's
recommendation for fiscal incentives to stimulate spending merits attention. He writes:

> What Japan needs to stimulate spending are targeted fiscal incentives.
> For example, a broad, two-year temporary investment tax credit that pays
> 20% of company outlays for equipment and structures between now and
> the middle of 2003 would substantially raise business spending by mak-
> ing such outlays 20% cheaper today than they would be after July 2003.
> A similar tax incentive for individual home-building could have a major
> effect on residential construction and on consumer durable spending.
>   The government could also temporarily suspend the value added tax,
> which is currently 5%, and announce that the tax will return at a 10% rate
> in the middle of 2003. Consumers would have a strong incentive to spend
> now, especially on consumer durables, because of the resulting 10% price
> rise that will occur in 2003. In effect, the Ministry of Finance could achieve
> a temporary 5% annual inflation for the next two years instead of assign-
> ing to the Bank of Japan the impossible task of using monetary policy to
> reverse the current negative inflation rate. (Feldstein 2001)

Just as a one-week sale at a department store encourages consumers to
buy this week, Feldstein's proposal should encourage businesses to spend
before the investment tax credit is terminated, and consumers to spend before the consumption tax cut is terminated. One concern about Feldstein's
proposal is that the government would be committed to a termination date.
Suppose the economy has not recovered by that date? It might be better to
trigger the termination according to some measure of economic recovery.
For example, it could be announced in advance that the fiscal incentives
would be automatically terminated as soon as actual real GDP is no longer
less than normal real GDP.

Currently, the U.S. federal government has neither a personal consumption tax nor a business-based consumption tax—a national retail sales tax
or a VAT. It might therefore seem that a temporary consumption tax cut to
combat recession cannot currently be implemented in the United States.
But this is not so. Alan Blinder explains how it might be feasible.

Blinder's Prescription for the U.S. Recession: A Temporary Cut in Sales Taxes

In an op ed article in the *New York Times*, September 28, 2001 titled "The Economic Stimulus We Need," Alan Blinder writes:

> Let Congress offer to reimburse the tax receipts lost by any state that agrees to cut its sales taxes over the next 12 months (up to some limit). Since almost every state levies a sales tax, this plan should be well received by both Republican and Democratic governors and legislatures throughout the country.
>
> A sales tax cut aims its medicine squarely at boosting consumer spending, which is the highest priority right now. Since most sales taxes are regressive, reducing them would benefit low-income families, many of whom live from paycheck to paycheck. Such people are likely to spend their gains quite promptly. But everyone who purchases taxable items would receive a tax cut.
>
> Since the proposed sales tax cut would be temporary, it would not damage the long-run budget outlook. As Alan Greenspan and many others have observed, fears that the surplus is disappearing have kept long-term interest rates too high for months. A stimulus program must not exacerbate those fears.
>
> The effectiveness of many types of tax cuts—like income tax cuts—is undermined by making them temporary, because most people base their spending decisions on more than this year's income. But the situation is just the reverse for a sales tax cut. The impact of a lower sales tax is actually enhanced by making it explicitly temporary, because doing so creates clear incentives (albeit small ones) to buy now rather than later. . . .
>
> A temporary sales tax cut would be politically attractive, economically effective and administratively simple to boot. The American economy is going to experience a recession, almost certainly. But if we act quickly and decisively, it can be a short one. (Blinder 2001)

Of course, as Blinder would surely agree, a temporary consumption tax cut would be easier to implement if the United States, like Japan and most Western European nations, had a federal value-added tax (or national retail sales tax). Some of the difficulties of implementing a temporary cut in state sales taxes have been noted. In an October 2, 2001 letter to the editor of the *New York Times* responding to Blinder's article, Alice Rivlin, a former director of the Office of Management and Budget, writes:

Alan S. Blinder's proposal for federally financed state sales-tax reduction is ingenious, but impractical. He is right that stimulating consumption, especially by low and moderate-income people, would help our shocked economy get back on track, but the stimulus needs to be quick, fair and uncomplicated. State sales taxes vary widely, and five states do not tax sales at all. A percentage point reduction might stimulate consumption in states with broad coverage, but would be less effective in states with narrow coverage and ineffective in states without a sales tax. Changing state tax laws would also require state legislatures to meet in 50 states. A rebate tied to workers' payroll taxes would be a quicker and fairer way of stimulating consumption.

A lengthier critique of a short (ten-day) sales tax "holiday" is given by Nicholas Johnson and Iris Lav of the Center on Budget and Policy Priorities. They write:

> The National Retail Federation and others have suggested that the federal stimulus package should include a "national sales tax holiday." . . . This would be a period of time, perhaps 10 days, in which states would reduce or eliminate their sales taxes. The federal government would compensate states for the lost revenue. The appeal of such a plan appears to be rooted in the sensible notion that the stimulus package should encourage spending by giving tax breaks to consumers. But on closer examination, a national sales tax holiday is found to have a number of significant problems that would prevent it from being implemented in a timely manner and would sharply limit its effectiveness.
>
> A federally designed sales tax holiday would take a number of months to enact, organize, and implement at the state level. . . . Each state legislature would need to meet to enact the plan for its state, but most are not in session until January or February. . . . Once state legislatures meet and enact the appropriate changes in state sales taxes, state revenue departments would need to write regulations or implementation guidance to adapt the parameters of the holiday to their own sales tax systems, each of which is unique, and would need to educate hundreds of thousands of retailers as well as the general public about the holiday. Retailers would have to be given time to reprogram their machines and train their employees. As explained below, it is not reasonable to expect that all of these steps— from federal enactment to full implementation at the state level—could be accomplished in many places before the spring of 2002. . . .
>
> Moreover, if consumers delay making major purchases to take advantage of the holiday, it could actually worsen the recession. If Congress enacts the sales tax holiday and consumers expect their state to imple-

ment the holiday in February or March of 2002, they could hold off making large-ticket expenditures until that time. . . .

To avoid adding to states' fiscal difficulties by forcing them to borrow
money at the time when many are already facing deficits, the federal
reimbursements would need to be distributed at the same time that the
holiday was occurring, despite the impossibility of knowing how much
the revenue losses will be. The federal reimbursement for such a holiday
would not be distributed in an even and fair manner among the states.
Five states . . . levy no sales tax at all, and so their residents would not
benefit. The other 45 vary widely in both sales tax rate and the base of
goods and services on which it is levied, so the benefits would vary widely
among residents of these states as well.

Better alternatives for using the stimulus package to boost consumer
spending exist. The most obvious ways are a rebate to low-income workers who are more likely to spend the rebate than high-income individuals,
and expansions of unemployment income benefits, which would replace
a portion of lost wages and are likely to be spent. . . . (Johnson and Lav
2001, 1218–1221)

Several of their criticisms apply only to a new proposal that is initially
conceived in the midst of a recession, requires a vote by Congress and a
subsequent voting in state legislatures, and must be implemented by states
and businesses for the first time. Blinder's September 28, 2001 proposal
may or may not have been too late to be successfully implemented in
time to help combat the 2001 recession. But it can certainly be ready for
the next recession. Once Congress enacts it, state legislatures will have
an opportunity to enact legislation specifying an automatic response triggered by the next recession, and to plan for the details of implementation;
in turn, businesses will know in advance that the plan has been enacted at
the federal and state level, and will have time to prepare their own implementation. As with many other programs by which the federal government transfers funds to the states, an equitable formula must be developed
that takes into account the differences in sales taxes among the different
states. For example, the five states without sales taxes could be reim-
bursed for cutting another tax.

Although some proponents have suggested brief holidays lasting just
ten days, note that Blinder, like Feldstein, recommends that the temporary
consumption tax cut last one full year. I would instead recommend that the
beginning and the end of the temporary consumption tax cut, as well as its
magnitude while in effect, be triggered automatically by the real GDP gap,
exactly as it triggers the automatic tax rebate proposed in chapter 2. Thus, it

is worthwhile preenacting a permanent policy—an automatic consumption tax cut—triggered by the real GDP gap. Even if Blinder's proposal cannot be implemented in time for the recession that began in 2001, it is a separate question whether it should be enacted as a permanent automatic fiscal policy that is ready to be triggered in any future recession.

Even if the United States had a national VAT or retail sales tax, one criticism of Johnson and Lav would still remain relevant: Would consumers postpone purchases anticipating the later triggering of the temporary sales tax cut? Note that the same question can be asked of private department stores: Do consumers postpone purchases waiting for special "sales" to be announced? Despite this possibility, most department store managers evidently believe that running special "sales" raises total spending at their stores, even if there is some shift in the timing of consumer purchases.

Note further that the same question can be asked of monetary policy. Do borrowers postpone borrowing, waiting for the Fed to cut interest rates, and even after the initial cuts, do they delay further, waiting for further cuts? Despite this possibility, most economists believe that countercyclical monetary policy is effective in stimulating borrowing and spending in a recession.

Early Advocates of a Temporary Consumption Tax Cut to Combat Recession

An early exposition of the case for a temporary consumption tax cut to combat recession was given by Branson in "The Use of Variable Tax Rates for Stabilization":

> The income-tax surcharge in 1968 did not sufficiently slow the growth of aggregate demand. Whatever the reason, this fact has led to renewed questioning of the usefulness of variable, or flexible, income-tax changes for stabilization purposes. It has also led to a search for, or at least some thinking about, alternative variable taxes that might prove more effective. . . . It is my conclusion that a variable sales tax on some subset of total durable goods, particularly those with longer-than-average product lives, may be the best place to begin a system of flexible taxes for use in achieving stabilization. (Branson 1973, 267)

Branson points out that a sales tax cut, like an income tax cut (or tax rebate), raises the real purchasing power of households; the sales tax cut reduces product prices so that consumers with the same income can buy more, while the income tax cut (or tax rebate) raises disposable income so consumers can buy more at the same prices. Hence, both tax cuts stimulate consumption through this income effect. But in contrast to an income tax cut (or tax rebate), a temporary consumption tax cut also has a price effect; it makes consumption goods cheaper while it lasts, thereby providing consumers an incentive to spend before the cut expires. This is similar to the effect on businesses of a temporary investment tax credit which makes investment goods cheaper while it lasts. He writes:

> *Significance of temporary price changes.* The variable investment tax credit involves the concept of an intertemporal price effect that may be particularly powerful in the case of temporary variations in taxes on expenditures. A temporary, or reversible, tax change can generate price effects over time by changing current prices relative to future prices. For example, imposition of a 10 per cent tax on automobile sales to consumers at the beginning of 1969, with the assurance that the tax would be lifted at the end of 1969, would have created a strong incentive for consumers to postpone auto purchases for a year. In general, these intertemporal price effects can make temporary variations in taxes on postponable expenditures a more powerful stabilization tool than temporary variations in income taxes. (Branson 1973, 271–272)

In their 1977 article analyzing the 1975 tax rebate, Modigliani and Steindel estimated a smaller impact of the rebate on consumer spending than other researchers (I discuss the 1975 rebate in chapter 7). It is not surprising that Modigliani, the originator of the life cycle theory of saving and consumption, is skeptical of the potency of temporary income tax cuts to induce a significant short-run response in consumption. But they made this important point at the end of their study:

> But, more important, the alternative to a *transitory* cut in income taxes is not a *permanent* one, which is simply not comparable since it implies a loss of revenue many times higher. Rather, the alternative is a change in some other tax, and preferably one that is made more, rather than less, effective by its temporary nature. One candidate would be a temporary reduction in sales and excise taxes, which should stimulate consumer spending fairly strongly while it lasted. The bulk of these taxes are paid at the state and local level, but reductions in them could be financed by increases in federal revenue sharing. We do feel that counter-cyclical tax policy is both possible and desirable, but as the life-cycle and permanent-income theories would predict, we find that the experiences of the last decade do not lend much support to the proposition that temporary changes in income tax liabilities or tax rebates are an efficacious method of rapidly changing consumer spending. (Modigliani and Steindel 1977, 201)

In an article advocating the conversion of the personal income tax to a progressive personal consumption (expenditure) tax in order to promote economic growth, efficiency, and fairness, Martin Feldstein notes the advantage of a temporary consumption tax cut for combating recession:

> A consumption tax would also be a more effective instrument of macroeconomic policy than our current income tax. A temporary cut in the consumption tax would stimulate demand in two ways. A fall in tax collections increases disposable income and thus increases consumption. (This is the mechanism by which our current income tax cuts are intended to operate.) In addition, a temporary cut in the rate of consumption tax would lower the net cost of current purchases relative to future purchases. This would tend to speed up the purchase of consumer durables, thus helping the consumption goods industries that are usually hardest hit in a recession and that income tax cuts are least effective in helping. (Feldstein 1976, 16)

The Formula for Automatically Triggering the Cut in the Consumption Tax Rate

This policy is symmetrical to the automatic tax rebate described in chapter 2. The policy provides an automatic cut in a consumption tax rate whenever real GDP is at least X percent below "normal" real GDP (the threshold X percent is either zero or positive), and the amount of the rate cut varies with the magnitude of this excess-GDP gap. The formula for the cut in the consumption tax rate is

$$Dt = g \ [Ygap - X]_{-1} \qquad (3.1)$$

where Dt = the reduction in the consumption tax rate (in percentage points),

$Ygap$ = percent gap of real GDP below normal real GDP,

X = the percent threshold that must be exceeded before the tax rate cut is triggered, and

g = the "power" coefficient.

Note that this quarter's tax rate cut depends on last quarter's $Ygap$ in excess of the threshold X, as indicated by the subscript -1 following $[Ygap - X]_{-1}$.

Congress must preenact the numerical values of X and g. To illustrate, suppose last quarter's $Ygap$ was 4 percent (Y was 4 percent below Y_n). Then for each of the three policies, this quarter's tax rate cut would be:

$$g \quad [Ygap - X]_{-1} = Dt$$

Policy T1: 1.0 [4% – 2%] = 2% (percentage points)
Policy T2: 2.0 [4% – 2%] = 4% (percentage points)
Policy T3: 2.0 [4% – 0%] = 8% (percentage points)

Suppose the normal (initial) consumption tax rate is 10 percent. Then under policy T1, the rate would be cut to 8 percent; under T2, to 6 percent; and under T3, to 2 percent. Note that policies T1 and T2 are "cautious" in that they have a threshold X of 2 percent ; the tax rate cut is triggered only if the $Ygap$ exceeds 2 percent. Also note that policies T2 and T3 are more "powerful" than T1 because g is 2.0 instead of 1.0.

If inflation is above target, however, (as in 1975 or 1982), the tax rate cut would equal only the percentage Z of the Dt given by formula (3.1). The percentage Z would be computed from the following formula:

$$Z = [100\% - \beta(p_{-1} - p^*)], \tag{3.2}$$

where $\beta > 0$.

Suppose last quarter's inflation rate p_{-1} is 7 percent, and Congress sets an inflation target p^* of 2 percent, and sets β equal to 8. Then $\beta(p_{-1} - p^*) = 8(7\% - 2\%) = 40\%$, so the percentage Z equals 60 percent, so the tax rate cut would equal 60 percent of the rate cut given by formula (3.1).

There are as yet no simulation studies of an automatic temporary consumption tax cut that captures the incentive effect on consumers to shift consumption to the recession period when the tax rate is temporarily low. At the end of chapter 2, I briefly described a simulation study by Fair (1999) using the indirect business tax (IBT) as his tax instrument. Fair, however, makes no attempt to estimate the incentive effect. His model incorporates only the income effect—the impact on after-tax income and hence consumption—resulting from changes in the IBT rate. Therefore, his study was reported in chapter 2, because his IBT rate is simply one way of altering household disposable income, like the tax rebate.

A Progressive Value-Added Tax (PVAT)

Implementation of a temporary consumption tax cut would be straightforward if the United States had a value-added tax (VAT). Under a VAT each business firm would be taxed on its sales revenue minus its purchases (including investment goods) from other firms. The subtraction of purchases of investment goods makes the VAT similar to a consumption tax. It is generally assumed that the VAT is reflected in the price of consumption goods. A central obstacle to enacting a VAT, therefore, has been concern about its regressivity.

But a VAT can be made progressive by coupling it with a VAT rebate implemented through the April 15 household income tax return. The VAT rebate must be an integral part of the VAT, enacted simultaneously. The following example shows how a progressive value-added tax (a PVAT) would work. The example uses a 10 percent VAT. To avoid a sudden increase in prices of 10 percent, the 10 percent VAT should be phased in gradually (for example, 2 percent per year for five years). Assume the five-year phase in is over and the VAT is now 10 percent.

Suppose the 10 percent VAT is coupled with the VAT rebate schedule shown in Table 3.1. For example, consider the first row of the table. A household with $20,000 of income plus transfers (including cash welfare and the earned income tax credit) would file its April 15 income tax return and then receive a $2,000 check from the U.S. Treasury (10 percent of its income plus transfers). Thus, a household's VAT rebate would be based on its income plus transfers as reported on its tax return. Note that a household's VAT rebate would not vary with its actual consumption expenditure. Hence, the rebate would not affect the household's incentive to spend versus save.

Assume the typical $20,000 household is estimated to have consumption expenditure of $20,000. Then its estimated VAT gross burden is $2,000 (10 percent of $20,000). Its VAT rebate of $2,000 would leave it with an estimated VAT net burden of $0. Note that a household's VAT rebate is not based on its actual expenditure, which is unknown, but on its income plus transfers. Thus, the table shows actual VAT rebates at each level of income plus transfers, but only *estimated* expenditure and gross and net burdens—the expenditure and burdens borne by a typical household with that particular income plus transfers. Empirical study would be needed to provide the numbers in the expenditure column, and therefore in the gross and net burden columns. Here, without empirical study, expenditure numbers are provided for illustration.

Now consider the second row of the table. A household with $40,000 of income plus transfers would receive a $3,500 check from the U.S. Treasury (8.75 percent of its income plus transfers). Assume the typical $40,000 household is estimated to have consumption expenditure of $39,000. Then its estimated VAT gross burden is $3,900 (10 percent of $39,000). Its VAT rebate of $3,500 would leave it with an estimated VAT net burden of $400, 1 percent of its income plus transfers of $40,000.

The rest of the table shows how the VAT rebate would gradually phase

Table 3.1

Rebates and Burdens Under a Progressive Value-Added Tax (PVAT)

Income plus transfers	VAT rebate	(Percent)	Estimated expenditure	Estimated gross burden	Estimated net burden	(Percent)
20,000	2,000	(10.00)	20,000	2,000	0	(0)
40,000	3,500	(8.75)	39,000	3,900	400	(1)
60,000	4,500	(7.50)	57,000	5,700	1,200	(2)
80,000	5,000	(6.25)	74,000	7,400	2,400	(3)
100,000	5,000	(5.00)	90,000	9,000	4,000	(4)
120,000	4,500	(3.75)	105,000	10,500	6,000	(5)
140,000	3,500	(2.50)	119,000	11,900	8,400	(6)
160,000	2,000	(1.25)	132,000	13,200	11,200	(7)
180,000	0	(0.00)	144,000	14,400	14,400	(8)

down to $0 as household income plus transfers rises to $180,000. The estimated VAT net burden would rise gradually from 0 percent of income plus transfers $(I + R)$ when $I + R$ is $20,000 to 8 percent when $I + R$ is $180,000; hence, over this range, which includes most households, the VAT plus rebate would be progressive. Above $180,000, the estimated VAT net burden (which would now equal the estimated VAT gross burden because there would be no VAT rebate) would continue to increase in dollars but would decline very gradually as a percentage of $I + R$.

A household must file an April 15 tax return to be protected from the VAT. Most low-income working households are already filing tax returns to receive the refundable earned income tax credit (EITC), so there would be little additional compliance or administrative burden for these households (the extra burden would come from reporting transfers received). The VAT rebate would provide an additional incentive for low-income households to file a tax return, thereby enabling the EITC to reach an even greater share of eligible working households. Households with no income receiving government transfer programs could be alerted to the new VAT rebate and assisted with filing a tax return through the administrative apparatus of these transfer programs. Persons who do not file in order to evade income taxes would, of course, receive no protection from the VAT.

An automatic temporary cut in this 10 percent PVAT would have the same countercyclical power to combat a recession as a temporary cut in an ordinary 10 percent VAT, even though the 10 percent PVAT raises less *net* revenue than an ordinary 10 percent VAT because of the VAT rebate. When GDP falls at least X percent below normal, automatically the VAT rate would be cut below 10 percent *while the VAT rebate would remain unchanged.*

Thus, with the PVAT, every household would receive exactly the same incentive to spend during the temporary tax cut as it would with an ordinary VAT because the price cut would be exactly the same. The temporary increase in the federal deficit would be exactly the same with the temporary PVAT cut as it would be with a temporary ordinary VAT cut.

Converting the Household Income Tax to a Household Consumption Tax

An automatic temporary consumption tax cut would also be relatively easy to implement if the United States adopted a fundamental tax reform: converting the income tax to a consumption tax (Seidman 1997). Under a personal consumption tax, each household would be taxed annually on its consumption rather than its income. To compute its consumption, each household would sum its cash inflows (wages and salaries, sale of assets) and subtract its nonconsumption cash outflows (purchase of assets, net increase in savings accounts). The difference would measure its consumption.

With a personal consumption tax, household consumption tax rates would be cut automatically whenever output falls sufficiently below normal, and this would be implemented through a prompt cut in withholding. Household consumption spending during that year would be taxed at rates that are temporarily below normal, thereby providing households an incentive to raise consumption.

Note that if the April 15 household tax were converted from an income tax to a consumption tax, the progressive value-added tax (PVAT) described in the preceding section would still be implemented in the same way: the VAT rebate would still depend on a household's income plus transfers, not its actual expenditure, so that the rebate would continue to have no effect on the household's incentive to spend versus save.

A Consumer Durable Tax Credit

Finally, Lewis and Seidman (2003) point out that a temporary incentive for consumer spending can be delivered by a temporary consumer durable tax credit (CDTC) that is analogous to an investment tax credit. For example, under a temporary 20 percent CDTC, households would claim an income tax credit equal to 20 percent of their expenditure on consumer durables.

4

Fiscal Discipline with NUBAR

(Normal Unemployment
Balanced Budget Rule)

The automatic fiscal policies proposed in chapters 2 and 3 imply that the federal budget will move automatically into deficit in recession. Does this mean that Congress should be generally unconcerned about running deficits, and permit a rising ratio of government debt to GDP? Not at all. These automatic fiscal policies to combat recession are fully compatible with imposing discipline on Congress when the economy is running normally. In fact, such discipline is necessary to enable the government to safely run temporary deficits in a recession.

For a half century, economists have recommended that Congress be pressured to maintain a "full employment" balanced budget, or even a "full employment" surplus—in other words, to set tax rates and spending rates so that, if the economy were at "full employment," the budget would be balanced (or in surplus). Automatic fiscal policies that automatically generate deficits in recession will be more acceptable to the public if Congress runs balanced budgets or surpluses when the economy is at "full employment," thereby maintaining a low ratio of government debt to GDP.

This chapter recommends that Congress enact a statute to implement this strategy that many economists have championed for a half century. There are just two wrinkles offered here. First, I recommend that "full employment" be replaced by "normal unemployment." Second, I recommend that Social Security and Medicare be separated from the rest of the budget: these programs should run annual surpluses to prepare for the retirement of the numerous baby boomers (Seidman 1999, 2000), and the normal unemployment balanced budget rule should apply to the rest of the budget. Hence, the federal budget plus Social Security and Medicare would run a surplus in a normal economy.

I call the recommended statute NUBAR: a normal unemployment balanced budget rule (Seidman 1990, chapter 4; 1998, chapter 5). NUBAR can be stated in one sentence: "Congress shall enact a *planned* budget for the coming fiscal year that technicians *estimate* will be balanced *if next year's unemployment rate is normal (the average of the preceding decade)*." The technicians should probably be the staff of the Congressional Budget Office (CBO) who already perform similar tasks for Congress.

I propose that NUBAR apply to the budget *excluding* Social Security and Medicare. Social Security and Medicare should be moved completely "off budget." Currently, Social Security is supposedly "off budget" but members of Congress, the president, and others often include Social Security when they make statements about the federal budget position. Social Security and Medicare should run annual surpluses to prepare for the retirement of the numerous baby boomers (Seidman 1999, 2000), and should be subject to long-term planning by the trustees and actuaries of the two programs. Thus, my NUBAR calls for the federal budget (excluding Social Security and Medicare) to be balanced. Hence, if these programs run surpluses, the government as a whole will be running a surplus in a normal economy.

Why have a balanced budget rule? I believe it is a good thing to have a properly constructed balanced budget rule for Congress to follow. The reason is straightforward: Legislators need fiscal discipline. They are naturally tempted to propose a cut in taxes, or an increase in spending, because both actions are attractive to voters. But a balanced budget rule brings some discipline. Legislators can only raise spending if they are willing to raise taxes, and can only cut taxes if they are willing to cut spending. The direct way to impose this discipline is to enact a balanced budget statute.

Many citizens believe any government should simply be required to balance its budget every year. According to this popular view, if a deficit begins to emerge, for whatever reason (including a recession), the government should be required to implement a prompt cut in spending or increase in taxes to restore balance. I call this an "always-balanced budget rule." Another name might be, "the no ifs, ands, or buts balanced budget rule," or "the no excuses balanced budget rule."

Most economists agree that this kind of rule would be dangerous. What happens to the economy, already in recession, if Congress is required to cut spending or raise taxes? Suppose Congress cuts government purchases. Then the producers of these goods suffer a fall in orders, and hence, cut production. Their employees earn less income, and in turn, cut their consumer spending. The recession deepens. Or suppose Congress cuts cash transfers. Then the recipients of these transfers have less to spend and producers observe a decline in demand. They cut production. Their employees earn less income, and in turn cut their consumer spending. Once again, the recession deepens. Finally, suppose Congress raises tax rates. Taxpayers have less after-tax income, cut their spending, and the result is the same: an intensification of the recession. Thus, no matter how Congress tries to eliminate the recession-induced deficit, it makes the recession worse. For more than half a century, economics textbooks have emphasized that an always-balanced budget rule is destabilizing: it risks turning a recession into a depression.

NUBAR Would Not Worsen a Recession

NUBAR would avoid turning a recession into a depression because of two key features. First, it applies to this year's *planned* budget for next year, not this year's actual spending and revenue. Second, it is *not* based on a *forecast* of next year's economy. Technicians are instructed to estimate spending and tax revenue on the assumption that next year's unemployment rate will be normal, whether or not they forecast a normal unemployment rate for next year.

If the technicians are accurate in their estimates about what spending and tax revenue will be if next year's unemployment rate is normal, and if next year's unemployment rate turns out to be normal, the budget will be balanced; if next year's unemployment rate turns out to be above normal (national output, income, and tax revenue below normal), the budget will run a deficit; and if next year's unemployment rate turns out to be below normal (national output, income, and tax revenue above normal), the budget will run a surplus. On average, but not in every year, the budget will be balanced. Of course, the technicians will make errors in particular years, but as long as some errors are positive and others are negative, on average the budget will be roughly balanced.

Suppose the economy drops into recession and NUBAR is in effect. Automatically, tax revenue falls and a budget deficit results. Moreover, if the automatic fiscal policies that I recommend in chapters 2 and 3 have been adopted, an even larger budget deficit is triggered by the recession. Under NUBAR, Congress is not required to immediately raise taxes or cut spending in the recession because NUBAR applies to the *planned* budget, not current spending and revenue.

Next, consider the budget that is planned in the middle of a recession for the coming fiscal year. To adhere to NUBAR, Congress must set spending and tax rates so that technicians estimate that the planned budget will be balanced *if and only if* the economy returns to a normal unemployment rate next year.

Suppose someone objects, "This year's recession is likely to drag on into next year so next year's actual budget will run a deficit." A NUBAR advocate should reply, "If next year the economy is still in recession, a budget deficit next year is what we want. If instead we planned a budget that would be balanced next year even if the economy is in recession next year, we would have to plan higher tax rates, and lower spending rates, than NUBAR requires. But these higher tax rates and lower spending rates would reduce total spending in the economy next year, making next year's recession worse. We want NUBAR to generate an actual deficit in recession, and an actual surplus in a boom."

NUBAR: The Full Employment Balanced Budget Rule with Two Wrinkles

NUBAR is not a new proposal. For half a century, economists have recommended that Congress try to balance the planned budget on the assumption that next year there is *full* employment."

There are, however, two minor wrinkles that make NUBAR differ slightly from the "full employment balanced budget rule." First, NUBAR avoids a debate about what is "full employment." Instead, NUBAR uses the normal unemployment rate as its benchmark. The normal unemployment rate is defined as the average of the preceding decade. "Normal" is not necessarily "optimal" or "full." Second, NUBAR will achieve an average budget deficit, over a decade, that is close to zero (not counting the surpluses that should be run in Social Security and Medicare), because it is based on a realistic unemployment rate—the actual average of the preceding decade. A full employment budget rule will achieve an average budget deficit, over a decade, that is much greater than zero if Congress defines "full employment" more ambitiously than normal employment. This last point requires clarification.

If the average unemployment rate over the preceding decade has been 6 percent, then NUBAR will require a planned budget that is estimated to be balanced on the assumption that the economy's unemployment rate will be 6 percent. There is no claim that 6 percent is "optimal" or "full"; it is simply realistic, "normal." A full employment balanced budget rule might require a planned budget that is balanced on the assumption that the economy's unemployment rate will be, say, 5 percent, or even 4 percent. But when the economy's unemployment rate turns out, on average, to be closer to 6 percent, this planned budget will result in a deficit. Thus, in practice, NUBAR will on average balance the budget, while a full employment balanced budget rule will not.

NUBAR is not a straightjacket. If a very severe recession occurs and even our automatic fiscal policies do not provide enough stimulus, NUBAR can and should be suspended so that emergency fiscal policies beyond the automatic fiscal policies can join monetary policy in preventing a depression. In such an economic emergency, Congress should be free to cut taxes and raise spending by more than NUBAR would allow in order to help raise total spending in the economy until a strong recovery is generated.

NUBAR and Countercyclical Fiscal Policy

Taylor (2000), who served on President George H. Bush's council of economic advisers during the 1991 recession, notes that because of the budget deficits and consequent rise in the ratio of government debt to GDP in the 1980s, there was great reluctance to propose fiscal stimulus to combat the 1991 recession. By contrast, in the 2001 recession, because of the shrinking of budget deficits and consequent fall in the ratio of government debt to GDP in the 1990s, Congress and the president were willing to enact a fiscal stimulus (the $600 rebate). Thus, willingness to use countercyclical fiscal policy in a recession depends on keeping the budget balanced, or even in surplus (including Social Security and Medicare) when the economy is normal. Adherence to a NUBAR statute in a normal economy would keep the ratio of government debt to GDP low; in turn, this should increase the willingness of Congress to enact countercyclical fiscal policies that entail temporary deficits during a recession.

5

A Fiscal Policy Advisory Board

This chapter proposes the establishment by Congress of a fiscal policy advisory board. Note the word "advisory." In contrast to the Federal Reserve Board of Governors, which actually controls monetary policy, the fiscal policy advisory board would advise Congress concerning the conduct of countercyclical fiscal policy. Its main functions would be to recommend to Congress the design of automatic fiscal policies to combat recession and the design of emergency fiscal policies in a severe recession. The members of the fiscal policy advisory board would be appointed for long terms (like the members of the Federal Reserve Board), have a small staff of economists, testify before Congress, meet with members of the administration and of the Fed, and prepare reports concerning countercyclical fiscal policy. Unlike the Fed, the fiscal policy advisory board would only advise Congress. Congress would retain full control of all fiscal policies.

My proposed advisory board differs from other proposals that would seek to improve countercyclical policy by removing some control of fiscal policy from Congress. After setting out the functions of my proposed advisory board, I will review two other alternatives to the fiscal policy advisory board just described: (1) Delegating some power over fiscal policy to the president, and (2) transferring some power over fiscal policy from Congress to a new fiscal policy board.

Why a New Advisory Board Focused on Countercyclical Fiscal Policy?

Would a new advisory board be worth establishing? After all, Congress currently gets plenty of advice and analysis. The budget and tax committees of the House and Senate have staffs, conduct hearings, obtain testimony from outside experts. The Congressional Budget Office provides technical studies of tax and spending programs. The Congressional Joint Economic Committee does studies. The president's Council of Economic Advisers produces an annual report that includes a review of fiscal policy. Isn't this enough?

The problem is that there is currently no institution that focuses exclusively and continuously on the design and operation of countercyclical fiscal policy. The House and Senate budget and tax committees are responsible for handling numerous other issues and objectives. They do not have the time or staff to worry about designing fiscal policies to combat recession until recession is upon them. Then legislation to combat the recession inevitably becomes entangled with measures to promote other objectives for taxes and spending, which usually involve partisan and philosophical differences among members of Congress.

Chapters 2 and 3 demonstrate that designing the best possible set of automatic fiscal policies is a challenging task. The specific automatic fiscal policies offered in these chapters may or may not be optimally designed for combating recession. Perhaps other automatic fiscal policies should be added to, or substituted for, some of these policies. For example, perhaps spending for public works projects in each region, or cash transfers to state governments to create public employment jobs, or temporary investment tax credits, should also be triggered. Perhaps they should only be triggered in a very severe recession. One responsibility of the fiscal policy advisory board would be to review all the alternatives.

Even if the policies offered in chapters 2 and 3 are judged optimal, many details need to be worked out—for example, the specific magnitude of the automatic rebate triggered by a particular output gap. Chapter 1 contends that preparation should also be made for emergency fiscal and monetary policies in the face of a severe recession. The assignment of the fiscal policy advisory board would be to work continuously on monitoring the design of automatic fiscal policies and preparing emergency fiscal policies for a severe recession. Initially, the board would formulate a set of automatic fiscal policies and recommend their adoption first by the House and Senate tax and/or budget committees, and then by the entire House and Senate. Thereafter, the board would monitor and reevaluate these policies, and from time to time recommend design alterations to the relevant House and Senate committees.

The establishment of a new fiscal policy advisory board would have several other benefits. The public would learn that monetary policy is not the only tool for countering recession. The public would ask not only what the Fed is doing, but also what the fiscal policy advisory board is recommending to Congress. In a recession, the board would focus on the most effective measures for combating recession, and oppose partisan attempts to use the recession as an excuse for adopting tax or spending policies that are really sought for other reasons, but are poorly designed to combat the recession. Finally, if the current automatic fiscal policies, along with monetary policy, seem unable to overcome a deep or prolonged recession, the board would recommend emergency fiscal policies designed solely to counter the recession rather than promote partisan or other objectives.

Prescribing Fiscal Discipline When the Economy is Normal

The focus of the fiscal policy advisory board would be to design policies to combat recession. But this requires paying attention to the ratio of public debt to GDP when the economy is normal.

As John Taylor (2000) notes, in the United States the large deficits and consequent rise in the debt/GDP ratio during the 1980s made it politically difficult for the government to enact a fiscal stimulus to combat the 1991 recession. The ratio of debt to GDP has figured prominently in the debate over whether and how much the Japanese government can use aggressive fiscal policy, as discussed in chapter 1. Even though, as explained in chapter 1, a money-financed fiscal stimulus would not increase the debt held by the public (excluding the central bank), large deficits per se will inevitably generate widespread concern. Moreover, many will no doubt count treasury debt held by the central bank when they evaluate the size of the debt/GDP ratio, even if such debt is officially excluded from "public debt" as I recommended in chapter 1.

Thus, to create a political climate receptive to aggressive fiscal expansion in an economic emergency, a government should "reload its fiscal cannon" whenever the economy is running normally, balancing its budget and even running surpluses, thereby achieving a low debt/GDP ratio. An advocate of aggressive fiscal policy in a recession, rather than being indifferent to the deficits and debt in a normal economy, should be especially determined to keep the government's fiscal house in order when the economic sun is shining.

Thus, the fiscal policy advisory board should make recommendations for the conduct of fiscal policy when the economy is normal in order to ensure the ability of fiscal policy to act against recession. The board might recommend NUBAR, together with the accumulation of large sums in the Social Security and Medicare trust funds, as described in chapter 4.

Recall from chapter 4 how this would work. Social Security and Medicare would be treated separately from the rest of the federal budget. The two social insurance programs would run surpluses every year and accumulate large funds to prepare for the retirement of the numerous baby boomers (Seidman 1999, 2000). Their financing and benefits would be based on long-term planning and projections prepared by actuaries and trustees. For the rest of the federal budget, the board might recommend that Congress enact a NUBAR—a normal unemployment balanced budget rule.

NUBAR states that Congress shall enact a *planned* budget for the coming fiscal year that technicians *estimate* will be balanced *if* the unemployment rate is normal (the average of the preceding decade). If Congress adheres to NUBAR, and the technicians are accurate, then if the economy has a normal unemployment rate, the budget (excluding Social Security and Medicare) will be balanced, and the surpluses in these two programs will be used to pay down the national debt. If the economy has a boom with a below-normal unemployment rate, the budget (excluding Social Security and Medicare) will run a surplus that can further pay down the national debt. If the economy has a recession and an above-normal unemployment rate, however, the budget (excluding Social Security and Medicare) will be in deficit. Part of the deficit will be due to the automatic stabilizers—the automatic fall in tax revenue and increase in transfers for unemployment insurance benefits; and part will be due to the new automatic fiscal policy. In a severe recession that overwhelms both monetary policy and the automatic fiscal policy, the board should advise Congress to take emergency discretionary action and suspend adherence to NUBAR in order to provide even greater stimulus through even larger transfers, tax cuts, and increases in government purchases.

To ensure the willingness of Congress to enact automatic fiscal policy to combat recession, the board should prescribe fiscal discipline in a normal economy. By running surpluses in Social Security and Medicare, and by adhering to NUBAR for the rest of the budget, fiscal discipline will be maintained, and the ratio of national debt to GDP will be kept low despite deficits that occur during recession due to the recession itself and the triggering of the automatic fiscal policy.

Alternative 1: Delegation of Some Power over Fiscal Policy to the President

One alternative strategy that has been proposed for improving fiscal policy has been to request that Congress delegate some power to the president. After serving as President Johnson's chairman of the Council of Economic Advisers, and experiencing the frustration of trying to get Congress to adopt a tax surcharge to reduce demand and hopefully reduce inflation, Arthur Okun wrote a book drawing on lessons from his experience. He offers this proposal:

Improving Fiscal Procedures

A decade ago, the bipartisan and distinguished Commission on Money and Credit displayed prophetic vision when it recommended that the

Congress delegate to the President discretionary authority to raise and lower tax rates within specified amounts, in specified ways, subject to congressional veto. A similar proposal—limited to tax reduction—was endorsed by President Kennedy in 1962, but not a single congressman was sufficiently impressed to introduce it as a piece of legislation.

President Johnson pointed to a more modest reform in January 1965, suggesting that Congress might amend its own rules to assure that a prompt verdict—up or down—would be forthcoming in response to a presidential request for a change in tax rates for the purposes of economic stabilization. In his valedictory economic report, President Johnson again called for a change in legislative procedures to assure against fiscal stalemate. In addition, he proposed that Congress, in extending the surcharge, should give discretionary authority to his successor to eliminate the surcharge ahead of schedule should military or economic developments make that appropriate. . . .

Congress appropriately treasures its constitutional prerogatives to alter our tax legislation. Given the repeated display of intense opposition to the delegation of authority, I am not optimistic about the near-term prospects for such a reform. But . . . our legislators must face up to the challenge either by improving their record or by delegating authority to the President. (Okun 1970, 118–119)

In the three decades since Okun's appeal for delegation of limited authority to the president, there has been no progress with this approach. This is not surprising. In many years, one political party has controlled the White House while the other has controlled Congress. It has probably become less, rather than more, likely that this strategy will succeed.

Alternative 2: A Fiscal Policy Board with Some Power over Fiscal Policy

A second alternative strategy that has been proposed for improving fiscal policy is transferring some power over fiscal policy from Congress to a new fiscal policy board. In a 1997 article titled, "Is Government Too Political?" Alan Blinder does not focus on countercyclical fiscal policy directly, but more generally argues for transferring some power to independent boards:

It is, of course, neither possible nor desirable to depoliticize government. Policymaking in a democracy must be political—that is, legitimized by popular support rather than by technical analyses. . . . But different arrangements for governance draw the line between political and techno-

cratic decisions in different places, and every society must choose where
that line should fall. . . .

Learning from the Fed. From January 1993 until June 1994, I worked
close to the political epicenter of the United States—on the president's
staff as a member of Council of Economic Advisers. From June 1994
through January 1996, I served as vice chairman of the Board of Governors of the Federal Reserve System, an independent agency created—not
coincidentally—during the Progressive Era, when reformers believed in
making government more "objective" and less "political." The contrast
was stark.

Regardless of who is president, life at the White House is fast-paced,
exhilarating, and—of necessity—highly political. Policy discussions may
begin with the merits ("Which option is best for the American public?"),
but the debate quickly turns to such cosmic questions as whether the chair
of the relevant congressional subcommittee would support the policy,
which interest groups would be for and against it, what the "message"
would be, and how that message would play in Peoria.

At the Federal Reserve, on the other hand, the pace is deliberate, sometimes plodding. Policy discussions are serious, even somber, and disagree-
ments are almost always over the policy's economic, social, or legal merits,
not its political marketability. . . . The Fed does not always make the right
call, but its criteria are clearly apolitical. And its decisions are arguably
better, on average, than those made in the political cauldron.

What accounts for the different styles of decision-making? It is not
that the Federal Reserve has smarter or more morally upright people in
authority. Rather, they labor under starkly different conditions. The White
House and Congress are supposed to be political venues. Where else should
a great democracy hash out its political differences? But the Fed is an
independent agency. Independent of what? Well, mostly of politics. Federal Reserve governors are presidential appointees, subject to Senate con-
firmation, but once they arrive at Fed headquarters they are neither obliged
nor expected to do the bidding of the president or Congress. The Federal
Reserve was designed to stand above the fray, insulated from politics,
making monetary policy on the merits. And it does, to a remarkable degree.

But what justifies assigning so much power to a small group of
unelected officials, nowadays mostly economists? Isn't that undemocratic?
The usual defense of central bank independence is more pragmatic than
philosophical: It works. . . .

As Fed vice chairman and since, I have often offered variants of this
defense of central bank independence. I believe it. But as I made the case,
a nasty little thought kept creeping through my head: the argument for
the Fed's independence applies just as forcefully to many other areas of

government policy. Many policy decisions require complex technical judg-
ments. . . . Yet in such cases, elected politicians make the key decisions.
Why should monetary policy be different?

   At first my inability to offer an intellectually coherent answer to this
question led me to question the justification for central bank independence. . . . But as I thought about the matter more deeply, the question
started to turn itself around. The justification for central bank independence is valid. Perhaps the model should be extended to other arenas.
(Blinder 1997, 116–117)

   In a 1999 "Economics Focus" article, "Fiscal Flexibility: Could Finance
Ministers Learn a Few Tricks from Central Bankers?" in *Economist* magazine, the case is made for consideration of an independent fiscal policy
board with some power over fiscal policy. The article notes that whereas it
is now generally accepted that monetary policy should be set by an independent central bank, fiscal policy still remains in the hands of politicians,
and most people would be disturbed by the idea that tax rates should be
adjusted by unelected individuals. But, contends the *Economist,* that possibility deserves serious consideration:

   It is now widely accepted that monetary policy is best set by an independent central bank, insulated from political pressures. But fiscal policy
   still remains in the hands of politicians. Indeed, most people would regard with horror the notion that tax rates might also be set by a band of
   unelected officials. Yet that is exactly what some economists are now
   calling for.
      For example, Alan Blinder, an economist at Princeton University and
   a former vice-chairman of America's Federal Reserve has argued . . . that
   the institutional framework around monetary policy should be extended
   to fiscal policy. . . . Tax changes also have consequences that stretch far
   into the future. But politicians' time horizons stretch only until the next
   election; all too often they are tempted to cut taxes ahead of an election,
   which can later cause the economy to overheat. Mr. Blinder concludes
   that the tax system would be simpler and more efficient if it were left to
   an independent agency, in the same way as monetary policy.
      This idea has now been adopted by the Business Council of Australia
   . . . as a way to make fiscal policy more flexible, while still maintaining
   discipline. At present fiscal policy is generally seen as less effective than
   monetary policy in steering the economy. This is partly because, in most
   countries, it takes ages to get parliamentary approval for changes in taxes,
   so tax rates cannot be altered as fast as interest rates. As a result, tax cuts
   in response to a slowdown have typically arrived too late. . . .

Some studies suggest that fiscal policy is better suited to steering nominal demand, because once implemented (where the delays currently lie), it affects the economy more swiftly than changes in interest rates. Furthermore, the effects of monetary policy tend to be spread less evenly across the economy than those of fiscal policy. For example, high interest rates and hence a stronger exchange rate squeeze manufacturers more than other producers.

Tuning up

Nobody is now suggesting a return to 1960s-style fiscal fine-tuning. But there would be advantages if fiscal policy could be made more effective. . . . The Business Council of Australia proposes that an independent body should be given the power to make small adjustments to tax rates in response to the state of the Australian economy without the need for parliamentary approval. This would both reduce the lags in fiscal policy and insulate it from political pressure. The government would still determine the size of the welfare state and the structure of the tax system (e.g., it would decide how progressive the income-tax schedule should be). It would also set a broad long-term goal for the budget deficit. The independent fiscal authority would then be given discretion to increase or reduce income-tax rates across the board within a narrow band of, say, a percentage point either side of existing rates. If it is felt the economy was overheating, say, it would raise taxes; if a recession loomed, it would cut them. . . .

The idea of an independent fiscal authority deserves serious consideration. It may seem radical and undemocratic. But that, remember, is what many governments once said of demands to make their central banks independent. (80)

Thus, the *Economist* suggests considering the creation of an independent board that would be given the power to make small adjustments to tax rates in response to the state of the economy without the need for approval by the legislature. Its independence would reduce the lags in fiscal policy and insulate it from political pressure. The government would still set the size and content of expenditures, the structure of the tax system, and long-term goals for the budget deficit. The independent fiscal authority would then be given discretion to increase or reduce income tax rates across the board within a narrow band.

Under this approach, the word "advisory" would be eliminated, and the title would be "fiscal policy board." Here is how the fiscal policy board might work (Seidman 2001). Congress and the president would continue to enact the annual budget. The fiscal policy board would implement periodic adjustments in taxes and government spending *relative* to the budget enacted by Congress. The *content* of the *adjustment package*—its relative components of specific taxes, transfers, and purchases—would be preenacted by Congress. The board would decide the *magnitude* and *timing* of the adjustment package. Its action would take effect without a vote of Congress unless Congress chooses to vote to override the board's decision.

An example will clarify how this would work. Congress would specify that any fiscal stimulus or restraint consist of 50 percent taxes, 20 percent transfers, and 30 percent government purchases. Thus, a package with a $100 billion stimulus would consist of a $50 billion reduction in taxes, $20 billion increase in transfers, and a $30 billion increase in purchases. Congress would then specify in great detail the content of the subcategories of the change in taxes, transfers, and purchases. For example, Congress might specify that the $50 billion reduction in taxes should consist of a $40 billion cut in personal income taxes, a $5 billion cut in corporate income taxes, and a $5 billion cut in excise taxes. Congress would then decide how the $40 billion of personal income tax cuts should be apportioned across income classes.

The fiscal policy board would meet regularly to decide changes in the magnitude of Congress's fiscal policy package of stimulus or restraint. Congress would preapprove the fiscal policy board's recommendation, which would then go into effect immediately without a congressional vote. Congress would, however, retain the power to vote to override any recommended adjustment by the board. It would be essential to institutionalize close communication and coordination between the fiscal policy board, the Federal Reserve board, and the U.S. Treasury.

The automatic fiscal policies proposed in chapters 2 and 3 are triggered by actual data—the GDP gap in the preceding quarter—rather than by a forecast of the GDP gap in the next quarter. If a forecast were sufficiently accurate often enough, automatic fiscal policies based on a forecast might perform better than automatic fiscal policies based on actual data, because the policies would stay ahead of the economy instead of lagging behind. I assumed that Congress would be unwilling to utilize a forecast. If Congress proves willing, however, then the fiscal policy board would seem to be the logical source for the "official" forecast. The board could use its own in-house econometric model, or base its official forecast on those prepared by external forecasters. This would, in effect, require Congress to transfer some power to the fiscal policy board, because its forecast would determine the triggering of funding. As described in chapter 9, Seidman (1975) suggested the use of an official forecast for a particular automatic fiscal policy, at a time when there was greater optimism about the forecasting ability of econometric models. Because there seems to be more skepticism today, in this book I do not ask Congress to enact an automatic fiscal policy that utilizes a forecast rather than actual data.

An "Economics Focus" article, "Remember Fiscal Policy?" in *Economist* magazine cites my *Challenge* article (2001) and restates its support for improving countercyclical fiscal policy:

> In any case, if counter-cyclical fiscal policy is to work, speed is crucial. To that end, Mr. Seidman discusses ways in which counter-cyclical fiscal policy, at least in America, could be made more automatic, either by having Congress pre-approve tax rebates that could be triggered by economic data, or by setting up an independent board (in its relationship to Congress, rather like the Federal Reserve) with powers to make limited changes to tax rates in response to economic circumstances. (The second approach was mulled over, favorably, on this page in 1999.) It all seems very ambitious. Politicians, whose privileges are at stake, will not be keen. But there is no denying that, now and then, arrangement such as this would be nice to have ready.
>
> At least governments should open their minds to the idea that fiscal option needs to be restored. Automatic or independent fiscal-policy adjustment (on top of so-called automatic stabilizers that operate in any case) may be difficult to develop. But once a country has achieved a reasonably sound long-term fiscal position, its government should regard that as an asset to be drawn upon. Surpluses are not an end in themselves. Budget balance on average, together with wide and well-timed fluctuations around the average according to circumstances, is clearly the policy to aim for. (64)

Establishing a fiscal policy board with some power over fiscal policy, rather than a fiscal policy advisory board that leaves full control of fiscal policy to Congress, may well be appealing to many economists (including me) and to many who are cynical about politicians and legislators. Perhaps in the future there might be sufficient political support for such a fiscal policy board. But in my judgment, the most urgent priority for improving countercyclical fiscal policy is to have Congress preenact automatic fiscal policies such as the ones proposed in chapters 2 and 3. A fiscal policy advisory board would focus on recommending specific automatic fiscal policies for Congress to consider enacting without challenging Congress's power over fiscal policy. It would therefore focus attention on the merits of the automatic fiscal policies. By contrast, a proposal today for the kind of fiscal policy board just described would divert attention from the merits of automatic fiscal policies, and congressional debate would inevitably center on whether Congress should relinquish some of its power over fiscal policy. I therefore propose a fiscal policy advisory board that leaves full control of fiscal policy with Congress, not a fiscal policy board that would obtain some actual power over fiscal policy.

Part II

6

Recent Empirical Studies Relevant to Countercyclical Fiscal Policy

This chapter considers recent empirical evidence on the power of counter-cyclical fiscal policy to combat a recession. The power of *temporary* income tax cuts or transfers has long been challenged by the permanent income and life cycle hypotheses of consumption. In the past decade, however, empirical studies have challenged the validity of the extreme versions of the permanent income and life cycle hypotheses. Although permanent or life cycle income remains important, it appears that current disposable income does, after all, also have an important impact on consumer spending. At the same time, empirical studies suggest that although monetary policy does have an important impact on aggregate demand, the magnitude of the impact is probably not strong enough to single handedly offset many cyclical downturns. The evidence suggests that monetary policy needs help. In this chapter, I review these studies.

In his *General Theory of Employment, Interest, and Money* (1936), Keynes suggested that consumption spending responds promptly and fully to changes in current income, and many early "Keynesians" of the 1940s believed that changing household taxes and transfers would produce prompt and large changes in consumption spending. For example, a tax cut or transfer of $100 might produce a prompt increase in consumption spending of $90. This belief led directly to an optimistic view of the ability of fiscal policy—implemented by cutting taxes or increasing transfers—to combat a recession.

But in the 1950s, two hypotheses about consumption behavior implied a pessimistic view about the power of temporary income tax changes to influence consumption. The permanent income hypothesis propounded by Milton Friedman contended that households keep their consumption geared to their "permanent" or normal income, so that temporary changes in income taxes or transfers will have little effect on current consumption. The life cycle hypothesis offered by Franco Modigliani contended that households try to achieve a steady path of consumption over a lifetime of work and retirement, so that consumption at any time is geared to lifetime income rather than current income, and therefore temporary changes in income taxes or transfers have little effect on current consumption. Upon receiving a temporary increase in disposable income, households "should" spread consumption spending smoothly over the remainder of their lives, thereby spending very little of it in the short run.

Thus, the permanent income and life cycle hypotheses caused many economists to be skeptical about the power of temporary changes in income taxes or transfers to significantly alter current consumption. But in the past decade the authors of several empirical studies have concluded that consumption seems to respond promptly and significantly to changes in current disposable income, even when these changes are due to temporary changes in income taxes and transfers. This new empirical work suggests that current as well as permanent or lifetime income affects current consumption, and that the power of fiscal policy, though not as large as early Keynesians assumed, is still large enough to warrant the use of temporary changes in income taxes and transfers to help combat a recession.

In reviewing the empirical work, it is crucial to keep in mind what matters for the effectiveness of countercyclical fiscal policy. The key question is this. Suppose households generally become aware that the government stands ready to give them a temporary income tax cut or transfer should the economy go into recession, and that the boost in disposable income will be renewed as long as the economy remains in recession but once the economy recovers it will be terminated. When the economy actually goes into recession, and the government actually cuts taxes or transfers, how will households respond? Will they spend a large fraction of the additional disposable income over the next few quarters? Or will they spend only a small fraction over the next few quarters? Unfortunately for the science of economics, we economists are unable to subject the actual economy to repeated episodes of exactly these experimental conditions. Instead, we must try to make inferences from the behavior of households under conditions that appear to have some relation to the experiment we are really interested in. Thus, in the studies that follow, economists analyze how consumers respond to changes in disposable income, to a change in income tax withholding, to income tax refunds, and to changes in the amount of payroll tax withheld for Social Security. Note that none of these is the precise experiment we are interested in. Thus, the results are suggestive, but cannot tell us definitively how consumers would react to the countercyclical fiscal policy that is the focus of this book. In chapter 6, I will examine the temporary income tax cut enacted to combat the 1975 recession, and in chapter 7, the $600 tax rebate enacted to combat the 2001 recession.

Romer's Review of Recent Empirical Work on
Consumption Behavior

In his text, *Advanced Macroeconomics*, David Romer presents a chapter that reviews both theory and recent empirical evidence on consumption behavior. He begins by giving an analysis of the permanent income hypothesis:

> This analysis implies that the individual's consumption in a given period is determined not by the income that period, but by income over his or her entire lifetime. . . . One implication is that a temporary tax cut may have little impact on consumption. . . . (Romer 2001, 332)

He then presents Robert Hall's corollary, the random walk hypothesis, which states that the expected value of next period's consumption equals this period's consumption:

$$C_t = C_{t-1} + e_t,$$

where the expected value of e_t is 0:

> This is Hall's famous result that the life-cycle/permanent-income hypothesis implies that consumption follows a random walk. (Romer 2001, 338)

Romer then describes an important study that challenges the empirical validity of Hall's random walk hypothesis:

> Campbell and Mankiw (1989) . . . use an instrumental-variables approach to test Hall's hypothesis against a specific alternative. The alternative they consider is that some fraction of consumers simply spend their current income, and the remainder behave according to Hall's theory. (Romer 2001, 341)

After giving some of the details of Campbell and Mankiw's analysis, Romer writes:

> Thus Campbell and Mankiw's estimates suggest quantitatively large and statistically significant departures from the predictions of the random-walk model: consumption appears to increase by about fifty cents in response to an anticipated 1 dollar increase in income, and the null hypothesis of no effect is strongly rejected. (Romer 2001, 342)

Mankiw's Review of Recent Empirical Work on Consumption Behavior

N. Gregory Mankiw reviews empirical studies on consumption behavior and comments:

> A large empirical literature . . . has addressed the question of how well households intertemporally smooth their consumption. Although this literature does not speak with a single voice, the consensus view is that consumption smoothing is far from perfect. In particular, consumer spending tracks current income far more than it should. (Mankiw 2000a, 120)

Mankiw looks at empirical studies that examine whether households keep their consumption steady ("smooth") despite fluctuations in their current disposable (after-tax) income, or instead adjust their consumption to changes in their disposable income. He says that although some economists think consumers "should" keep their consumption smooth, most of these studies conclude that consumer spending tracks current disposable income far more than "it should." For example, Campbell and Mankiw (1989) estimate that roughly half of income goes to households that consume according to current income, and half to households that consume according to permanent (normal) income. Parker (1999) examines income changes resulting from Social Security taxes and reports that the elasticity of expenditure on nondurable goods with respect to a decline in take-home pay is roughly one-half. Souleles (1999) studies the impact of predictable income tax refunds and concludes that consumption increases by at least 35 percent of a refund within three months. Mankiw says imperfect smoothing occurs because some consumers may not have "rational expectations" and may simply extrapolate their current income into the future because it is the only definite information available (Tversky and Kahneman 1973); and some may face borrowing constraints, as indicated by the finding that some engage in "buffer-stock saving" to prepare for emergencies (Carroll 1997), and by the fact that many households have virtually zero wealth (Wolff 1998). He says that a simple conclusion is inescapable: many households do not have the financial means to smooth consumption, and the prevalence of these low-wealth households explains why consumption tracks current disposable income. The empirical evidence implies that "temporary tax changes have large effects on the demand for goods and services" because an important share of the population are "spenders who live paycheck-to-paycheck." Mankiw concludes:

> Reflecting on these facts, one cannot help but be drawn to a simple conclusion: many households do not have the financial wherewithal to do the

intertemporal consumption-smoothing assumed by much modern macroeconomic theory.... Acknowledging the prevalence of these low-wealth households helps explain why consumption tracks current income as strongly as it does. (Mankiw 2000a, 121)

Shapiro and Slemrod's Study of the 1992 Reduction in Withholding

Matthew Shapiro and Joel Slemrod (1995) provide surprising evidence that even a temporary cut in income tax withholding that must be made up the following April 15 with a higher tax payment may significantly affect consumption during the period when withholding is cut. Note that this degree of responsiveness to disposable income is not necessary for the automatic tax rebate proposed in chapter 2 to work. That rebate is not made up the following April 15, or any time in the foreseeable future. Thus, even if consumers did not respond to the 1992 cut in withholding examined by Shapiro and Slemrod, they might well respond to the automatic tax rebate. However, if they even respond to the 1992 withholding change, this indicates that they are remarkably responsive to current disposable income, and will therefore almost surely respond to the automatic tax rebate.

Shapiro and Slemrod describe the 1992 withholding "experiment." In his State of the Union Address on January 28, 1992, with the economy recovering very slowly from recession and an election looming in November, President Bush indicated that he would issue an executive order reducing withholding rates for income taxes. The president's executive order directed employers to reduce income taxes withheld in paychecks issued after February 28, 1992. Bush argued in his State of the Union Address that the withholding cut would provide "money that people can use to help pay for clothing, college, or to get a new car." However, the executive order did not change the tax each household owed for 1992 so that each household would have to pay more to the IRS on April 15, 1993 to make up for the reduced withholding. "Rational" households should save the extra take-home pay to make the extra tax payment on April 15, 1993, contrary to the hope of President Bush. Thus, this withholding cut is an example of a *very* temporary tax change.

Shapiro and Slemrod report the results of a survey of consumers' stated intentions. They surveyed a sample of individuals one to two months after their withholding changed, asking them whether they would spend or save the extra take-home pay. They added several questions to the April 1992 *Survey of Consumers* conducted by the Survey Research Center (SRC) of the University of Michigan, a monthly telephone survey of about 500 people.

After asking several questions about what the household usually does with a tax refund, they ask their key question:

> The federal government *has* recently changed the amount of income tax that is being withheld from paychecks. On average, the change in withholding should *increase* your take-home pay by about $25 per month, or by a total of about $250 for all of 1992. It also means that next year your tax refund will be about $250 less than otherwise, or you will have to pay about $250 more in taxes next year than otherwise. How do you think you will use the extra $25 per month—do you think you will *spend most* of it, *save most* of it, use *most* of it to *repay debts*, or what? (What do you think you will do with *most* of the extra money?) (Shapiro and Slemrod 1995, 282)

According to Robert Barro's "Ricardian equivalence" hypothesis (1974), almost everyone should answer: "I will save it all so I can use it to pay the additional tax next April 15th." Yet Shapiro and Slemrod report that nearly half of the respondents said they intended to spend most of it. Barro's hypothesis fails empirically even for a tax cut that must be made up in less than a year. This survey data provides a direct refutation of Barro's hypothesis. To my knowledge, neither Barro nor anyone else who endorses his hypothesis has provided any empirical evidence whatsoever that people actually think the way he believes they should. It is possible that some respondents may have been aware that President Bush hoped that they would spend it, and that this influenced their answer. It seems implausible, however, that many actually thought, "I'll say I'm going to spend it because the president wants me to spend it, but I'll really save it to pay tax."

Slemrod and Shapiro draw this conclusion:

> When President Bush announced in his 1992 State of the Union Address that he would reduce the amount of tax withheld from paychecks, few economists expected that it would provide much stimulus to the economy. Their reasoning was that few taxpayers would interpret the change in withholding as an increase in lifetime resources; the increased after-tax income in 1992 would be offset by a decreased net tax transaction with the government in the spring of 1993. Consumption would be increased only by those who were liquidity-constrained in 1992 and expected to be unconstrained in 1993.
>
> The results of this paper shed doubt on both presumptions. Forty-three percent of those who responded to a telephone survey said they would spend most of the extra take-home pay. Such a high percentage suggests

that the program would be moderately effective in stimulating aggregate consumption. . . . We could uncover no relationship between indicators of liquidity constraint and the tendency to spend the extra income. . . . Hence, our results do not support the theory that liquidity constraints explain a high marginal propensity to consume out of transitory income. Yet our findings do support the notion that a substantial fraction of consumers simply spend their current paychecks. (Shapiro and Slemrod 1995, 281)

Souleles's Tax Refund Study

Nicholas Souleles uses micro data from the U.S. Bureau of Labor Statistics' Consumer Expenditure (CEX) Surveys from 1980 to 1991 to estimate the response of household consumption to income tax refunds. Before describing his study in detail, one crucial point should be made at the outset: his study significantly underestimates the one-year or even half-year impact of refunds on consumption spending because it does not look beyond one quarter.

> This paper examines the response of household consumption to a particular type of income that is both predictable and transitory—income tax refunds. Since a refund depends on events in the previous calender year, it is predictable income as regards consumption in the year of its receipt. Consequently, under the life-cycle theory consumption should not increase on receipt of a refund. In addition to testing the canonical model of consumption, this paper provides estimates interpretable as the marginal propensity to consume (MPC) out of refunds. Since federal tax refunds now amount to over $80 billion per year (averaging well over $1,000 per refund), these estimates are of interest in themselves. More generally they bear on the impact of even preannounced and temporary changes in fiscal policy. (Souleles 1999, 947)

Note that Souleles calls an income tax refund "predictable." But I doubt that the typical household actually "predicts" the amount of its refund in advance, and this makes Souleles's study all the more relevant to our countercyclical fiscal policy. Until its tax return is filled out (sometime between January 1 and April 15), a typical household doesn't have any idea about the amount of its refund (or even whether it will receive one at all), and therefore won't be able to adjust its consumption in advance. For most households, the filling out of the tax return generates a "surprise": discovery that the household must write a check for $X, or instead, that it will soon receive a refund of $Y. Since the amount of the refund is a surprise to the typical household upon completion of its tax return, it is therefore similar to our temporary tax cut or transfer triggered by a recession. If the household is to receive a refund of $Y, it now has two choices: raise spending promptly by a significant fraction of the refund, or raise spending very little. Souleles's study sheds light on what households actually do upon filing for a refund.

He runs a regression in which the left-hand dependent variable is the change in household i's real consumption (in levels) between quarter I (January through March) and quarter II (April through June) of year y, $[C^{II}_{iy} - C^{I}_{iy}]$. On the right-hand side are a set of demographic variables (the age of the household head and changes in the number of adults and in the number of children) that "help control for the most basic changes in household preferences," year dummies to "help control for aggregate shocks and interest rates across time," and finally, the household's income tax refund (usually received in March, April, or May). The regression estimates the impact of a household's tax refund on the household's consumption.

Souleles says that according to the IRS, about three-fourths of the 100 million or so tax filers each year receive refund checks. He then provides a fact that will be crucial to his study: In each year about 80 percent of refunds were mailed out in the three months of March, April, and May. He presents a table indicating that between 1980 and 1991, his sample period, 25 percent of the total annual refund expenditure of the U.S. Treasury was paid in March, 27 percent in April, and 27 percent in May. Based on this fact, Souleles assumes that the typical refund is received at the end of the first quarter (March) and the first two-thirds of the second quarter (April and May), and seeks to test the hypothesis that receipt of a refund causes a household to raise its second quarter consumption above its first quarter consumption.

The data are drawn from the CEX surveys for 1980 to 1991. In the CEX survey households are interviewed four times, three months apart (though starting in different months for different households). In each interview the reference period for expenditure covers the three months before the interview. Note that each household is reporting its quarterly consumption for the preceding *three* months. Thus, the expenditure data enables Souleles to calculate how much a household raises its consumption from the first quarter of a year to the second quarter.

He points out that the CEX asks about the value of federal tax refunds received by the household in the twelve months before the interview month, and concedes that there appears to be a substantial underreporting: only about half of households report a refund, whereas according to the IRS three-fourths of tax filers receive refunds. Note that the CEX does not ask for the refund received in the preceding three months, but rather, in the preceding *twelve* months. Souleles admits that this complicates the analysis. Here is how he tries to address this problem.

Because most refunds are received between March and May, Souleles makes the assumption that the refund for each household is received between March and May. This assumption enables him to line up the receipt of a rebate between March and May of year y for a given household, with the change in consumption from the first to the second quarter of that same year y for that same household. If all refunds were received from March to May, and if every household waited exactly one month to consume out of its refund, and thereafter consumed nothing more from its refund, then the line up would work perfectly. The refunds received from March to May would be consumed from April to June so that all consumption would occur in the second quarter, none in the first, and none thereafter. The dependent variable, $C^{II}_{iy} - C^{I}_{iy}$, would reflect the impact of the refund, and the coefficient of the refund, β_2, would measure the marginal propensity to consume (MPC) out of the refund. Unfortunately, in practice households are not so cooperative and this implies the possibility of a significant divergence between the estimated β_2 and the MPC. Souleles explains:

> To illustrate, suppose the sample consists of three people who each receive a $1 refund; one person receives her refund in March, another receives it in April, and a third receives it in May. Suppose each person immediately consumes the entire refund, i.e. the true MPC = 1. Then, in the dependent variable, $C^{II}_{iy} - C^{I}_{iy}$, [second quarter consumption minus first quarter consumption], the $1 consumed in March goes into the $- C^{I}$ term, and so partly offsets the $2 spent in April and May that go into the C^{II} term. The estimated β_2 [the coefficient of the refund variable in his regression equation] would therefore be 1/3 (normalizing by the number of people), attenuated by a factor of $(2/3 - 1/3) = 1/3$ compared to the actual MPC. (Souleles 1999, 952)

Thus, Souleles contends that the true MPC is significantly greater than the estimate he obtains from his regression for β_2, the coefficient of the refund variable. So how will he infer the MPC from his estimated β_2? He writes:

> Generalizing beyond this example, one can calculate an "attenuation factor" p from the distribution of aggregate refund disbursements: $p_{iy} = p^{II}_{iy} - p^{I}_{iy}$, where p^{I}_{iy} is the proportion of the refunds disbursed during i's refund reference period that were disbursed in quarter I of year y. Multiplying the refund regressor by these factors should largely undo the attenuation. (Souleles 1999, 952)

In his example, he would multiply his estimated β_2 by 3 to obtain his estimate of the MPC.

By contrast, if households wait exactly one month before consuming out of their refund, then all consumption occurs in the second quarter and none in the first, so the MPC equals β_2. The intermediate case, a two-week delay between receiving the refund and consuming out of it, requires an intermediate adjustment.

Souleles reports his estimate of the MPC:

> To correct for the timing attenuation, the refund regressor is weighted by the attenuation factor p. The resulting coefficients can be interpreted as MPCs. . . . The response of total consumption is quite large at 0.64. That is, almost two-thirds of every extra dollar of refund is spent within a quarter. . . . Allowing for a two-week delay after disbursement results in smaller yet still substantial coefficients, about double the original coefficients. . . . The estimate for total consumption bounds from below the MPC at about 0.35. Even this amount is greater than most previous estimates of the impact of fiscal policy. (Souleles 1999, 955)

Souleles draws these conclusions from his study:

> This paper has found significant evidence of excess sensitivity in the response of households' consumption to their income tax refunds. Further, some of the sources of this sensitivity were identified. In particular, liquidity constraints appear to play an important role, because the nondurable consumption of constrained households increased at the time of refund receipt, far more than for unconstrained households. However, more than liquidity constraints are at play, because durable expenditures by the unconstrained also responded substantially; and the response of nondurables extended later into the year, after refund receipts. Furthermore, the response in durables by the unconstrained is not easily explained by standard models of durables or self-control, because liquid households could have bought their durables before receiving their refunds. There was also some evidence of a disproportionate response to larger refunds, counter to some views of mental accounts. . . .
>
> Having rejected the null hypothesis of the life-cycle theory, the paper estimated under a simple alternative hypothesis the marginal propensity to consume out of refunds. The response of total consumption was found to be at least 35 percent of refunds within a quarter, up to over 60 percent. Given the large aggregate value of tax refunds, these results imply rather substantial macroeconomic effects of refunds, and more generally of fiscal policy. (Souleles 1999, 956)

One concern one might have with Souleles's study is whether the CEX data on tax refunds and on consumption spending are accurate enough for his purpose. There are two key pieces of information that each household must provide in their response to the survey. First, it must report any income tax refund(s) it received over the preceding twelve months. Second, each household must report its consumption expenditures in various categories over the preceding three months.

The first piece of information would seem to be easy for a household to ascertain. The household need only look back at its checkbook and see if it deposited any checks from the U.S. Treasury. Even here, as Souleles reports above, there appears to be substantial underreporting of refunds in the survey, because only about half of households report receiving a refund, but U.S. Treasury data says that three-quarters of households in fact receive a refund.

The second piece of information would seem to be hard for a household to ascertain if it tries to do so by a direct accounting of each item of expenditure. After all, a household makes numerous expenditures over three months. For some expenditures it uses a credit or debit card, for others it writes checks, and for others it uses cash. It seems likely that the typical household might make large errors in reporting its consumption expenditures if it tries to tally up its many individual purchases.

If the only information sought were total consumption expenditure, this might be computed with much greater accuracy by a subtraction method using cash-flow accounting as recommended for the administration of a personal consumption (expenditure) tax (Seidman 1997). The household would add all cash inflows (wage and salary, withdrawals from investment funds or savings accounts, etc.) and subtract nonconsumption cash outflows (deposits into investment funds or savings accounts, etc.); the result equals its consumption spending. Under the CEX survey, however, households are not instructed to use this method for determining their consumption.

Despite the likelihood of large errors in the consumption data, the data may be accurate enough for Souleles's purpose, and his main conclusions may nevertheless be valid, because Souleles has a very large sample of individuals, and there is no reason to suspect that individuals are biased in their reporting. With several thousand individual observations, Souleles is able to get reasonably precise estimates; in his main equations for total consumption, the estimated standard error for his refund variable is a small fraction of the point estimate, so that his estimates are highly statistically significant. It seems likely that the sample is large enough, and the typical household's calculation accurate enough, so that he has estimated the relationship between refunds and consumption spending with reasonable accuracy.

Finally, it is important to emphasize a point made at the beginning of this section: Souleles's study significantly underestimates the one-year or even half-year impact of refunds on consumption because it does not look beyond one quarter. Thus, if a household receives a refund in May and consumes the whole refund in July, this consumption escapes his study because his dependent variable is $C^{II}_{iy} - C^{I}_{iy}$, the increase in consumption from the first quarter of the year to the second quarter of the year. Yet surely if there is spending out of refunds, a good portion of it is likely to occur with some delay. Some households will spread it evenly over several months. Others may wait a few months and then spend it all; for example, think of the household that earmarks its May refund for a summer vacation trip in August. By finding substantial spending of refunds in the second quarter alone, Souleles's study implies that the full spending out of refunds over a half year, and especially over one full year, is likely to be large.

Parker's Payroll Tax Withholding Study

Jonathan Parker uses the household-level consumption data from the Consumer Expenditure Survey (CEX) to test whether expenditures on nondurable goods respond to changes in Social Security tax withholding. At first glance it may seem that Social Security withholding changes too infrequently to provide much evidence on how households respond. For example, the combined (employer plus employee) payroll tax rate has been 12.4 percent for many years. But Parker explains how it can be done:

> When an individual's income earned in a calender year reaches the maximum taxable amount, the individual's take-home pay increases because Social Security taxes are no longer withheld from his or her paycheck. In January of the following year, when withholding begins again, take-home pay falls again. . . . Under the null hypothesis, household consumption should not respond to these changes in tax rates since they are expected. . . . (Parker 1999, 959)

Note that Parker calls the tax rate changes in the 1980s "preannounced," and calls the end-of-year increment to take-home pay "expected." But I doubt that the typical household in the 1980s actually anticipated the "preannounced" rate changes in advance; more likely the household was surprised when its withholding changed, altering its take-home pay. Similarly, it is doubtful that the typical household knows the exact month its end-of-year take-home pay will increase; and if it doesn't know the month, it doesn't know the amount of its end-of-year increment in take-home pay.

This makes Parker's study all the more relevant to countercyclical fiscal policy. Since the amount of the increment in end-of-year take-home pay is a surprise to the typical household, it is therefore similar to our temporary tax cut or transfer triggered by a recession. If the household's take-home pay increases $Y, it now has two choices: raise spending promptly by a significant fraction of the refund, or raise spending very little. Parker's study sheds light on what households actually do upon receiving a surprise increase in take-home pay.

Parker then previews his conclusion:

> This study finds that households do change their consumption expenditures in response to the predictable fluctuations in income induced by the Social Security tax system. A predictable, 1–percent increase in after-tax income in a three-month interval contemporaneously increases expenditures on nondurable consumption by around a half of a percent. To put this in perspective, since nondurable consumption averages about 40 percent of income, expenditures on nondurable goods rise 20 cents for each dollar of predictable increase in income. Several steps are taken to reduce the possibility that the results are spurious or that differential seasonal patterns of consumption across wealth levels are driving the results. (Parker 1999, 959–960)

Parker contends that his study has four advantages over other studies:

> First, the income changes caused by Social Security are calculated at the household level and are exogenous to the household. The predictable change in income is thus not highly correlated with labor supply or family size. Such a correlation reduces the power of many previous tests. Second, the predictable changes in income are large and easily identifiable. Income changes due to the tax cap are around 9 percent of net income. Measurement error in the income change is relatively small because the income change is calculated from the *level* of individual labor income, not its growth rate. (Parker 1999, 960–961)

These first two points seem correct, but his next point is less persuasive:

> Third, the CEX provides comprehensive data on many different types of consumption expenditures at the household level. Many previous microeconomic studies have employed only a (noisy) measure of food consumption. (Parker 1999, 961)

The CEX probably is better than relying solely on household data on food consumption. But, as I suggested above in discussing Souleles's study, the accuracy of the consumption data reported by households is still a matter of concern. Parker continues:

> Finally, because this test has a large time-series dimension (167 three-month periods) and individual-level measures of change in income (including a control group), it avoids the poor performance of tests using short panels with common sources of expected change in income. . . .
> (Parker 1999, 961)

He runs a regression of the change in consumption of individual h in quarter t against a set of variables that includes the percent increase in income due to Social Security taxes. According to the permanent income/life cycle hypothesis, the coefficient of this variable should be zero—there should be no change in consumption this quarter relative to last because the increase in income due to Social Security taxes was entirely predictable and smoothing should have already occurred. To control for seasonal effects (in the fall, most families spend more due to the holidays), he includes dummy variables for each month. Here is what he finds:

> The first entry in [the table] reports the estimated response of consumption to predictable changes in income from ordinary least squares estimation of equation (3) on the entire sample. . . . The response of consumption is highly statistically significant and implies that when a household's Social Security payments fall so that income rises by 10 percent, nondurable consumption rises by 5.4 percent. (Parker 1999, 963–964)

After presenting his analysis of the data, he concludes:

> Contrary to the basic life cycle/permanent income hypothesis, consumption reacts in an economically significant manner to predictable changes in tax rates: the elasticity of expenditures on nondurable goods with respect to the predictable declines in income that are studied is around one-half. . . .
> This paper and other recent evidence against pure consumption smoothing have potentially far-reaching implications. If expected changes in taxes influence contemporaneous consumption behavior, then fiscal stabilization, such as that undertaken by President Bush in 1992 or that provided by automatic tax stabilizers, is likely to have important effects on consumption. (Parker 1999, 970)

Browning and Collado versus Souleles and Parker

At first glance, a recent study by Browning and Collado appears to conflict with the studies of Souleles and Parker. They begin by citing Souleles's and Parker's studies. They write:

Here we present Spanish panel data [between 1985 and 1995] evidence that provides an alternative investigation of the link between income and expenditure within the year. The Spanish data has two principal advantages over the other data on expenditures. First, this is the only large panel data set that gives information on expenditures over more than four quarters. . . . The second major advantage of the Spanish data is an institutional feature of the Spanish economy. This is that a majority of full-time workers receive extra payments in the summer and winter of each year. . . . The usual practice for workers who are in a bonus-payment scheme is to receive one-fourteenth of their annual pay in most months and one-seventh in the bonus months. Thus for some workers the path of earnings over the year varies in a large and predictable way. (Browning and Collado 2001, 682)

They then preview their findings:

Contrary to Shapiro and Slemrod (1995) . . . Parker (1999) and Souleles (1999) we do not find any effect of anticipated changes in income on expenditure patterns over the year. In particular, the paths of expenditure patterns over the year for those who receive the bonus payments are indistinguishable from the patterns of those who do not receive a bonus. (Browning and Collado 2001, 682)

After presenting the details of their study, they draw these conclusions:

We have used a unique expenditure panel data set from Spain to examine whether the demands of households react to predictable and large changes in household income within the year. We find that for a sample of households in which the husband is in full-time employment at all interviews of the panel, there is no evidence of any synchronization between the income flow in the year and expenditures in the year. . . . On the face of it, our empirical finding appears contrary to those of earlier investigators, particularly Parker (1999) and Souleles (1999). (Browning and Collado 2001, 689)

They say they doubt that the difference in countries is the reason for the difference in results:

We are reluctant to advance this as an explanation of the differences, particularly since Spain had a much less developed personal credit market than the United States in our sample period. (Browning and Collado 2001, 690)

They then offer a way to make sense of the differing results:

> Our preferred reconciliation of our results with earlier work builds on the suggestion that households using bounded rationality procedures will not bother to adjust optimally to small income changes since the utility cost of doing so is small. This is consistent with our findings since the income changes we consider are large (a doubling from one month of the next rather than, say, the 9 percent increase for Parker) so that treating the changes as unanticipated would impose a large welfare cost. Additionally, the mechanics of the income changes we exploit are transparent and occur in the same form year after year whereas the changes that Parker and Souleles consider are relatively small and variable fluctuations that come at different times of the year. Thus the benefits of making the optimal expenditure calculations in our income scheme are large and the costs are small, and for the Parker and Souleles income processes the converse is the case. This bounded rationality explanation is also consistent with Hsieh (1999), which are particularly relevant for our explanation. Recall that Hsieh finds that the same households overreact to (relatively small) tax refunds but do not react to (large and highly predictable) payments from the [Alaska] Permanent Fund, exactly as this hypothesis would predict. (Browning and Collado 2001, 690)

What are the implications of this study for our countercyclical fiscal policy? As Browning and Collado emphasize, the bonuses are a regular part of the compensation scheme and are announced in advance, and workers can easily anticipate both the amount and timing of the upcoming bonuses. By contrast, the temporary tax cut or transfer proposed in chapter 2 is triggered by a recession, and the amount depends on the severity of the recession. Hence, the typical worker cannot anticipate either the amount or the timing. Thus, in contrast to the Spanish bonuses, the temporary tax cut or transfer is a surprise for the typical recipient.

Souleles's Study of the Reagan Tax Cut

In a recent paper, Souleles studies consumer response to the Reagan tax cuts of the early 1980s using household data from the CEX surveys for 1982 and 1983:

> The Economic Recovery Act [ERTA], enacted in August, 1981, phased in the cuts over three years, with withholding rates decreasing by about 5% in October 1981, another 10% in July of 1982, and a final 10% in

July of 1983. Since the second and third phases of these cuts, in 1982 and 1983, had been pre-announced, the resulting increases in take-home pay were predictable at the time of their receipt. Hence, under the canonical Life-Cycle/Permanent-Income [LC/PI] model, consumption should not have responded to the tax cuts at those times [Footnote: Under the canonical model consumers should respond to news about their future tax liability, not to (previously expected) actual changes in withholding cash flows. Tax liabilities, which pertain to the entire calendar (tax) year, declined as of January of the two years at issue (by 5% each time, cumulatively), before the actual declines in withholding in July. Moreover, these declines were expected even before the start of the tax year, at least as early as the enactment of ERTA in 1981]. (Souleles 2001, 1)

Note that Souleles calls the Reagan tax rate changes "predictable." But I doubt that the typical household actually predicted the amount of its increase in after-tax income; more likely the household was surprised when its income tax withholding changed, altering its take-home pay. This makes Souleles's study all the more relevant to countercyclical fiscal policy. If the household's take-home pay increases $Y, it now has two choices: raise spending promptly by a significant fraction of the refund, or raise spending very little. Souleles's study sheds light on what households actually do upon receiving a surprise increase in take-home pay.

Based on the analysis of household response to the change in disposable income resulting from the tax cut, Souleles provides an estimate of the marginal propensity to consume out of current disposable income:

> In addition to testing for excess sensitivity, this paper provides estimates interpretable as the marginal propensity to consume [MPC] out of predictable income. These estimates bear on the expansionary effect of even pre-announced changes in fiscal policy, particularly changes in withholding and payroll taxes. The results can be contrasted with similar estimates of the response of consumption to changes in social security taxes in Parker (1999) and to changes in lump-sum federal tax refunds in Souleles (1999). (Souleles 2001, 2)

The Reagan tax cut was implemented by cutting the withholding rates. How does the magnitude of the response to a cut in withholding compare with the response to lump-sum income tax refunds which Souleles studies in his 1999 paper? He writes:

> The consumption response is larger than previously estimated for tax refunds and more concentrated in nondurables. These differences have im-

portant implications for the structure of tax changes, in particular for choosing between varying withholding rates versus varying "lumpy" final payments and refunds. (Souleles 2001, 2)

Later, he elaborates on this distinction:

> Under the LC/PI model, different types of income are fungible, so results for refunds should apply equally well to smaller but prolonged increases in disposable income due to reductions in withholding. However, outside of the model, it might matter what fraction of a tax change is implemented via changes in withholding versus lump-sum changes in final tax payments and refunds (including changes in rebates and credits, etc.). Katona and Mueller argued long ago that more of a given increase in income is likely to be saved if the increase is received in a single large payment than if it is received in small amounts spread out over time.

After giving a detailed account of his analysis of the CEX household data for 1982 and 1983, Souleles draws this conclusion:

> This paper found significant evidence of excess sensitivity in the response of consumption to the Reagan tax cuts. This response is counter to the canonical LC/PI model since the resulting increase in take-home pay was predictable. Most of the response came in nondurables, including disproportionate spending on summer-time trips. The overall MPC for nondurables was estimated to be around 0.6 to 0.9, though with correspondingly large standard errors. The source of the excess sensitivity remains an open issue. The standard candidate sources, notably liquidity constraints and unobserved household heterogeneity, do not appear to explain the results. (Souleles 2001, 18)

In this study, Souleles analyzes the response to a change in income tax withholding. Recall that in his 1999 study described above, he analyzed the response to income tax refunds. He then makes an interesting comparison that is relevant to the design of countercyclical fiscal policy:

> The results also have important implications for the structure of tax changes, in particular for choosing between changes in withholding versus changes in lump-sum final tax payments or refunds (including changes in credits and rebates, etc.). The response here to changes in withholding is larger than that in Souleles (1999) for refunds, and more concentrated in nondurables. The response is more similar to that in Parker (1999) for

changes in social security payroll taxes. More generally the conclusions are consistent with the behavioral view that more of a given increase in income is likely to be spent if the increase is received in small amounts and spread out over time, than if it is received in a single large payment. (Souleles 2001, 19)

Shapiro and Slemrod's Study of the 2001 Tax Rebate

At first glance, the Shapiro and Slemrod study of the 2001 rebate seems to find a smaller response than the rest of the recent empirical literature, including their 1995 study. They asked survey questions to households in August and September about their plans for the tax rebate mailed by the U.S. Treasury in July, August, and September ($600 per family).

> We find that only 21.8 percent of those receiving the rebate reported that it would lead them to mostly increase spending. This propensity to spend is remarkably low, both from a theoretical perspective and when compared to previous estimates. (Shapiro and Slemrod 2002, 1)

I would immediately note that spending "only" 21.8 percent would be very helpful in combating a recession. Their statement gives the impression that respondents intended to spend 21.8 percent of their total rebate dollars, but this inference is unwarranted. To see why, examine the exact wording of their key question:

> Earlier this year a Federal law was passed cutting income tax rates and expanding certain credits and deductions. The tax cuts will be phased in over the next ten years. This year many households will receive a tax rebate check in the mail. In most cases, the tax rebate will be $300 for single individuals and $600 for married couples. Thinking about your (family's) financial situation this year, will the tax rebate lead you mostly to increase spending, mostly to increase saving, or mostly to pay off debt? (Shapiro and Slemrod 2002, 5)

Note that they do *not* ask the respondents what *percent* of their rebate they intend to spend. Now consider a simple hypothetical example. Suppose every household intends to spend 40 percent of its rebate and use 60 percent to pay off debt. Then 0 percent would report that the rebate leads them "mostly to increase spending," and 100 percent would report that the rebate leads them "mostly to pay off debt." Yet in this example, the percent of total rebate dollars spent would be 40 percent, not 0 percent.[1] In retrospect, it might have been better to ask respondents what *percent* they intended to spend, save, and use to pay off debt. Because the percent was not asked, the study does *not* obtain information on the percent of total rebate dollars that respondents intend to spend (or on the marginal propensity to consume).[2]

They are puzzled by their finding:

> The lower propensity to consume we find cannot be attributed to our survey methodology. In 1992, we fielded a similar survey question to measure the propensity to consume from the 1992 changes in income tax withholding. Both the 1992 and 2001 survey questions were included as modules on the University of Michigan Survey Research Center's monthly Survey of Consumers, so the procedures for drawing the sample were the same in both surveys. For the 1992 withholding change, we find that over forty percent of households would spend the extra current income from a reduction in withholding, despite the fact that the increase in take-home pay would be offset by either a lower tax refund or higher final payment (Shapiro and Slemrod 1995). While that behavior is inconsistent with unconstrained optimization, it is quite consistent with the broad range of evidence that a high fraction of income goes to households who act myopically or liquidity constrained with respect to changes in income. Because the methodology used to study the 2001 rebate closely mirrors that of the 1992 study, the surprising results of the 2001 study appear to represent a genuine departure from past behavior and are not an artifact of our methodology or the specific details of the survey. We cannot, though, definitively rule out the possibility that subtle differences in wording between the surveys affected the responses. (Shapiro and Slemrod 2002, 22)

There is, in fact, a potentially important difference in the wording of the key question that may have biased the 2001 study. Here is the exact wording of the 1992 key question:

> The federal government *has* recently changed the amount of income tax that is being withheld from paychecks. On average, the change in withholding should *increase* your take-home pay by about $25 per month, or by a total of about $250 for all of 1992. It also means that next year your tax refund will be about $250 less than otherwise, or you will have to pay about $250 more in taxes next year than otherwise. How do you think you will use the extra $25 per month—do you think you will *spend most* of it, *save most* of it, use *most* of it to *repay debts*, or what? (What do you think you will do with *most* of the extra money?) (Shapiro and Slemrod 1995, 282)

The 2001 key question (see above) begins with the phrase "Thinking about your (family's) financial situation." This phrase does not appear in the 1992 key question. This phrase may have influenced some respondents to answer either "save" or "pay off debt." Suppose instead that the phrase had been "Thinking about the needs of your family." Such a phrase might do the reverse. On reflection, perhaps the question should have omitted the introductory phrase, and simply have read: "What percent of the tax rebate will you spend? What percent will you save? What percent will you use to pay off debt?"[3]

Another problem with the 2001 question is the phrase "this year." Because the survey was conducted in August, September, and October 2001, some respondents may have interpreted "this year" to mean "before the end of this calender year." If these respondents planned to spend it in early 2002, they may not have answered "spend." In retrospect, perhaps the question should have been: "What percent do you intend to spend *within a* year?"

Shapiro and Slemrod also report on a follow-up survey conducted in March and April 2002 as a module in the University of Michigan Survey Research Center's monthly Survey of Consumers. They state (p. 17) that "the survey has a partial panel structure, where forty percent of respondents each month are reinterviewed six months later." They give the exact wording of the key question:

> Last year a Federal law was passed cutting income tax rates and expanding certain credits and deductions. Some tax cuts took effect last year and others will be phased in over the next nine years. Last year many households received a tax rebate check in the mail. In most cases, the tax rebate was 300 dollars for single individuals and 600 dollars for married couples. Did the tax rebate lead you mostly to increase spending, mostly to increase saving, or mostly to pay off debt? (Shapiro and Slemrod 2002, 16–17)

They state:

> In this survey, 24.9 percent of the respondents reported spending the rebate. (Shapiro and Slemrod 2002, 16)

Again, I would immediately note that spending 24.9 percent would have been very helpful in combating the recession. But note that once again they do *not* ask respondents what *percent* they spent, so we cannot infer the percent of the total rebate dollars spent. They are, however, neutral in presenting the three options (there is no longer the introductory phrase, "Thinking about your (family's) financial situation.)"

The question they ask is very difficult for any respondent to answer accurately. Suppose you were asked what you did with your 2001 rebate? How would you figure it out? You probably remember depositing the rebate check in your bank. But then what? You may recall the moment you wrote a check to pay down your home equity loan, and think, "That's what I did with the rebate." Or you may recall the moment you used your credit card to buy a new TV, and think, "That's what I did with the rebate." Or was it the morning you went shopping at your mall? Was that your rebate? To answer the question accurately, you must compare your actual spending to a hypothetical—what you would have spent had there been no rebate. You may recall the moment you think you used the rebate for activity X, but the real issue is how much more did you spend, having received the rebate, than you would have spent had you not received the rebate. To give the correct answer, you have to know what you would have done had there been no rebate. Are you sure you know this?

I believe, then, that the jury is still out on the impact of the 2001 tax rebate. A decision must await the kind of empirical studies of behavior described in this chapter.

Empirical Evidence on the Power of Monetary Policy

But if monetary policy can handle any recession, then why bother with fiscal policy? The Seidman and Lewis study reported in chapter 2 showed that in the Fair econometric model, monetary policy alone was not strong enough to effectively combat a severe recession. I now review empirical evidence concerning the power of monetary policy. The evidence comes from simulations with macroeconometric models. By citing results from these models, I explicitly reject the proposition that the "Lucas critique" invalidates results generated by simulation with such models. In chapter 11, I examine the "Lucas critique" in detail.

Klein (1991) describes the conference that led to the table below (see Table 6.1) using macroeconometric models vintage late 1980s:

> During the second half of the 1970s leading model builders in the United States came together for repeated seminars that culminated in a series of research papers . . . published in a single book volume in 1976. . . . There was such enthusiastic response among leading U.S. model builders when asked if they would participate in a new round of comparisons that it was easy to decide to resume operations. The results of the second phase are reported in this volume. . . . Most of the material in this volume is concerned with comparisons among *mainstream* models, which are largely or basically natural evolutions of the original group from the late 1970s. (Klein 1991, preface v)

Table 6.1

Percent Increase in Real GNP From a One Percentage Point Cut In *r*

	1975.1	1975.2	1975.3	1975.4	1976.4	1977.4
BEA	0.16	0.38	0.62	0.89	1.93	3.06
DRI	−0.02	0.05	0.17	0.31	1.04	1.87
FAIR	0.06	0.18	0.31	0.43	0.79	0.90
IND	0.22	0.55	0.79	1.01	1.95	2.51
LM&A	0.12	0.38	0.66	0.93	1.91	1.78
MICH	0.01	0.21	0.44	0.67	1.22	1.28
WEFA	0.09	0.20	0.36	0.44	0.77	0.88
FRB	0.07	0.16	0.37	0.57	1.59	2.93
Average of the eight models	0.09	0.26	0.47	0.66	1.40	1.90

Source: P46, Table A2.5, [2B], in Lawrence R. Klein (ed.), *Comparative Performance of U.S. Econometric Models* (New York: Oxford University Press, 1991).

Klein and Adams describe the simulations:

> Early in the meetings of the model comparison seminar, the philosophy of model comparisons was the topic of some extensive discussion. It was thought that comparison would require some standardization, but the model operators were reluctant to tamper with the structure of their models or even with the way they were used. Although it rapidly became clear that the alternative simulations would have to be prescribed quite precisely, it was decided to "let the models be models." This phrase was understood to mean that the model operators would use the models in the way they typically did. . . .
>
> The approach of this work was to compare alternative "disturbed" model solutions to a base solution. Each model operator was instructed to prepare a so-called "tracking solution" that would approximately reproduce history over the period 1975.1 to 1984.4. (Klein and Adams 1991, 18–19)

Although the simulation period began in 1975.1, the experiments were performed at the end of the 1980s (the book was published in 1991), so these are the results of macroeconometric models vintage late 1980s. To perform the experiment of reducing the short-term interest rate 1 percentage point (100 basis points) below the baseline path, each model had to adjust its monetary variables each quarter to achieve the target path for the short-term interest rate: a path of numerical values 1 percentage point below the historical value in each quarter. To do this, models that contained a Federal Reserve reaction function had to suspend that function. These reaction functions are estimated equations showing how the Fed historically adjusts the short-term interest rate in response to economic variables such as the unemployment rate and the inflation rate.

Consider the implications of the numerical values of the "average of the eight models." If the interest rate is cut 1 percentage point in 1975.1, and held 1 percentage point below its baseline value in subsequent quarters, real output increases 0.09 percent in the first (same) quarter, 0.26 percent in the second, 0.47 percent in the third, 0.66 percent in the fourth, 1.40 percent in the eighth, and 1.90 percent in the twelfth. Note that the Fair model, used in the Seidman and Lewis study described in chapter 2, is reasonably representative of the response in the eight mainstream models.

According to the rough approximation known as "Okun's law," suppose a 2 percent fall in real output generates a 1 percentage point rise in the unemployment rate. Then imagine a severe recession that reaches its trough in four quarters, reduces output in the fourth quarter 6 percent below its trend value, and raises the unemployment rate 3 percentage points (for example, from 6.5 percent to 9.5 percent, as in the early 1980s) above its normal value. What cut in the interest rate must occur immediately in the first quarter and be maintained for four quarters in order to cut the severity of this recession in half, so that output falls only 3 percent below trend and the unemployment rate rises only 1.5 percentage points (for example, from 6.5 percent to 8.0 percent)? Using the average value for these eight models, a 1 percentage point cut in the short-term interest rate would raise real output 0.66 percent in the fourth quarter. To cut the severity of the recession in half, output must be raised 3 percent so that it falls only 3 percent instead of 6 percent below trend in the fourth quarter. But this requires a prompt cut in the interest rate of 4.5 percentage points that is maintained for four quarters (3%/0.66% = 4.5). For example, if the short-term interest rate were initially 6 percent, it would have to be cut immediately to 1.5 percent, and held at 1.5 percent for four quarters, to cut the severity of this recession in half. Of course, such a huge sudden cut by the Fed would frighten the public—a reaction not captured by the models—and it is therefore extremely doubtful that the Fed would ever attempt such a sudden cut. In the 2001 recession, the Fed took a full year to cut the interest rate in eleven small decrements from 6.50 percent to 1.75 percent.

Thus, based on these eight models, monetary policy cannot handle a severe recession on its own. It needs help from countercyclical fiscal policy.

Conclusion from the Empirical Studies of Consumption

It is easy to summarize the findings of recent empirical studies on the response of household consumption to changes in disposable income: the response is prompt and substantial.

There are two studies that, at first glance, seem to run counter to the other studies. The first finds no response to a regular annual preannounced bonus that can easily be anticipated by the typical person; but this study has no relevance to countercyclical fiscal policy where the timing and amount of the increment to disposable income depends on whether and when a recession occurs, and how severe it is. The second is a consumer survey that seems to find only a moderate response to the 2001 tax rebate; but the wording of the key question in the survey biases a respondent toward answering "pay down debt" because it begins with the phrase "Thinking about your (family's) financial situation" before asking the respondent what he plans to do with the rebate.

The results of these recent studies are, of course, consistent with the hypothesis that consumption is *partly* influenced by permanent (lifetime) income. But the studies find that current disposable income also matters significantly. The impact of current disposable income is large enough and reliable enough to support the use of temporary changes in taxes and transfers for stabilization.

Notes

1. Symmetrically, suppose every household intends to spend 60 percent of its rebate and use 40 percent to pay off debt. Then 100 percent would report that the rebate leads them "mostly to increase spending," and 0 percent would report that the rebate leads them "mostly to pay off debt." Yet in this example, the percent of total rebate dollars spent would be 60 percent, not 100 percent; the marginal propensity to consume of every household would be 60 percent, not 100 percent.

2. Suppose the 20 percent who say they will "mostly spend" actually spend 80 percent of the rebate, and the 80 percent who say they will "mostly not spend" actually spend 20 percent of the rebate, then 32 percent of the total rebate dollars will be spent (because $.2(80\%) + .8(20\%) = 32\%$). In fact, if all we know is that 20 percent say they will "mostly spend," it is possible for the percent of the total rebate dollars spent to be as high as 46 percent (if the 20 percent who "mostly spend" actually spend 100 percent, and if the remaining 80 percent spend 33 percent, save 33 percent (34%), and use 34 percent (33%) to pay off debt, then 46 percent of total rebate dollars would be spent, because $.2(100\%) + .8(33\%) = 46\%$; conversely, it is also possible that the percent of total rebate dollars spent could be less than 20 percent.

3. Also, another difference between the 1992 and 2001 wording may have influenced some respondents not to answer "increase spending," but instead to answer "pay off debt." The 2001 question asks whether the respondent will mostly "increase spending," whereas the 1992 question asks whether the respondent will "spend most of it." The word "increase" appears in the 2001 question but not the 1992 question. Some 2001 respondents might have thought, "I don't plan to use the rebate to *increase* spending, just to *maintain* spending despite the recession," and consequently did not select "increase spending." It is true that in the 2001 question the word "increase" also appears with saving. But it does *not* appear with "pay off debt."

7

The Tax Rebate in the
1975 Recession

It is frequently asserted that "discretionary" fiscal policy—fiscal policy that requires Congress to enact a stimulus package—is impractical because it takes too long for Congress to act. However, discretionary fiscal policy responded promptly to the recession of 1975. *From the time a consensus emerged that recession posed a greater threat than inflation* (January 1975), it took just three months for Congress to enact a tax cut (end of March), and only another month for the increase in household disposable income to occur through the first tax-rebate checks from the treasury (checks were sent out in April, May, and June). A key element of the package was a one-time rebate of 1974 income tax: each household received a check equal to 10 percent of its 1974 personal income tax up to a maximum of $200 per household.

Despite the promptness of discretionary fiscal policy in the 1975 recession, it is surely better to have a preenacted fiscal package that is triggered automatically. With an automatic trigger, rebate checks would have been mailed out in the first quarter, rather than the second quarter, of 1975. In the 2001 recession, Congress promptly enacted a $600 per household rebate in July, but in the fall of 2001, with the recession deepening, Republicans and Democrats deadlocked, each promoting their preferred stimulus package. In my view, the central importance of the history of the 1975 rebate is that it teaches us how to preenact an automatic fiscal policy today.

Why go all the way back to the 1975 recession? First, the countercyclical rebate I proposed in chapter 2 was born in that recession. Second, fiscal stimulus was not attempted in the 1982 recession because that recession was intentionally generated by the Federal Reserve under chairman Paul Volcker in order to reduce inflation. Third, fiscal stimulus was not attempted in the 1991 recession because the huge budget deficits of the 1980s had significantly raised the ratio of government debt to GDP, so fear of further debt ruled it out politically. I will discuss the 2001 rebate in the next chapter.

The Deepening Recession

Otto Eckstein analyzes the impact of fiscal policy in the 1975 recession in his book *The Great Recession* (1978). Eckstein was the principal builder of the Data Resources Incorporated (DRI) macroeconometric model and his analysis is based on simulations with that model. In a chapter titled "How We Escaped Depression," Eckstein reports that in 1973–74 the economy was hit with a food price explosion, an oil embargo, gasoline lines and a quadrupling of the price of foreign oil, double-digit interest and inflation rates, and a severe stock market decline. He writes:

> The energy crisis was the single largest cause of the Great Recession. Without it, even given all the preceding problems, the economy would have suffered no worse than a year of a small GNP decline in 1974, and would have seen 1975 as the first year of recovery. But when the energy crisis, with its gasoline lines and the quadrupling of the price of foreign oil, was superimposed upon an already highly vulnerable economic situation, it was sufficient to turn the beginnings of recovery into the sharpest decline of the postwar period. (Eckstein 1978, 124)

Before the decade was out, economic textbooks appeared (for example, Robert Gordon's first edition of his intermediate macroeconomics text which appeared in the late 1970s) presenting a simple aggregate demand/aggregate supply diagram to explain how an economy could experience a burst of inflation *and* recession simultaneously—"stagflation." The increase in the world price of oil shifted up the aggregate supply curve, because the height of a supply curve reflects the cost of production, and that cost had been raised by the world oil price increase engineered by the OPEC oil-producing nations of the Persian Gulf. Thus, the intersection of aggregate supply and aggregate demand moved "northwest" up the demand curve, indicating a higher price—inflation—and a lower output—recession. In 1974, however, there was some confusion about how recession and inflation could occur together because most economists were accustomed to thinking of shifts in demand, not supply, as the driving force behind changes in the macroeconomy.

Because of the even greater severity of the 1982 recession, which generated an unemployment rate of 9.5 percent for both 1982 and 1983, it is often forgotten how serious the 1975 recession appeared to be as it unfolded. Here is Eckstein's account:

> In the winter months of 1974–75, the U.S. economy was on the path to depression. Between September 1974 and March 1975, production fell by

12.4%, payroll employment was reduced by 2.36 million individuals, unemployment rose from 5.5% in August to an 8.9% peak in May. The real gross national product fell at an annual rate of 10% in the winter quarter. . . . Real business fixed investment declined at an annual rate of 19%. The American economy was a vast factory that was closing down. . . .

During those six months [the last quarter of 1974 and the first quarter of 1975], the rate of decline was of the same order of magnitude as the beginnings of the Great Depression of the 1930's. Back then, production was down 16.7% in the first year and real business fixed investment dropped 17.8%. . . . In 1930, unemployment rose from 3.2% to 8.9%. The sense of panic, while certainly intensified by the collapse of the stock market in late 1929, was not so different from the feelings of households and businesses in the winter of 1974–75. The food price explosion, the oil embargo, double-digit interest and inflation rates, a stock market decline of 35%, and new unemployment insurance claims of nearly one million a week represented a bundle of bad news sufficient to frighten anybody.

But whereas 1930 was only the first of three years of sharp declines, the winter of 1974–75 was followed by an early and vigorous recovery. . . . How did the economy get off the path to depression? What brought the great postwar economic crisis to such a quick end? The DRI econometric model can as easily be used for this cliometric exercise as for the analysis of the causes of the crisis. (Eckstein 1978, 128–129)

Eckstein then attributes the early recovery to five factors: (1) No further external shocks (such as food or oil prices); (2) automatic transfers like unemployment insurance and other income maintenance transfers; (3) a shift in monetary policy toward lower interest rates; (4) improved availability of credit; and (5) a major shift in fiscal policy. I will, of course, concentrate on the contribution of this last factor: the fiscal stimulus package enacted in March 1975 and implemented in the second quarter (April, May, June) of that year.

Which Gets Top Priority: Inflation or Recession?

But with the recession intensifying in the second half of 1974, why did it take until March 1975 for a fiscal stimulus package to be enacted by Congress and signed into law by the president? The reason is straightforward: Inflation was also soaring in 1974, and throughout the entire year most conservatives and Republicans felt that containing inflation should have the highest priority. In contrast to today, in 1974 most conservatives believed that balancing the budget was a key element in containing inflation and should be achieved by raising taxes as well as cutting spending; moreover they were alarmed at the prospect of cutting taxes and running deficits to counter a recession while inflation was roaring. Of course, this willingness to raise taxes to restrain inflation, and this fear that cutting taxes might lead to intolerable deficits, was jettisoned by most conservatives when Reagan came to power in 1981 championing a new "supply-side economics" that placed the highest priority on cutting tax rates. But it is impossible to understand the Ford administration's behavior in 1974 without understanding the economic perspective of conservatives that prevailed prior to 1980.

It took until January 1975 for most conservatives to reluctantly conclude that combating a now severe recession deserved a higher priority than containing inflation. Once Republicans joined Democrats in assigning top priority to fighting the recession, it took just three months to enact the fiscal stimulus. In his book, *Economic Policy and the Great Stagflation* (1979), Alan Blinder described how Republicans concentrated on inflation throughout 1974. When President Nixon resigned in August under threat of impeachment, Gerald Ford became president. Blinder writes:

> The economic problems facing the new President were perhaps the most severe ones for this country since the Great Depression. And the devilish combination of inflation and recession probably put any President, no matter who he was, in a "no win" situation. In these dire circumstances Gerald Ford, a veteran Congressman who had never sought national office, was thrust into the White House. It may be that not even the wisdom of Lincoln could have unearthed a successful economic policy in these times; and the new President himself confessed that he was a Ford, not a Lincoln.
>
> Mr. Ford made his first major economic address on August 12, 1974, just a few days after assuming office. At the time inflation was roaring along at double-digit rates and the economy had experienced 2 consecutive quarters of negative real growth in GNP—thus satisfying the popular definition of a recession. As was probably inevitable given the political climate, the new President decided to take his chances on inflation fighting, stating flatly that, "My first priority is to work with you to bring inflation under control. Inflation is domestic enemy number one." He further pledged to fight inflation through reduced federal spending. . . .
>
> The period surrounding the much ballyhooed White House "Summit Conference" on inflation in September gave the new President many well-publicized opportunities to express his sincere intention to battle the in-

flationary dragon—opportunities he did not squander. . . . In an address to a joint session of Congress in early October, President Ford [requested] that Congress place a tight ceiling on federal spending and enact a 5% temporary income tax surcharge on corporations and upper-income families. (Blinder 1979, 148–149)

Ever since Reagan came into office championing supply-side economics in 1981, most conservatives have opposed any increase in income tax rates under any circumstances. But in 1974 President Ford and many other Republicans supported a temporary income tax increase to contain inflation. Thus, although many Democrats supported a tax cut in 1974 to combat recession, most Republicans opposed it because of their worry about worsening inflation.

Blinder concedes that in October 1974 President Ford did not know that real output would plunge during 1974:4 and 1975:1; few economic forecasters predicted such a sharp decline. But data was available showing that real GNP had declined for three consecutive quarters and that the fourth quarter would almost certainly show another decline. Blinder continues:

As late as Thanksgiving the President [Ford] held to this hard line against inflation despite a badly deteriorating economy. While he reiterated his advocacy of an increase in unemployment benefits, he still requested budget cuts and listed inflation as his number one concern. But 2 weeks later, in a speech to the Business Council in Washington, this attitude began to soften. Mr. Ford admitted that recession was a serious problem, though he denied that the country was in an "economic crisis." And he added these words of warning to the business leaders: "If there are any among you who want me to take a 180 degree turn from inflation fighting to recessionary pump priming, they will be disappointed."

By January 13, 1975, the economic slide had worsened dramatically, and President Ford's attitudes had changed accordingly. In a televised address to the nation, he conceded that it was time to "shift our emphasis from inflation to recession," though he added that "in doing so, we must not lose sight of the very real and deadly dangers of rising prices." Instead of the tax increase he had requested just 3 months earlier, Mr. Ford now called upon Congress to enact a $16 billion tax reduction—including a $12 billion reduction for consumers (mostly through a rebate of 1974 taxes) and a $4 billion cut for businesses (mostly in the form of an increase in the investment tax credit). However, at the same time he called for a moratorium on further federal spending, threatening to veto any new spending proposals that the Congress sent him. (Blinder 1979, 150)

Thus, in a period of stagflation, with the economy plagued by both inflation and recession, there will inevitably be disagreement about which should get the highest priority. It took until January 1975 for Republicans to join Democrats in giving highest priority to fighting the recession. Once that consensus was formed, it took only three months to forge a fiscal stimulus package and enact it into law, even though Congress was controlled by the Democrats and the president was a Republican.

Prompt Political Compromise over the Content of the Fiscal Package

It is remarkable how quickly Republicans and Democrats forged a compromise stimulus package once the Republican president shifted his top priority from inflation to recession at the beginning of January. Here is how it happened. On the front page of the December 23, 1974 issue of the *New York Times* there appeared an article with this title, "10% Tax Reduction to Spur Economy is Urged on Ford," and with this subtitle: "Brimmer asks $13-Billion Cut—Congressional Unit and Heller Also Plead." Perhaps not coincidentally, adjacent to the article the *Times* placed a picture of a smiling President Ford starting up a chair lift at his Vail, Colorado ski vacation. The article reads as follows:

> A former member of the Federal Reserve Board has proposed to President Ford and Congressional leaders a quick, one-time-only $13-billion stimulus for the economy through a 10 percent reduction in Federal income taxes due next April. The proposal was made in the form of letters to the President and other leaders by Andrew F. Brimmer, who left the reserve board earlier this year and is now teaching at Harvard. He disclosed it in an interview. Government officials have privately expressed interest in the idea. . . . Under the Brimmer proposal, everyone's tax liability on 1974 income would be reduced by 10 percent, regardless of the amount that had been withheld. . . . In many cases taxpayers would swing from owing taxes to receiving a refund. With individual income-tax liabilities estimated at $132 billion, the plan would mean that taxpayers as a whole would have $13.2 billion more to spend in the early months of this year. Taxpayers can get refunds as early as February. . . .
>
> "I think most of it would be spent," Mr. Brimmer said. "And this spending is needed to restore production."
>
> Other advantages cited by Mr. Brimmer include the following:
>
> • The stimulus would be for next year only, when the economy is in a recession. It would not lead to a permanent loss of revenues, nor would it pump

up the economy with new government spending programs that would be difficult to "turn off."
* It would partly correct what many regard as the "unjust" impact of inflation, which tends to push people into higher tax brackets as their income rises."

On January 13, 1975, President Ford unveiled his plan. It was described in a front page *New York Times* article as follows:

> President Ford, announcing a drastic turn in his economic policies in a nationally televised address, proposed tonight a $16-billion income tax cut that would include a rebate to individuals of up to $1,000 from their payments on 1974 income. The proposed rebate, amounting to 12 per cent of tax payments for 1974, would come in two equal installments, one in May and one by September, the President said. . . . There was a tone of reluctance in the President's speech . . . a reluctance at recommending an enormous Federal deficit as a result of the tax cut. "I have fought against deficits all my public life," he said. Yet he made a sharp turn from mild October 8 proposals—which counted inflation, not recession, the major danger. . . . (*New York Times* January 14, 1975)

The Democrats, who held a majority in both houses of Congress, had been calling for fiscal stimulus for many months. But they contended that President Ford's formula would distribute too much rebate to the affluent relative to the nonaffluent. On February 6, less than a month after the president made his tax-cut proposal, the key committee of the House of Representatives enacted an alternative. The action was reported on the front page of the *Washington Post*:

> The House Ways and Means Committee approved yesterday a $20.2 billion anti-recession tax cut, including $8 billion in rebates that would be mailed out by the Treasury late this spring. The rebates would generally be 10 per cent of 1974 income taxes—the ones payable this April 15—but could not go above a maximum of $200 per tax return, nor in most cases below a minimum of . . . $100. The only taxpayers who would get less than the minimum would be those whose total taxes were less; they would simply get back everything they had paid. The one other complication is that the maximum would decline for those with total incomes over $20,000. They would get back less than $200 per return. They would all, however, get at least the minimum of . . . $100. (*Washington Post* February 7, 1975)

Shortly thereafter the House enacted the committee's bill. A month and a half later, on March 22, the Senate enacted a bill quite similar to the one enacted in the House. To reconcile the two bills as quickly as possible, a conference committee with representatives from both houses promptly met. The House Ways and Means rebate, as described above, prevailed. Two additional provisions were added to benefit two groups helped little by the rebate: A one-shot $50 payment for Social Security beneficiaries; and a "work bonus" for workers with children that has come to be known as the earned income tax credit (EITC), equal to 10 percent of wages up to a maximum of $400 (when wage income reaches $4,000), then phasing down to zero when income reaches $8,000 (an annount of the origin of the EITC is given in Hoffman and Seidman 2003). In just one week both houses of Congress had ratified the conference committee bill, and sent it to the president who immediately signed it into law on March 29. Despite the fact of a Republican president and a Democratic Congress, the entire process of formulating, compromising, and enacting the tax cut was completed in three months.

The Tax Reduction Act of 1975

Blinder describes the components of the stimulus package that was finally enacted at the end of March:

The Tax Reduction Act of 1975, the centerpiece of fiscal policy during the recession, included the following major elements:

1. A *one-time* rebate of 1974 taxes, amounting to just under $8 billion.
2. A reduction in personal income taxes for *1 year* of about $12 billion, accomplished mostly through reduced withholding and subsequently extended.
3. A *one-time* payment of $50 to each recipient of social security benefits, amounting to about $1.7 billion.
4. A so-called "earned income credit" (a type of negative income tax) of about $1 billion, also for 1 year, and also subsequently extended.

[The table below] details the effects on personal disposable income (in current dollars) of the various provisions of the 1975 tax cut and its extension into the first half of 1976.

	Tax rebate	Other tax cuts	Social security	Earned income	Total
75:2	31.2	8.5	6.7	0	46.4
75:3	0	12.3	0	0	12.3
75:4	0	11.9	0	0	11.9
76:1	0	14.2	0	1.9	16.1
76:2	0	14.0	0	1.6	15.6

In addition, there were small temporary cuts in corporate income taxes and large temporary increases in the investment tax credit. In total, the fiscal package moved the high employment budget from approximate balance in 1975:1 to a deficit of $29 billion in 1975:3 [I omit 1975:2, which was distorted by the huge rebate]. . . . (Blinder 1979, 151)

Eckstein gives this account of the fiscal stimulus package:

The combined fiscal policy measures injected $22.8 billion into the economy. Much of the stimulus was of a one-time nature, including a personal tax rebate of $8.2 billion and $1.7 billion in payments to social security recipients. The larger part of the fiscal package was enacted to be effective through the balance of the calendar year; and after some political controversy, these elements were subsequently retained. The more permanent measures included $7.8 billion in personal tax reductions accomplished with changes in the tax withholding schedules, a small negative income tax for the working poor, an increase in the business investment tax credit, and corporate tax reductions offset by the repeal of the oil depletion allowance. In addition, Federal grants to state and local governments were increased to create 320,000 new public service jobs. (Eckstein 1978, 130)

Eckstein's Estimate of the Impact of the Fiscal Stimulus on the Economy

What was the impact of this fiscal stimulus on the economy? To answer this question, Eckstein uses the DRI model to estimate what path the economy would have followed without the fiscal stimulus. He simulates the model with and without the fiscal stimulus package, and reports:

Without the massive injection of tax rebates in the spring of 1975, the economy would have stayed on a downward course in the second quarter. Real GNP would have declined at a 6.2% annual rate compared to small positive growth under actual policies. Real GNP would have risen at an average rate of 8% in the second half of 1975; yet the level of real GNP would have fallen short of its historical path by 3.8% in the third quarter and 3.0% in the final quarter (Eckstein 1978, 130)

The DRI model predicts that there will be a lag between an increase in disposable income and the consequent increase in consumption spending. Its consumption equations, fitted to U.S. time series data, detect such a lag. Thus, according to its consumption equations, a significant portion of the rebate that households received in the second quarter of 1975 was initially saved rather than spent. According to these equations, it took several quarters for most of the rebate to be spent:

> The full impact of the stimulus was not immediately felt. A large portion of the tax rebates and tax cuts was saved, pushing the personal savings rate to 10.6% in the second quarter of 1975, compared with 8.8% in the alternative. The proportion of incremental disposable income channeled into savings was 45% in the second quarter, 29% in the third quarter and 23% in the last quarter of 1975. Without the tax reductions, real consumption would have averaged 3.2% below the actual levels in the final three quarters of 1975. Real consumption of durables would have dropped 7.8% below its historical path. (Eckstein 1978, 132)

Perhaps the easiest way to appreciate the magnitude of the impact of the stimulus package is to focus on its reduction in the unemployment rate:

> The fiscal stimulus was the pivotal factor in reversing unemployment during 1975. The unemployment rate peaked at 8.9% in the spring and dropped to 8.4% by the end of the year. Without the tax cuts and emergency public service employment programs, the unemployment rate would have climbed to 9.3% in the second quarter and peaked at 9.6% in the final quarter of 1975. (Eckstein 1978, 133)

Eckstein draws this lesson from the Great Recession concerning fiscal policy:

> *The Keynesian theory of fiscal policy received strong support during the Great Recession.* The tax cut of 1975, which was imposed under trying conditions, was spent promptly and fully, with the extra retail spending fully matching the tax cut in just five months. (Eckstein 1978, 149–150)

Modigliani and Steindel's Estimate of the Impact of the 1975 Rebate

Modigliani, the originator of the life cycle hypothesis of consumption, and his coauthor Steindel analyze the rebate using the MPS (MIT/Penn/Social Science Research Council) model that Modigliani helped to develop:

> The quantitative characteristics of this consumption sector can be illustrated by its predicted total expenditure response in the first year after a $10 billion tax reduction. If the reduction takes the form of a one-time

rebate, consumer spending is predicted to rise by $7 billion during the
first year. (Modigliani and Steindel 1977, 180)

Thus, the MPS model predicts that consumer spending in the year following a one-time rebate will equal 70 percent of the rebate. How is this
estimate made? They explain:

[It] is simply the difference between the actual forecast of the model and
an alternative forecast computed on the assumption that there had been
no rebate—subtracting from the second-quarter disposable income the
amount of the rebate. (Modigliani and Steindel 1977, 181)

Further, they present the time pattern of spending. The rebate paid out in
1975.2, expressed at an annual rate (in 1972 dollars), was $25.6 billion.
The result is as follows:

**Effects of the 1975 Tax Rebate on Consumer Spending Predicted by the
MPS Model** (the rebate was $25.6 billion in 1975.2 in 1972 dollars; consumer
spending is in 1972 dollars)

	1975.2	1975.3	1975.4	1976.1	1976.2	1976.3
MPS predicted effect of rebate on consumer spending ($billions)	9.1	3.8	2.9	2.2	1.4	0.9
MPS predicted effect of rebate, cumulated as percent of rebate	35.5	50.4	61.7	70.3	75.8	79.3

Thus, the MPS model predicts that over a third (35.5 percent) of the rebate
was spent in the first quarter, half (50.4 percent) in the first two quarters, 61.7
percent in the first three quarters, and 70.3 percent in the first year.

Thus far, their results are similar to Eckstein's using the DRI model. But
having presented these numbers, and having stated that these are the effects
of the rebate that are "predicted" by their MPS model, they then *overrule
their own model* by making a controversial assumption. They note that in
1975.2, the MPS model forecasts a level of consumption spending that is
$5.0 billion higher than the actual level. Modigliani and Steindel simply
assume that the error for consumption in 1975.2 is due *entirely* to over-

predicting the power of the rebate. Although the model predicts that the rebate raises consumption $9.1 billion, Modigliani and Steindel (182) assert that because the model's consumption forecast is $5 billion too high, the "true" or "actual" effect of the rebate was only $4.1 billion. They assert: "Clearly, this figure [$4.1 billion] provides an estimate of the 'true' effect of the rebate on expenditure." In each quarter, they attribute the *entire* error of the MPS consumption forecast to a *presumed* equal error in the MPS model's predicted effect of the rebate. They therefore present another row as their estimate of the effect of the rebate.

From this point on, *they overrule their MPS model*, and refer only to their own estimates rather than to the MPS model's predicted effects. Thus,

	1975.2	1975.3	1975.4	1976.1	1976.2	1976.3
Modigliani/Steindel estimate of effect of rebate on consumer spending ($billions)	4.1	3.5	1.2	6.8	3.5	2.6
Modigliani/Steindel estimate of effect of rebate cumulated, as percent of rebate	16.0	29.7	34.4	60.9	74.6	84.8

they assert that in the first quarter, 1975.2, consumption increased by only 16 percent of the rebate, despite the fact that the MPS model predicts that consumption increased by 35 percent of the rebate. *Their estimate is less than half of the effect predicted by their own MPS model.*

A discussant of their paper, Thomas Juster, challenges their controversial assumption:

> The authors estimate consumption patterns without rebates . . . by using prediction errors from a simulation that ignores the existence of temporary tax changes. But that procedure holds up only if the equation is perfectly specified; otherwise errors arise from a combination of causes, only one of which is the omitted transitory tax change. (Juster 1977, 207)

Juster then makes this observation:

> Interestingly enough, their preferred equation has a time path for the rebate part of the 1975 tax cut that is not credible, as they themselves point

out: it implies that the effect of the rebate accelerates through time, being larger in the fourth through the sixth quarters after the rebate than in the first through the third quarters. (Juster 1977, 207)

To see Juster's point, compare the row of dollar amounts showing the MPS predicted effect of the rebate with the row of dollar amounts showing the Modigliani/Steindel estimate of the effect of the rebate. The MPS row shows a plausible pattern of a monotonically declining impact of the $25.6 billion rebate on consumer spending, from $9.1 billion in the first quarter, 1975.2, to $0.9 billion in 1976.3. By contrast, the Modigliani/Steindel row shows an implausible pattern, with the impact on consumer spending declining over the first three quarters from $4.1 billion to $1.2 billion, but then inexplicably jumping to a peak value of $6.8 billion in 1976.1 before once again declining.

I summarize the Modigliani/Steindel study this way. They report that the MPS model, like the DRI model, predicts that a third of the rebate is spent in the first quarter, and two-thirds in the first year. They argue, however, that their own model's estimate should be overruled, based on their controversial assumption that the model's prediction error in 1975.2 is due entirely to the model's overestimate of the power of the tax rebate. Like Juster, I do not find this assumption to be persuasive. I therefore give more weight to the results from the MPS model itself, and note that it is similar to Eckstein's results from the DRI model.

Blinder's Estimate of the Impact of the 1975 Rebate

Blinder presents an innovative approach to estimating the impact of the 1975 rebate:

> I come now to the important question of whether the effectiveness of the tax cuts of 1975 and 1976 was undermined by their explicitly temporary nature and, if so, to what extent. The discussion is divided into three sections. The first section reviews the reasons why the implications of the pure permanent income (or life-cycle) theory must be modified, reasons that make the issue an empirical one, not to be decided on *a priori* grounds. . . . The second section presents the basic ideas of the model to be estimated in as nontechnical form as possible. The empirical results are presented and analyzed in the third section. (Blinder 1979, 155)

Blinder explains why the actual impact of a tax rebate is probably larger than predicted by the permanent income or life cycle hypothesis:

But there are a number of reasons to believe that the pure permanent income theory systematically *understates* spending from a temporary tax.

A first reason for why surtaxes may affect spending more strongly than indicated by pure theory is that the concept of *consumption* to which the theory applies differs from the *consumer spending* that is relevant to aggregate demand [Footnote: *Consumption* is obtained from *consumer spending* by subtracting purchases of consumer durables and adding back the imputed service flow from the existing stock of durables]. The theory may be correct in predicting little effect of a temporary tax on *consumption*, yet there could be a strong effect on aggregate demand if consumers "save" their tax rebates by purchasing durable goods. . . .

A second reason is that some households may have their spending constrained by limitations on borrowing that are usually ignored by the permanent income theory. Such constrained households may react strongly to even temporary income changes. Thus the aggregate MPC [marginal propensity to consume] for a temporary tax is a weighted average of the low MPC's of unconstrained households and the high MPC's of constrained ones. . . .

Third, . . . consumer behavior depends on what people *believe* rather than on what the government *announces*. If consumers disbelieve the government when it tells them that a tax hike is only temporary, then the spending response will be greater than that predicted by pure theory [Footnote: The point has rather less cogency for tax cuts, but here too consumers may believe them to be more permanent than the government says.] It is the *perceived* duration of the surtax, not the *declared* duration, that is relevant from the standpoint of the permanent income theory. . .

Finally, we must recognize the possibility that households may be more shortsighted than the rational long-term planners envisioned by the theory, or, what amounts to the same thing, may have very high discount rates. If they are shortsighted, then temporary fluctuations in disposable income may have substantial effects on spending.

Notice that all four of these caveats point in the same direction: toward a greater MPC from temporary tax changes than would be predicted from the pure life-cycle theory. (Blinder 1979, 155–156)

Blinder then makes several points that will guide his own empirical study:

The theoretical and empirical review of the previous section leads to three conclusions that influenced the design of my own research. First, the "zero effect" hypothesis . . . is really outside the reasonable range: even the purest form of the permanent income hypothesis suggests that a temporary tax change will have *some* short-run effect. Second, if we consider a long enough period (e.g., a period equal to the planning horizon of the consumer), then *every* tax will be fully effective, regardless of how temporary or permanent it is. This conclusion follows simply because consumers *eventually* will spend almost all of any income change. Thus, if we want to inquire into the "effectiveness" of a temporary tax, it is crucial to specify the time horizon over which this "effectiveness" is to be judged. Third, and finally, both theory and evidence suggest that it is inappropriate to run a contest between two polar cases such as "zero effect" and "full effect," however these two extremes may be formulated. There is every reason to believe that the truth, as so often happens, lies between the two extremes. (Blinder 1979, 158)

Blinder presents his empirical work in his book, but a revised presentation of the same empirical work appears in his 1981 article in the *Journal of Political Economy.* I will focus on his exposition in that article. Blinder's method is to separate changes in income due to temporary tax changes from changes in income due to other reasons, and to try to estimate the impact of each separately. Although the details of his empirical work are complex, his strategy is straightforward: Instead of regressing consumption against disposable income from all sources the way the standard models (such as DRI and MPS) do, he regresses consumption against what disposable income would have been ignoring temporary tax changes, and against temporary tax changes. Thus, in contrast to the standard models, he obtains one estimate for the impact of temporary tax changes on consumption, and another for the impact of changes in disposable income from other sources. He relies on the temporary tax changes in 1968 and 1975 to provide his estimates.

Blinder emphasizes that his estimates are subject to large standard errors because of the paucity of temporary tax changes in his sample. With this caveat, Blinder reports finding small responses to both permanent and temporary tax changes (his Table 4). For example, suppose there is a permanent tax cut of $100 per year. It might seem that in the first quarter a consumer would raise her annual rate of consumption spending by, say, $80 or $90 per year, and this would be maintained in every future quarter. Yet Blinder estimates that in the first quarter the consumer would raise her annual rate of consumption spending by only $34. This response to a "permanent" tax change seems very low, unless, of course, the consumer is either unaware of the permanency of the tax cut, or refuses to believe that the tax cut is really permanent and therefore responds cautiously. Blinder's estimate for the response to the rebate is even smaller: in the first quarter the consumer would raise her annual rate of consumption spending by only $16.

Perhaps because responses to both permanent and temporary tax changes seem low in absolute amount, Blinder emphasizes the relative rather than the absolute responses. He summarizes his results this way:

> Though the standard error is unavoidably large, the point estimate suggests that a temporary tax change is treated as a 50–50 blend of a normal income tax change and a pure windfall. Over a 1–year planning horizon, a temporary tax change is estimated to have only a little more than half as much impact as a permanent tax change of equal magnitude, and a rebate is estimated to have only about 38 percent as much impact. (Blinder 1981, 47)

It is important to note the first phrase in his summary: "Though the standard error is unavoidably large." The reason it is unavoidably large is that there have been relatively few temporary tax changes. In his sample, Blinder has only the temporary changes in 1968 and 1975. This is the reason, of course, that the standard models (such as DRI and MPS) make no attempt to estimate the response to temporary tax changes, but acquiesce in the assumption that a change in disposable income, regardless of its source, has the same impact on consumption. Blinder and other economists are right to be skeptical of that assumption. But unless temporary tax changes become more frequent, economists will be unable to provide estimates of the impact that have small standard errors. Blinder's strategy is a good one in theory, and his point estimates are a useful contribution, but the inevitable large standard errors of his estimates should always be kept in mind.

Poterba's Estimate of the Impact of the 1975 Rebate

How does Poterba's study differ from the others? All of the earlier studies use quarterly data. He writes:

> My analysis differs from previous studies in using monthly consumption data to exploit the pronounced intraquarter pattern of the 1975 rebate. (More than three-quarters of the rebate were received in May.) This higher frequency data is also attractive because finding that spending rises in the month when tax payments change is strong evidence of a link between current income and consumption. (Poterba 1988, 414)

Like Blinder's study, Poterba's has only two temporary tax changes to include in his sample, the 1968 surtax and the 1975 rebate. He explains his strategy this way:

I estimate the effect of the rebate and the surtax following recent econometric studies of the stochastic permanent income hypothesis. . . . These studies demonstrate that in the presence of rational expectations and perfect credit markets, the change in the logarithm of real per capita consumption (c_t) should not be predictable from lagged information. Since both the rebate and surtax were announced at least a month before the change in tax payments, they should have been incorporated into consumption before they affected cash flow. The tax changes therefore should not help forecast the change in consumption between one month and the next. (Poterba 1988, 414)

Poterba runs the following regression on monthly data from 1959.6 to 1987.9 (339 observations):

$$c_t = a_0 + a_1 c_{t-1} + g[Dtax_t/c_{t-1}] + e_t$$

where c_t is the change in the logarithm of real per capita consumption, and $Dtax_t$ is the change in the real per capital rebate level in month t. Data for the 1975 rebate come from monthly treasury data on personal tax payments. For the 1968 surtax, Poterba uses quarterly data from the *Survey of Current Business* that he distributes equally across months. He says that "after scaling $Dtax_t$ by lagged per capita consumption, the coefficient g measures the amount of additional consumption that results from a $1 rebate." After estimating this equation, he adds several other explanatory variables to the right side of the equation (real per capita wage and salary income, short-term nominal interest rates, and stock market returns), and then estimates the augmented equation. He presents a table with separate estimates for the effect of the 1968 surtax and the 1975 rebate. He reports this result for the impact of a rebate on consumption spending in the month the rebate is received:

The results differ somewhat across specifications, but suggest that consumption spending rises by between 12 and 24 cents per dollar of temporary tax rebate. (Poterba 1988, 414–415)

Two comments are warranted. First, there are only a few months of data with a tax rebate, so it is hard to get an estimate that does not have a large standard error. Remarkably, he does get an error less than half the size of his point estimate for nondurable spending. But he admits that "the standard errors for most of the estimates are nevertheless large."

Second, Poterba estimates the impact of the rebate only in the same month, and ignores any impact in future months; this omission implies that he underestimates the full impact of the rebate over several months. In contrast to Poterba's equation, most macroeconometric models include a distributed lag of disposable income, so that a change in disposable income this quarter is assumed to raise consumption spending over several quarters. But Poterba's equation detects only the change in consumption in the month a rebate check is received. Suppose, for example, that if a consumer receives a rebate of $100 in May she raises consumption $20 in each of five months from May through September. Poterba's equation picks up only the $20 in May. His equation predicts a $20 increase in May. It seems likely that the paucity of data makes it difficult to estimate a distributed lag. It is important to keep in mind, however, that by omitting a distributed lag, Poterba's one-month effect probably significantly understates the full effect (over the next few quarters) of a rebate on consumption spending.

Conclusion

Based on a careful reading of the studies of the 1975 tax rebate, I conclude that the rebate was reasonably effective in helping to combat the 1975 recession.

8

The Tax Rebate in the
2001 Recession

In June 2001, President Bush signed into law a tax cut containing a rebate of $600 per married couple ($300 per single person). The rebate was the one element of the tax cut that received strong bipartisan support (by contrast, the majority of Democrats opposed the rest of the tax cut). The U.S. Treasury mailed these checks out in July, August, and September. The reason for mailing out rebate checks that summer, rather than reducing tax owed the following April 15, was to promptly stimulate consumer spending to counter the slowdown that was occurring in the U.S. economy.

The Origin of the Bush Tax Cut

There is an important parallel between the Bush tax cut of 2001 and the Reagan tax cut of 1981. Neither was conceived as a means to stimulate spending to counter a recession. When candidate Bush announced his tax plan in December 1999, there was no recession in sight; the U.S. economy was enjoying a half decade of strong growth with low inflation. What was in sight were rivals for the Republican presidential nomination, especially Steve Forbes, who were committed to across-the-board cuts in income tax rates because they believed the public, especially its most productive citizens, were overtaxed, and that low tax rates would provide incentives for people to supply more labor and capital and produce a stronger economy over the long run. George W. Bush shared this belief in "supply-side economics" and conservative philosophy. Bush proposed cutting the current five bracket rates, 15 percent, 28 percent, 31 percent, 36 percent, 39.6 percent, to four: 10 percent, 15 percent, 25 percent, and 33 percent.

Similarly, when candidate Reagan proposed his across-the-board income tax cut in 1980, his reasons were the same: to unleash the supply of labor and capital over the long run, not to stimulate demand in the short run to counter a recession. In 1981, Reagan prevailed and his across-the-board cuts in income tax rates were enacted. Only after the tax cut was signed into law in mid-1981 did the economy plunge into a recession that proved more severe than the 1975 recession. In the fourth quarter of 1981, real GNP fell 5.3 percent, and in the first quarter of 1982 it fell 5.1 percent. The unemployment rate, which had remained below 7.5 percent through mid-1981, jumped to 8.6 percent by January 1982, 9.5 percent by June, and peaked at 10.8 percent in December. The recession had been engineered by the Federal Reserve, chaired by Paul Volcker, in an attempt to break the back of inflation which had hovered near 10 percent. Painfully, the severe recession did its job, and the inflation rate was below 5 percent by 1982. With inflation down, the urgent problem now was to stimulate spending in order to prevent the recession from turning into a depression. And at just this crucial moment, the Reagan tax cut began to phase in, providing good old-fashioned Keynesian demand stimulus to an economy that badly needed it. Keynesian stimulus from the Reagan tax cut is perhaps the primary reason the U.S. economy recovered more rapidly than western European economies that had undergone a similar monetary disinflation.

During the 2000 presidential campaign, the economy appeared strong, and the two presidential candidates, George Bush and Al Gore, debated long-run economic issues. Bush and the Republicans argued that cutting income tax rates from top to bottom would provide economic growth in the coming decade. Gore and the Democrats countered that it would be better to preserve the income tax revenue from the affluent to pay down the national debt and strengthen the Social Security and Medicare trust funds for the challenge they would face when the numerous baby boomers retired.

The Weakening Economy

But as election day approached in the fall, the U.S. economy began weakening. Republicans narrowly retained control of both houses of Congress while capturing the presidency in a very close election. During the transition, president-elect Bush remarked that the prospect of a recession made it all the more important to promptly pass his tax plan, implying that the administration was willing to append a Keynesian argument to its central arguments for its tax plan: supply-side economics and the "over-taxation" of the affluent. Democrats resented this sudden convenient conversion to Keynesian economics.

In the 1960s, Democrats and liberals had been ardent champions of using fiscal policy—tax cuts or increases in government spending—to stimulate a weakening economy, even though this meant running budget deficits in the short-run. We saw in chapter 7 that as soon as the OPEC oil-shock recession began in 1974, Democrats were the first to call for tax cuts to stimulate the economy, and President Ford and the Republicans resisted until January 1975. Until 1980, many (though not all) Republicans had resisted the Keynesian argument for running deficits in a recession, and viewed it as a devious method of justifying increased government spending. But with Reagan's election in 1980, the roles of the parties reversed. "Supply-side" Republicans now made the cutting of tax rates their first priority; balancing the budget would have to come second. The result was a decade of huge deficits and a disturbing rise in the ratio of national debt to GDP. In 1990, President George H. Bush angered many conservatives in his own Republican Party by compromising with the Democratic Congress to both cut spending and raise taxes in order to reduce the budget deficit. The hostility of antitax conservatives weakened Bush's support in his campaign for reelection, and contributed to the election victory of Democrat Bill Clinton. In the 1990s, the Democrats became the party that set the higher priority on reducing deficits. Secretary of the Treasury Robert Rubin set out a schedule for deficit reduction, and in return Chairman of the Federal Reserve Alan Greenspan agreed to stimulate the economy with low interest rates. This mix of tight fiscal and easy monetary policy seemed to work, and the second half of the 1990s witnessed strong economic growth with low inflation. During the 2000 presidential election, many Democrats had naturally defended this policy of fiscal discipline, and viewed with alarm the tax cut plan of George W. Bush which they saw as a rerun of "Reaganomics" that would lead to deficits and debt.

In response to the administration's sudden adoption of a Keynesian argument for their tax plan, many Democrats resisted. They correctly pointed out that this was not the real reason Bush had proposed his tax plan. To maximize resistance to Bush's tax plan, many Democrats declared that the Federal Reserve could handle any recession threat by lowering interest rates. Monetary policy alone could do the job. Thus, in 2001 quite a few Democrats resisted the Keynesian prescription to use fiscal policy as well as monetary policy to combat the economic slowdown.

The Origin of the Tax Rebate

But not all Democrats took this view. They opposed the Bush permanent tax cut, with its benefits skewed to the affluent, and instead offered a temporary tax rebate with equal dollar benefits for households of all incomes. The following two op ed pieces reflected the approach adopted by many Democrats.

In a January 28, 2001 op ed piece in the *Philadelphia Inquirer,* I write:

> *In A Recession, Think Tax Rebates, Not Across-the-Board Cuts in Taxes*
> In testimony on Thursday before the Senate Budget Committee, Alan

Greenspan took us back to the last time Congress enacted a tax cut specifically aimed at combating a recession.

Confronted with a deepening recession in January 1975, the President and Congress responded promptly to stimulate consumer spending. President Gerald Ford proposed a stimulus package in January, the House passed the bill in late February, the Senate approved it in March, and the president signed later that month.

The key element of the Tax Reduction Act of 1975 was a 10 percent rebate of each household's 1974 personal income tax up to a maximum of $200 per household—sending nearly $8 billion from the Treasury to households from late April to mid-June. More than three-quarters of the rebate checks were received in May.

In his 1978 monograph analyzing "the great recession" of 1975, Harvard economist Otto Eckstein used the DRI model to compare how the economy performed with the stimulus package to how it would have performed without it. He concluded that the stimulus played a key role in mitigating the recession. According to the DRI simulations, in the absence of the stimulus, output would have declined at a 6 percent annual rate in the second quarter of 1975 instead of holding steady; and the unemployment rate would have been 9.6 percent at the end of 1975 instead of being 8.4 percent.

Eckstein concluded that "the Keynesian theory of fiscal policy received strong support during the Great Recession. The tax cut of 1975 . . . was spent promptly and fully, with the extra retail spending fully matching the tax cut in just five months."

Congress should immediately begin drafting a tax rebate similar to the one enacted in 1975. If Congress follows the sensible design of the 1975 rebate, each household will receive a rebate equal to X percent of its 2000 Federal income tax up to a maximum of $Y dollars per household, and each Social Security recipient will receive a one-time benefit supplement of $Z dollars.

Technicians should advise Congress on the numerical values for X, Y, and Z that will provide the appropriate degree of stimulus for the economy. As in 1975, it will take at least a month to agree on the exact content of the rebate. By then, there will be clearer evidence on whether the economy has actually entered a recession. If so, the rebate should be enacted promptly.

If not, the rebate should be kept on the shelf, ready if and when the economy actually enters a recession. Ideally, Congress should enact permanent legislation that would automatically trigger a rebate whenever the economy enters a recession, automatically renew the rebate periodically as long as the economy is in recession, and automatically terminate the rebate once the economy emerges from recession.

A temporary tax rebate, not a permanent across-the-board cut in tax rates, is the appropriate response to an economic recession. President Bush's proposal to cut income tax rates permanently, top to bottom, should be judged on its long-term implications for the federal budget, the economy, and the distribution of economic welfare. If enacted, the Bush tax-rate cut will not be terminated when the recession (if it occurs) ends, so it should only be enacted if its long-term effects are judged desirable. Nor is the Bush rate cut well designed to stimulate consumer spending to counter a recession because a large share of the dollars will go to affluent families who have a lower propensity to spend (and a higher propensity to save) than the average family. Thus, Congress should put the temporary anti-recession rebate on a separate fast track for prompt enactment, while taking more time to consider the long-term implications of the permanent Bush rate-cut proposal.

Although Alan Greenspan and the Federal Reserve have generally done a good job steering the economy, they need help in a recession. Greenspan was at the helm in 1990 when the economy last fell into recession, and the economy remained sluggish for nearly two years despite the Fed's attempt to counter it. If a recession occurs, the Fed will lower interest rates and this will stimulate some borrowing and spending. But for many households, a tax rebate will do more to increase their spending than lower interest rates.

The best argument for leaving a recession to the Fed is not that the Fed can easily handle a recession, but the fear that Congress will enact a stimulus that cannot be reversed once the recession is over. This fear is fully justified with respect to an across-the-board rate cut. But it is unwarranted with respect to a tax rebate which requires another congressional vote to renew it. Congress should get ready to give the Fed the right kind of help if recession comes: a tax rebate.

In a February 1, 2001 op ed piece in the *New York Times*, Richard Freeman, professor of economics at Harvard, and Eileen Appelbaum, research director at the liberal Economic Policy Institute, write:

Instead of a Tax Cut, Send Out Dividends

Imagine arriving home at the end of the workday to find a $500 check from the government waiting for you in the mail. Even better: Imagine a prosperity dividend, paid to every American man, woman, and child, thanks to a record budget surplus. . . . Our current surplus is America's return on 10 years of good economic performance, to which all of us have contributed. The government should declare a dividend—a one-time payment that would give a quick lift to the economy, spur consumer spending and help fight off a potentially deep recession. . . .

But for this kind of stimulus to work, it should meet three criteria.

First, it should be large enough to matter in an economy as large as ours. A tax-free $500 check to every permanent resident would transfer roughly $140 billion from the government to the private sector—enough to make a difference.

Second, the stimulus should automatically end once the economy is back on track. The prosperity dividend meets this criterion because it is a one-time payment from the government to the people.

And third, the stimulus should be targeted to people who need it. The prosperity dividend would be distributed equally to everyone living permanently in the United States. But it would mean the most to low- and middle-income families with young children. (A married couple with two children would receive a total of $2,000). These families would be likely to spend all or most of the dividend on goods and services. If they were in financial distress, they could use it to pay down credit card debts. . .

A prosperity dividend check to every person in America is a fair and efficient way to spend a part of the surplus that all Americans helped produce while stimulating the economy quickly without tying government's hands for the future.

In fact, the Bush tax plan contained one element that was compatible with the proposals in these op ed articles. Under the income tax schedule then in effect, the tax rate that applied to the first dollars of taxable income was 15 percent. Although the Bush plan emphasized the cut in the top marginal tax rates, it also contained a proposal to create a new 10 percent tax bracket that would apply to the first $12,000 of taxable income for a couple filing jointly, and the first $6,000 for a single person; thereafter, the household would enter the 15 percent tax bracket. This cut of 5 percentage points (15 percent to 10 percent) on the first $12,000 of taxable income for a couple meant a $600 tax cut; on the first $6,000 for a single person, a $300 tax cut. All taxpayers of all incomes pay the first bracket rate on their first dollars of taxable income, so all couples with taxable income above $12,000 would receive an equal dollar tax cut—$600, under the Bush plan (and all singles with taxable income above $6,000 would receive a $300 dollar tax cut). Clearly, this one element of the Bush plan was very similar to the proposals in the op ed articles and appealed to many Democrats.

A front page story on March 24, 2001 in the *New York Times* by reporter David Rosenbaum read:

Democrats Back Immediate Tax Cut Proposed by G.O.P. Disputes on the Details. Tying Plan to Bigger Reduction Promised by Bush Stands in Way of Consensus

The idea of a $60 billion tax cut this year to stimulate the economy gained strength in Congress today, but new questions arose about whether a consensus could be reached on the details. Senator Tom Daschle of South Dakota, the Democratic leader, and Senator Kent Conrad of North Dakota, the top Democrat on the Budget Committee, called news conferences to announce their strong support of a plan for an immediate tax cut announced Thursday by Republican Senators.

But Mr. Daschle and Mr. Conrad said they could not go along with the intention of Republicans to tie the $60 billion tax cut for 2001 to Congressional approval of the across-the-board rate reductions proposed by President Bush. The rate cuts have been approved by the House but face uncertain prospects in the Senate.

"Why not take what we already agree on, in the name of expeditious response to the economic concerns raised by leaders in both parties," Mr. Daschle said, instead of holding "that piece hostage to the larger questions involving the tax cut that have been debated now for several months." . . .

Senator Joseph I. Lieberman, Democrat of Connecticut, plans to offer a proposal next week to send a rebate check to all taxpayers. The advantage in that approach is that people would get a chunk of money quickly. The problem is that the last record the Internal Revenue Service has of most taxpayers is their 1999 tax returns, and millions have moved, divorced or died since those returns were filed. . . .

On March 27, the Senate Democratic leadership introduced bill S629 aimed at providing an immediate stimulus to the economy. They issued the following sheet describing the key features of the bill:

Senate Democratic Immediate Tax Cut Fact Sheet (March 27, 2001)

The Senate Democrats propose an immediate tax cut for all taxpayers to help keep the economy growing. The bill has two components: 1) A one-time tax refund check for all people who pay income and payroll taxes; 2) An immediate and permanent cut in the 15 percent income tax rate for all income taxpayers, creating a new 10 percent bracket.

Tax Cut Checks to Provide Economic Stimulus

The bill would dedicate $60 billion of the fiscal year 2001 non-Social Security and non-Medicare surplus to provide tax refund checks to help keep the economy growing.

Eligibility: People who had income or payroll tax liability in 2000 would be eligible to receive a tax cut check. Taxpayers who were claimed as dependents would not be eligible. The tax cut checks would be computed independently of eligibility for the earned income or child tax credit. Taxpayers who erroneously do not receive checks would be able to file a claim for the monies.

Amount: Eligible couples would receive a tax cut check of $600. Singles would receive $300.

Timing: The IRS would rely on address and tax information from 2000 returns and W-2 information for those people who do not file returns. From historical experience and discussions with former officials, we would expect the tax cut checks to begin to be mailed about two months after enactment. Therefore, if the bill is passed in April, people would begin to receive the checks in July.

Creating a New 10 Percent Bracket

A portion of the 15 percent bracket that *all* income taxpayers face would be cut to 10 percent as the President has proposed. For married couples the first $12,000 in taxable income would be taxed at the new 10 percent rate. For singles, the new 10 percent rate would apply to the first $6,000 in taxable income. The only difference between the Democratic proposal and the President's plan is the timing of the tax cut. The President's proposal is phased-in slowly over several years. The Democratic proposal accelerates the timing. The full amount of this tax cut would begin to flow as soon as the IRS and employers are able to change the income tax withholding tables. We estimate that the tables would be changed by about July 1, 2001.

Eligibility: All income tax payers would be eligible for the new 10 percent rate.

Amount: The full year impact of this permanent tax cut would be $600 for a couple and $300 for singles. In 2001, the withholding tables would be changed for six months of the year. Taxpayers would, therefore, receive half of the total amount in 2001. For married couples, this would mean $300 in 2001 and singles would receive $150.

Combined Impact on Average Taxpayers

In 2001, the typical couple would receive $600 from the one-time tax check. In addition, the couple, if they pay income taxes, would receive an additional $300 in 2001 from the new 10 percent bracket. The couples total tax cut in 2001 would therefore be $900. In 2002 and beyond, the couple would receive $600 from the rate cut. Additional tax cuts, such as from marriage penalty relief, would be debated in the context of the overall budget.

Cost
While awaiting official revenue estimates from the Joint Tax Committee, we assume that the one-time checks will cost roughly $60 billion. The new 10 percent tax bracket would cost about $400 billion over eleven years. The total cost would therefore be about $460 billion excluding interest (which would likely add about $125 billion). Most of the $60 billion in one-time checks would be incurred in fiscal year 2001. However, some of the checks for late filers would not be sent until late 2001 and fall into fiscal year 2002. Most of the cost of the rate reduction would be deferred until fiscal year 2002. However, changes in withholding tables during July, August, and September of 2001 would affect revenues for fiscal year 2001. (Senate Democratic Leadership 2001)

Thus, the Democratic proposal accepted the President's 5 percentage point cut (15 percent to 10 percent) on the first $12,000 (for a couple), but added an additional one-time refund check of the same amount, $600 (for a couple), that would go to all people who pay payroll tax as well as income tax.

In his March 28, 2001 article in the *New York Times,* Rosenbaum writes:

Seeking a political edge on the question of tax cuts, Democrats introduced legislation in the Senate today that would give all taxpayers a $300 rebate check this year and give most of them an additional $150 by withholding less money from their paychecks in the second half of the year. Some Democrats said this proposal, whose cost they put at $60 billion, would relieve the pressure on them to vote for the across-the-board tax-rate reduction over 10 years that President Bush favors. . . .

On the question of rebates, [the Republicans] accused the Democrats of distorting the idea Republicans first broached last week of allocating $60 billion from the budget surplus for an immediate tax cut. Republicans insist that the one-time stimulus be combined with long-term tax reduction. . . . Democrats, meanwhile, were upbeat after months of uncertainty about how to respond to the Bush tax plan.

"We're mystified as to why the Republicans will not take us up on our offer" to lower taxes by $60 billion this year, said Senator Tom Daschle of South Dakota, the Democratic leader.

"Is it possible," Mr. Daschle said, "that the Republicans have just met the first tax cut they don't like, or is it that tax relief for everyone is being held hostage by their commitment to a massive tax cut for the very few?" . . .

Under the Democratic plan, the government would send a $300 check to everyone who paid income or payroll taxes in 2000. A couple would get $600.

In addition, the lowest income tax rate, 15 percent, would be reduced to 10 percent on the first $6,000 of taxable income for an individual and $12,000 for a couple filing jointly. That would mean a tax reduction in the second half of this year of $150—$300 for a couple—which would reflect the lower withholding from paychecks beginning July 1.

The front page story on the same day (March 28) in the *New York Times*, written by reporter Frank Bruni, reads:

Bush Says Rebate Isn't a Substitute for His Tax Plan. Warns against Quick Fix. As One-Time Cut Gains Backing in Senate, President Says It Isn't Enough to Help
President Bush urged lawmakers today not to let the momentum in the Senate for a one-time rebate serve as a substitute for his 10-year tax-cutting plan that he values at $1.6 trillion, saying that the immediate measure would not do nearly enough to revive the economy.

The Passage and Implementation of the Rebate

The final tax act, passed by Congress over Memorial Day weekend near the end of May, reflected the fact that the Republicans controlled both Congress and the White House. The Democrats' proposal to enact an *additional* one-time check to people who pay payroll tax as well as income tax was omitted. However, the president's 5 percentage point cut on the first $12,000 (for a couple) instead of being implemented through small changes in withholding rates and a final adjustment on April 15, 2002, would instead be implemented more promptly just as the Democrats proposed: checks would be mailed out by the U.S. Treasury quickly (between July and September of 2001), $600 per couple ($300 per single person). The Joint Committee on Taxation summarized the final provision in its May 26, 2002 summary of the tax act:

New 10-percent rate bracket
The conference agreement creates a new 10-percent regular income tax bracket for a portion of taxable income that is currently taxed at 15 percent, effective for taxable years beginning after December 31, 2000.

The 10-percent rate bracket applies to the first $6,000 of taxable income for single individuals ($7,000 for 2008 and thereafter), $10,000 of taxable income for heads of households, and $12,000 for married couples filing joint returns ($14,000 for 2008 and thereafter). . . .

Rate reduction credit for 2001

The conference agreement includes a rate reduction credit for 2001 to deliver the benefit of the new 10-percent income tax rate bracket during calender year 2001. Under the conference agreement, taxpayers would be entitled to a credit in tax year 2001 of 5 percent (the difference between the 15-percent rate and the 10-percent rate) of the amount of income that would otherwise be eligible for the new 10-percent rate. Thus, the maximum credit will be $300 in the case of a single individual, $500 in the case of a head of household, and $600 in the case of a married couple filing a joint return. This credit is in lieu of the 10 percent rate bracket for 2001.

Most taxpayers will receive this credit in the form of a check issued by the Department of the Treasury. It is anticipated that the Department of the Treasury will make every effort to issue all checks before October 1, 2001, to taxpayers who timely filed their 2000 tax returns. Taxpayers who filed late or pursuant to extensions will receive their checks later in the fall. (U.S. Joint Committee on Taxation 2002)

On June 7, 2001 President Bush signed the tax bill into law. In his article in the *New York Times* on June 8, reporter David Sanger writes:

President Bush fulfilled a major promise of his campaign for president today, signing into law the most sweeping tax cut in two decades, which he called "the first major achievement of a new era."

Mr. Bush signed the $1.35 trillion tax cut—which provides for soon-to-be mailed rebate checks of $300 to $600 for almost every income-tax payer—amid the kind of presidential pomp he usually disdains: a formal ceremony in the East Room with a Marine Corps band playing "Hail to the Chief." . . .

The Rebate Checks

Next month, the Treasury Department begins mailing checks to all income-tax payers not claimed as a dependent on someone else's tax return.

How much	And when	
	Last two digits of Social Security number	Taxpayer should receive check the week of
Single or married filing separately with over $6,000 in taxable income, $300	00–09	July 23
	10–19	July 30
	20–29	Aug. 6
	30–39	Aug. 13
Head of household	40–49	Aug. 20
with over $10,000	50–59	Aug. 27
in taxable income, $500	60–69	Sept. 3
	70–79	Sept. 10
	80–89	Sept. 17
Married filing jointly	90–99	Sept. 24
with over $12,000 in taxable income, $600		

In early July, millions of taxpayers received the following letter from the IRS:

Notice of Status and Amount of Immediate Tax Relief

Dear Taxpayer:

We are pleased to inform you that the United States Congress passed and President George W. Bush signed into law the Economic Growth and Tax Relief Reconciliation Act of 2001, which provides immediate tax relief in 2001 and long-term tax relief for the years to come.

As part of the immediate tax relief, you will be receiving a check in the amount of $600.00 during the week of _____ . Your amount is based on information you submitted on your 2000 federal tax return and is just the first installment of the long-term tax relief provided by the new law. The amount of the check could be reduced by an outstanding federal debt you owe, such as past due child support or federal or state income taxes.

You need to take no additional steps. Your check will be mailed to you. You will not be required to report the amount as taxable income on your federal tax return . . . the amount of your check will be the lesser of $600, 5 percent of your taxable income, or your income tax liability.

Some Democrats were unhappy with the inclusion of the reference to the long-term tax relief that most Democrats had opposed. They felt the only relevant information was the rebate amount and the date it would be received. Some questioned the need for any advance notice at all.

As noted above, unfortunately not everyone received the rebate. The Republican Congress and the White House rejected the Democrats attempt to include people who paid payroll tax but not income tax. Amy Hamilton describes a report issued by the liberal Citizens for Tax Justice (CTJ). The CTJ estimated that 34 million people who file tax returns would get no check at all, and another 17 million would get only partial rebates, averaging about half the full amounts of $600 (couple), $500 (head of household), and $300 (single). Hamilton writes:

CTJ's figures work precisely with estimates released June 6 by the House Ways and Means Committee. The rebate is a crude application of the new 10 percent tax rate to 2001 income, and it is structured as a credit against 2001 tax liability. So that it can be paid mid-2001 before income for 2001 is known, it is calculated by reference to income in 2000 that would fall into the 10 percent bracket. . . . Because the rebate is based on 2000 income, no repayment is required even if 2001 income would not earn a rebate in the amount paid.

The Ways and Means Committee estimates that 130 million tax returns will be filed by the end of this calendar year, and that 34 million of those returns will show no income tax liability—that is, those filers pay no income tax at all. As a result, no refund check will be issued to those 34 million . . . because there is no income tax liability to refund.

The remaining 96 million returns have tax liability and will receive refunds. Of those, 79 million will receive the maximum check amounts ($600, $500, or $300). Seventeen million will get a smaller check, equal to 5 percent of their taxable income. (Hamilton 2001, 1826)

A humorous and insightful account of the rebate is provided by tax attorney Alvin Lurie in "Funny Money? No, Funny Tax Rebate—And a Larger Largesse Than $600."

The tax rebate checks now showing up in taxpayers' mailboxes must seem to many like an unexpected check from a rich uncle. That's easier to understand than the total improbability of getting a check from Uncle Sam that one didn't ask for, certainly didn't expect, and doesn't really understand. The incomprehensibility of such an unprecedented windfall from Washington is underscored by a recent news item . . . reporting that in the two-week period ending July 31, 2001, 8.6 million people called the IRS with questions about the so-called rebate of their 2001 income tax!

No wonder. It is a head-scratcher, even for us tax professionals, many of whom would be hard-pressed to explain its workings in words our clients can understand. It's not really a 2001 tax rebate. It's not based on any tax paid for 2001. It's even possible for people who will owe no 2001 federal income tax to get this "rebate" of their taxes, and they will nevertheless be entitled to keep it. But illogical as that may seem, indeed unbelievable to those cynics who know better than to believe "checks are in the mail," from the IRS, taxpayers seem to be having no trouble suspending belief, taking their money, and, yes, running with it. . . .

Make no mistake. This is not funny money we're talking about. The rebate mechanism may be pretty funny (as in "odd"); but the dollars being pumped into folks' pockets are very real and fully expected by economists to further support the consumer spending binge that has been such an important antidote to the feared fall into recession. . . .

Rube Goldberg would have loved this rebate. So should your clients. This once, their checks really are in the mail. (Lurie 2001, 1487–1488)

The economy continued to deteriorate. On August 27, in his front page "Outlook" column in the *Wall Street Journal*, reporter Greg Ip takes note of the willingness of a top Bush economic adviser, Lawrence Lindsey, to utilize Keynesian countercyclical policy:

Economic Odd Couple: Keynes Meets Bush
   The federal budget surplus is rapidly shrinking. That's a good thing, but you wouldn't know it from the debate in Washington, where the standard recession-fighting prescription is endangered by a newfound obsession with the Social Security surplus. Most economists accept that, at least in theory, the government should offset contracting private activity in downturns by reducing its tax take and by boosting spending, a policy advocated by British economist John Maynard Keynes in the 1930s. . . .
   On Wall Street, where you'd think preserving surpluses would score points, instead it's considered a really bad idea. "If the economy needs help today, fiscal stimulus may well be a better bargain than mindless fealty to an accounting fiction about Social Security and Medicare trust funds," remarked Neal Soss, Credit Suisse First Boston's chief econo-

mist. Jan Hatzius of Goldman Sachs adds that President Bush's defense of the Social Security surplus may very well stand in the way of a sensible, countercyclical fiscal policy. After all, a temporary on-budget deficit would be a price well worth paying for averting a recession.

But don't let last week's rhetoric in Washington fool you. Keynesianism is not dead. It's enjoying a revival in some of the oddest places. The International Monetary Fund, whose austerity prescriptions are often blamed for deepening the late-1990s Asian crisis, praises the U.S. tax cut as "appropriate and timely." . . .

But Keynesianism's oddest standard bearers are President Bush and the supply sider who advises him, Lawrence Lindsey. Mr. Lindsey once labeled Keynes' advocacy of counter-cyclical fiscal policy "utopian." But last month, he said it was only common sense economics, not only to let the budget deteriorate in a slowdown, but to push it along with a tax cut. He compared Democratic critics of the tax cut to Herbert Hoover, who raised taxes in 1932. . . . If, as many economists think, the 2001 tax cut has come just in time to head off recession, it may give Keynesian fine-tuning its biggest jolt of credibility in decades.

In the political arena, many members of both parties seemed to forget the common sense Keynesian prescription: In an economic boom, run surpluses and pay down debt, but in a recession, run deficits to stimulate the economy. Many Democrats criticized the president for letting the non–Social Security surplus vanish, and blamed his tax cut. Many Republicans agreed that the non–Social Security surplus should be restored, but by cutting wasteful government spending on domestic programs.

There were, however, some liberals and conservatives who recognized that trying to preserve a surplus in the regular budget in the face of a recession is bad economics. On August 29, 2001 liberal Robert Reich, secretary of labor during the first term of the Clinton presidency, wrote a *Wall Street Journal* editorial page article entitled "Surplus Silliness":

> The more fundamental oddity is that both parties have grasped so tightly the orthodoxy of fiscal austerity. Republicans who a few months ago proudly proffered the supply-side mantra that the bush tax cut would spur economic growth over the long term are suddenly squirming over the possibility that their budgets may go into the red in the short term. Democrats who used to celebrate Keynesian deficits as means for stimulating the economy during downturns and simultaneously accomplishing liberal objectives for enhanced public spending are suddenly sounding pious demands that the budget be balanced every year and that the Social Security surplus remain untouched.

Welcome to the magic world of fiscal restraint as an end in itself. Both parties have bought into the budget numbers racket—a zero-sum game that confers enormous power on green-eyeshade actuaries in the Congressional Budget Office. . . . Meanwhile, the American public—though confused and bored—nonetheless has come to accept the premises that the Social Security surplus must not be "raided," that balance in the remainder of the budget is always better than an imbalance, that revenues should always exceed expenses, and that debt is bad. Politicians, either ignorant or fearful of the truth, play along. Much of the financial press accepts the gospel as given. And thus the gap between public understanding and economic reality widens.

Back to basics for a moment. The purpose of fiscal policy is to accomplish two objectives. The first is to complement monetary policy in making full use of the nation's productive capacities. This may mean running deficits when the economy is shrinking and when neither business nor consumer spending is adequate to the task of maintaining adequate aggregate demand.

Similarly, on September 10, 2001 conservative columnist William Safire wrote a *New York Times* op ed article, "Jimmy That 'Lockbox'":

Here is a bedrock principle about the role of government in the economy: When prosperity booms, the government should apply a brake by running a surplus. Conversely, when recession looms, the government should press the accelerator by running a deficit. That subtraction or addition to aggregate demand is called "raising Keynes." Thus, when happy days are here, government should surely slow the growth of spending; when harder times are on the way, the feds should spend more and tax less. . . .Only in boom times is "deficit" a dirty word; when air is hissing out of the balloon and a deficit becomes temporarily desirable, "surplus" becomes the dirty word.

On September 1, my letter appeared on the editorial page of the *New York Times*:

The Rebate Helps. Do It Again
Paul Krugman ("Greenspan Stands Alone," column, Aug. 31) is right that Alan Greenspan, the Federal Reserve chairman, needs help in fighting the looming recession. Congress could provide such help with additional temporary tax cuts.

This quarter, from July through September, millions of taxpayers are receiving $600, $500, or $300 rebates, depending on family size. Some are saving their rebates, others are spending them now, and still others will spend most of their rebates before the year ends.

Congress should immediately enact a repeat of the rebate for the next quarter. The United States Treasury has the mailing addresses ready—new checks could go to the same addresses in the same sequence.

Most technicians advise that a larger stimulus is needed, so Congress should double the size of each check. The rebate should be repeated every quarter until the latest economic data show that a strong economic recovery has begun.

In an article written on September 10 (and appearing in the September 11, 2001 issue of the *Wall Street Journal*), reporter Jacob Schlesinger provides a good summary of the prevailing attitudes toward fiscal stimulus:

Finding a Fix for the Declining Economy: Government's Options Include Spending, Cutting Rates and Taxes

With unemployment rising and the stock market slumping, politicians are nearing a panic, howling for the government to do *something* to stop the economic decline. Of course, it isn't like policymakers have been sitting idly by. The Federal Reserve has cut interest rates seven times this year, while President Bush and Congress approved an emergency tax rebate. Those measures may well turn out to be sufficient to prevent a recession. But with each passing day of scary data, patience inside the Beltway is wearing thin, especially for those folks running for re-election next year. Fed Chairman Alan Greenspan and his central-bank colleagues have a clear course: They will likely keep cutting interest rates. Here is a look at the more complex set of options facing the White House and Capitol Hill:

Q: Politics aside, does it really make economic sense to do anything?

A: Until recently, conventional wisdom told us no. The experts concluded that the wheels of government—outside the Fed—worked too slowly to give any short-term assistance, and by the time federal action kicked in, the economy would be recovering anyway, risking overstimulation. "I don't think the government really has the power to prevent recessions," says Murray Weidenbaum, who was chairman of President Reagan's Council of Economic Advisers. Yet most economists—liberal and conservative alike—grudgingly admit that the answer may indeed be "yes," saying this year's tax rebate was well-timed, thus reviving interest in short-term measures.

Q: So what are the choices?
A: The most likely to succeed is fiscal stimulus—either spending increases or further tax cuts. That is, the federal government pumps more money into the economy. . . .

Q: What is the best kind of tax cut?
A: One that is likely to be spent quickly. For that, it is probably best to give as much money as possible to lower-income and middle-income families. Strapped for cash to meet basic expenses, they are most likely to spend their full check. . . ."

September 11, 2001

Then came September 11, 2001, a day that will never be forgotten. Terrorist hijackers crashed commercial planes into the two towers of New York City's World Trade Center, destroying them and killing three thousand people; and into the Pentagon in Washington, D.C., killing hundreds. The attack completely altered the economic debate. Confronted with a national emergency, Congress abruptly turned away from trying to preserve the current surplus, and focused instead on providing the spending needed to strengthen national security against the terrorist threat, and stimulate the economy that had been shocked by the attack.

In a *New York Times* op ed article "A Post-Disaster Economy in Need of Repair," (September 30, 2001) Robert Rubin, secretary of the treasury during the Clinton administration and known for his emphasis on long-term fiscal discipline, explains how to preserve that discipline while providing short-term stimulus:

> I live and work in New York City, and the terrible tragedy on Sept. 11 has had a tremendous impact on the lives of so many people I know. . . .
>
> Each measure in a stimulus package must have a substantial effect in the short term, the greatest impact for the money spent, and no cost in the later years. The third criterion is crucial. While our strategy needs to be geared to the changed economic situation at hand, the laws of economics have not changed, and the fiscal discipline that was so enormously important over the last eight years is still extremely important now. Since the short-term fiscal position has changed dramatically, it is all the more important to preserve our already diminished long-term fiscal health. Market interest rates affect business investment and, more important, mortgage rates, which in turn affect housing prices and mortgage refinancing, and hence consumption. And market rates now—as well as general confidence—can be significantly influenced by expectations about our longer-term fiscal strength. Despite eight federal rates cuts, longer-

term bond market interest rates have come down very little, which many ascribe, in part, to our diminished long-term fiscal condition following the passage of last spring's tax cut.

I believe all these considerations should guide our work going forward on specific stimulus measures. Business investment has declined because of great excess production capacity. For most companies, low levels of investment now are not the result of cash position or financing capacity, but an absence of demand.

To increase demand, the most effective measures would be tax rebates to low- and middle-income working people—including those who pay Social Security taxes but not income taxes—who have the highest propensity to spend. . . .

In the October 1 issue of the *Wall Street Journal,* reporter Greg Ip writes in his Outlook column, *For Quick Stimulus, Cut Personal Tax Rates:*

With momentum growing for a big fiscal-stimulus package, businesses have been quick to press for what they didn't get in the first Bush tax cut: lower corporate-tax rates and more generous investment write-offs. But whatever the long-term merits of such policies, it's unlikely that a tax cut for businesses will provide the quick shot of adrenaline the slumping U.S. economy needs. . . . Instead, short-term stimulus calls for temporary, not permanent, tax breaks—and preferably for consumers, not businesses. . . .

Advocates of cuts for business say those address the biggest source of weakness in the economy: plunging investment. But experts are doubtful. "Investment spending at this stage is not going to go up even in response to cuts in interest rates or to decreases in taxes," says Massachusetts Institute of Technology economist Olivier Blanchard, who has written extensively on both fiscal policy and investment. Spending on buildings and equipment is falling because business already has too much of both— indeed, just 76% of industrial capacity is in use, the lowest level since 1983. . . . Tax cuts won't get airlines to order more planes or hotels to rehire workers; a resumption of travel would. In other words, stimulating spending and making Americans feel secure would be more effective than reducing corporate-tax rates as a way to boost economic growth.

But how? One option is another tax rebate. While the $40 billion of rebate checks sent out since July haven't turned around the economy, they appear to have kept retail sales from shrinking. And the rebate's effectiveness may have been damped by the exclusion of millions of lower-income households that pay little or no income tax. Christopher Carroll, an economist at Johns Hopkins University in Baltimore who studies consumption and saving, believes that to maximize the amount of consumer-tax cut that's spent, "you want to direct it a much as possible at low-income or low-wealth people." He says there is considerable evidence that poor households spend more of an increase in their incomes than rich households. Many conservative economists argue that for a tax cut to spur households to spend it has to be permanent. Consumers tend to average the impact out over their lifetimes, they say, so a one-time rebate does little to alter their spending plans. But Mr. Carroll says lower-income households, which tend to spend most of what they earn, will increase consumption even with a temporary tax cut. . . .

The revival of Keynesian fiscal policy is evidenced in an op ed article in the *Wall Street Journal* (October 10, 2001) by a long-time opponent, Milton Friedman, who expresses his frustration over its revival:

Crude Keynesianism has risen from the dead. On all sides, there are calls for fiscal stimulus to "provide the quick shot of adrenaline the slumping U.S. economy needs" (to quote from this newspaper's Outlook column on October 1). . . .

I believe this is a great mistake. Let me count the reasons why:

1. The economic slowdown to date has been relatively mild. Unemployment is still at levels that more often accompany prosperity than recession, let alone depression. Sept. 11 was a major shock psychologically, but its direct economic effect—perhaps $25 billion to $100 bilion—is a pin prick in a $10 trillion economy. . . .

2. The Fed is already providing a "quick shot of adrenaline," having cut the federal funds rate from 6.5% to 2.5% in the past nine months, the final one percentage point drop after Sept. 11. Monetary growth (M2) for the past year has been close to 10%, a rate of growth that if long continued would assure a sharp rise in inflation. By historical standards, the Fed's behavior was pre-emptive and aggressive. . . .

3. Fiscal stimulus also takes time to have any effect. Anything passed now is not likely to affect actual spending or tax receipts until after the economy has already started to recover, and to come full flood only when the economy is expanding. Talk about locking the stable door after the horse is stolen.

4. More fundamentally, does fiscal stimulus stimulate? Japan's experience in the '90s is dramatic evidence to the contrary. Japan resorted repeatedly to large doses of fiscal stimulus in the form of extra government spending, while maintaining a restrictive monetary policy. The result: stagnation at best, depression at worst, for most of the past decade. That

has also been the experience in the U.S. and other countries that have tried
to use government spending to jump-start the economy. . . .
5. Cutting taxes now would promote private spending rather than government spending and provide a supply-side incentive. That is highly
relevant for the long run, but not for cyclical stimulus. Here, too, time
delay is crucial. The effect of the tax reductions is likely to come into
effect when the economy is already on the mend.

Shapiro and Slemrod's Study of the 2001 Tax Rebate

In the fall of 2001, University of Michigan economists Shapiro and
Slemrod released the results of a survey of consumer intentions for the
2001 tax rebate. Their study received substantial media coverage, and
may have influenced the debate in Congress against enacting a second
rebate. They asked survey questions to households in August and September about their plans for the tax rebate mailed by the U.S. Treasury
in July, August, and September, and reported that "only" 22 percent
said they intended to mostly increase spending; most said they intended
to use the rebate to pay down debt or save. I would immediately emphasize that spending 22 percent of the rebate would be very helpful in
combating the recession, but their word "only" got media attention.

As I explained in my critique of their study in chapter 6, I believe their
key survey question was seriously flawed. Here is the wording of their key
question:

> Earlier this year a Federal law was passed cutting income tax rates and
> expanding certain credits and deductions. The tax cuts will be phased in
> over the next ten years. This year many households will receive a tax
> rebate check in the mail. In most cases, the tax rebate will be $300 for
> single individuals and $600 for married couples. Thinking about your
> (family's) financial situation this year, will the tax rebate lead you mostly
> to increase spending, mostly to increase saving, or mostly to pay off debt?
> (Shapiro and Slemrod 2002, 5)

Note that they did *not* ask the respondent what *percent* of their rebate
they intend to spend. Now consider a simple hypothetical example. Suppose every household intends to spend 40 percent of its rebate and use 60
percent to pay off debt. Then 0 percent would report that the rebate leads
them "mostly to increase spending," and 100 percent would report that the
rebate leads them "mostly to pay off debt." Yet in this example, the percent
of total rebate dollars spent would be 40 percent, not 0 percent; the marginal propensity to consume of every household would be 40 percent, not 0

percent. In retrospect, it might have been better to ask respondents what *percent* they intended to spend, save, and use to pay off debt. Because the percent was not asked, the study does *not* obtain information on the percent of total rebate dollars that respondents intend to spend (or on the marginal propensity to consume).[1]

Their key question began with the phrase, "Thinking about your (family's) financial situation." This phrase may have influenced some respondents to answer either "save" or "pay off debt." Suppose instead that the phrase had been "Thinking about the needs of your family." Such a phrase might do the reverse. On reflection, perhaps the question should have omitted the introductory phrase, and simply have read: "What percent of the tax rebate will you spend? What percent will you save? What percent will you use to pay off debt?"

Their key question used the phrase "this year." Because the survey was conducted in August, September, and October 2001, some respondents may have interpreted "this year" to mean "before the end of this calender year." If these respondents planned to spend it in early 2002, they may not have answered "spend." In retrospect, perhaps the question should have been: "What percent do you intend to spend *within a* year?"

Shapiro and Slemrod did a follow-up survey in March and April 2002 as a module in the University of Michigan Survey Research Center's monthly Survey of Consumers. Here is the exact wording of their key question:

> Last year a Federal law was passed cutting income tax rates and expanding certain credits and deductions. Some tax cuts took effect last year and others will be phased in over the next nine years. Last year many households received a tax rebate check in the mail. In most cases, the tax rebate was 300 dollars for single individuals and 600 dollars for married couples. Did the tax rebate lead you mostly to increase spending, mostly to increase saving, or mostly to pay off debt? (Shapiro and Slemrod 2002, 16–17)

They state:

> In this survey, 24.9 percent of the respondents reported spending the rebate. (Shapiro and Slemrod 2002, 16)

Their question is very difficult for any respondent to answer accurately. Suppose you were asked what you did with your 2001 rebate? How would you figure it out? You probably remember depositing the rebate check in your bank. But then what? You may recall the moment you wrote a check to pay down your home equity loan, and think, "That's what I did with the rebate." Or you may recall the moment you used your credit card to buy a new TV, and think, "That's what I did with the rebate." Or was it the morning you went shopping at your mall? Was that your rebate? To answer the question accurately, you must compare your actual spending to a hypothetical situation—what you would have spent had there been no rebate. You may recall the moment you think you used the rebate for activity X, but the real issue is how much more did you spend, having received the rebate, than you would have spent had you not received the rebate. To give the correct answer, you have to know what you would have done had there been no rebate. Are you sure you know this?

I believe, then, that the jury is still out on the impact of the 2001 tax rebate. A decision must await the kind of empirical studies of behavior described in chapter 6.

Fall 2001: Political Deadlock over a Stimulus Package

Unfortunately, the fall of 2001 witnessed a partisan political deadlock in Congress over a fiscal stimulus package. The deadlock underscores the need to have automatic fiscal policies, as proposed in chapters 2 and 3, preenacted and in place, ready to be triggered by the state of the economy without the need for new Congressional legislation. On January 20, 2002, my op ed article appeared in the Wilmington, Delaware *News Journal,* explaining the deadlock of fall 2001 and proposing another larger rebate:

> *Just Triple the Tax Rebate*
>   Since passing the $600 tax rebate in June, Congress has fiddled while the economy has slowly burned. In an admirable bipartisan action last June, Republicans and Democrats agreed to instruct the U.S. Treasury to mail tax rebate checks—$600 each—to most American households. With speed and competence, the U.S. Treasury got the checks in the mail in July, August, and September, and the extra cash helped many households maintain their consumer spending.
>   But after this promising bipartisan response to the economic downturn, Congress has reverted to partisanship and has accomplished nothing for the economy. The House Republicans, led by Congressmen Armey and Thomas, decided to use the recession as an excuse to pass a new tax bill favoring wealthy individuals and corporate contributors. Angered by House Republican partisanship, the Senate Democrats countered with a bill to fund several of their long-term priorities such as health insurance. The result has been a rerun of the 2000 election-year debate about long-term priorities, and political gridlock. Meanwhile the economy has stagnated and unemployment has risen.

The Federal Reserve has just cut interest rates again but it is running out of ammunition. This year the Fed has reduced the federal funds rate in eleven steps from 6.5 percent to 1.75 percent, but the interest rate cannot be cut below 0 percent. The Fed badly needs help from Congress, but Fed Chairman Alan Greenspan understandably does not want to alarm the public by openly calling for help.

Instead of trying to negotiate a compromise bill full of partisan measures, it is not too late for the House and Senate to table these measures for the future, and simply triple last June's rebate. The Treasury can have checks in the mail—this time $1,800 per household—in February, March, and April. The Treasury has the mailing addresses ready—new checks could go to the same addresses in the same sequence. Taxpayers who paid payroll tax but not income tax should this time be added to the list to receive a rebate. Prior to September 11, a doubling of the rebate would have been an appropriate response to the weakening economy. Because of the economic impact of September 11, Congress should triple the size of each rebate check.

But do rebates work? It is true that one survey last September found that households reported spending only about 20 percent of their rebate as of September. This is consistent with studies of past experience. In the three months following a tax rebate, households spend perhaps 20 percent. But in the year following a rebate, they spend over 50 percent. Most economists agree that the economy will need more spending throughout 2002. As long as 50 percent of the rebates paid out are spent by the end of 2002, the rebates will be just the medicine the economy needs. If the economy unexpectedly recovers so strongly in 2002 that inflation threatens, the Fed can easily raise interest rates to contain the boom.

Ever since the Great Depression, most economists have taught that when a recession threatens, the government's top priority should be to stimulate household and business spending, not to try to maintain budget surpluses. During a recession, the government should borrow money in order to send rebate checks to households, maintain all its regular spending programs, and expand its spending for countering terrorism. Once the recession is over and the economy is recovering strongly, then the government should make sure that it runs budget surpluses and uses its surpluses to pay off the debt that it incurred during the recession. Tax rebates are inherently temporary. They are sent out only when the economy is weak. Once a strong sustained recovery is underway, Congress and the President should return to the task they accomplished during the 1990s: reducing the deficit until it eventually becomes a surplus and using the surplus to pay down the debt incurred fighting the recession.

So Congress should immediately end the partisan gridlock over a stimulus package. Once again, as in June, let Democrats and Republicans come together quickly to enact a large tax rebate to stimulate consumer spending, and agree to postpone debate over permanent partisan economic measures to a later date.

In early 2002, the economy began to show signs of recovery, and a consensus soon developed that no further stimulus was needed. At the time of this writing in mid-2002, the recovery seems to be continuing, but the pace is weaker than many had hoped. I still believe that another rebate in early 2002 would have helped strengthen the 2002 recovery.

To summarize: In 2001, countercyclical monetary and fiscal policy were implemented. Over the year, the Federal Reserve cut the federal funds rate (in eleven decrements) from 6.50 percent to 1.75 percent. And Congress enacted a $600 rebate that was mailed out to households in July, August, and September. These countercyclical policies surely helped combat the 2001 recession.

Note

1. If 20 percent say they will "mostly spend," it is possible for the percent of the total rebate dollars spent to be as high as 46 percent (if the 20 percent who "mostly spend" actually spend 100 percent, and if the remaining 80 percent spend 33 percent, save 33 percent [34 percent], and use 34 percent [33 percent] to pay off debt, then 46 percent of total rebate dollars would be spent, because .2[100%] + .8[33%] = 46%).

9

Early Studies of Automatic Fiscal Policy

This chapter reviews four early studies of automatic fiscal policy: Phillips (1954), Pack (1968), Duggal (1975), and my own (Seidman 1975). Further progress, as noted in the introduction, was interrupted by the classical counterrevolution. The policy analyzed by Phillips, Pack, and Duggal is actually more complex than the policy I propose in chapter 2. Their policy has three components: "proportional," "integral," and "derivative," in Phillips's terminology, which I will explain below. By contrast, my chapter 2 policy utilizes only the proportional component.

Their studies suggest that my simpler policy may be only a first step toward the optimal design of an automatic fiscal policy, and provide support for my chapter 5 proposal to establish a fiscal policy advisory board that would work continuously on monitoring and improving the design of automatic fiscal policies.

Phillips's Study of Stabilization Policy in a Simple Model

Before he became famous for his empirical study relating wage increases to the unemployment rate, which came to be known as "the Phillips curve," A.W. Phillips wrote an important article on countercyclical policy. In this article, he analyzed the use of three automatic countercyclical policies to which he gave the names proportional, integral, and derivative. Based on his analysis, he contended that a combination of all three policies might better stabilize a macroeconomy than any one policy alone. To analyze the stabilization problem, Phillips turned to the engineering literature.

> The following treatment is an application of the general principles of automatic regulating systems and closed-loop control systems, in the analysis of which notable advances have been made in recent years. (Phillips 1954, 294)

He begins by setting out his model of the economy. He assumes that output adjusts to demand, but with a lag. This lag makes stabilization challenging, because countercyclical policy can only react to the most recent value of output, but output is still in the process of adjusting to demand. He assumes that the greater is the discrepancy between output and demand, the faster is the speed with which output moves toward demand. In turn, the change in output changes demand. He investigates the problem of restoring output as rapidly as possible to its target value after it is displaced from that value by a demand shock. He writes:

> Stabilisation policy consists in detecting any error and taking correcting action, by altering government expenditure, taxation, or monetary and credit conditions, in order to change demand in a direction which tends to eliminate the error. (Phillips 1954, 293–294)

Phillips first considers a proportional policy, essentially the policy I have proposed in chapter 2, which he explains with an example:

> As an example, a proportional correction factor of 0.5 would mean that if production was 2% below the desired value the authorities concerned would attempt to directly stimulate demand by an amount equal to 1% of production (excluding the further increase which would be induced through the multiplier effects), and as the error was gradually reduced as a result of this action they would decrease the . . . policy demand proportionately. (Phillips 1954, 294–295)

Phillips considers how the policy would work if there were a sudden drop in demand. He presents a figure illustrating the path of the economy. For his simple model, and for the particular shock he investigates (a sudden permanent cut in demand), he draws this conclusion:

> Two defects of a proportional stabilisation policy are immediately apparent. First, complete correction of the an error is not obtained, since the correcting action continues only because the error exists. . . . The second defect of a proportional stabilisation policy is that it tends to cause a cyclical fluctuation in the time path of production, this fluctuation being the greater, the stronger the policy and the longer the time lag involved in applying it. (Phillips 1954, 296)

To remedy the first shortcoming of a proportional policy, he proposes an integral policy:

> An integral stabilisation policy is one in which the potential policy demand at any time is made proportional in magnitude and opposite in sign

to the cumulated error up to that time, i.e., to the time integral of the error instead of to the magnitude of the error. (Phillips 1954, 297)

He contends that the integral policy will remedy the first defect of the proportional policy because, as long as any error persists, the cumulated error or time integral must be continuously increasing, and with it the magnitude of the required corrective action. He says, however, that there is a catch.

It will be found, however, that in thus avoiding the first defect of a proportional correction policy, the second defect, the introduction of cyclical fluctuations, is greatly aggravated, and for this reason integral correction is rarely used alone in automatic control systems. (Phillips 1954, 297)

Phillips then recommends adding a derivative policy:

A better method is available which not only eliminates the fluctuations, but also reduces both the maximum size of the error and the time taken to obtain complete correction. This method is to add to the potential policy demand, as determined by the proportional and integral relationships, a third element, proportional in magnitude and opposite in sign to the rate of change, or time derivative, of production. The effect of this is to make demand lower than it would otherwise have been whenever production is rising, and higher than it would otherwise have been whenever production is falling, so tending to check movements in either direction without affecting the final equilibrium position. (Phillips 1954, 301–302)

Phillips then presents figures in which the three policies utilized together do a good job of returning output to its value prior to the particular demand shock he imposes on his simple economy. He offers these concluding comments for the use of fiscal and monetary policy that respond automatically to recent economic data according to simple rules:

Proposals have sometimes been made for improving the stability of the economic system by "building in" additional regulating mechanisms. In the British Government's White Paper on Employment Policy reference is made to a scheme for influencing consumption spending by varying the rates of social-insurance contributions above or below the standard rates by amounts depending on the percentage by which the actual employment is above or below the average percentage over a period of years. On the basis of the figures given in the White Paper to illustrate how the scheme might operate, this would introduce a proportional regulating mechanism with a correction factor of about 0.2. [Footnote: Professor

Meade has a suggested a scheme, operating through special monthly taxes and credits related to the level of employment, which would have similar effects. With the scales of taxes and credits suggested by him the proportional correction factor would be about 0.4. . . .] If schemes of this sort could be administered successfully they would undoubtedly improve the stability of the system considerably, and would probably be more effective than attempts to forecast conditions a year or more ahead and adjust an annual budget accordingly.

Monetary policy would be a more convenient instrument for stabilising an economy. Some may doubt whether it is a sufficiently powerful instrument; but if the right type of stabilisation policy is being applied continuously, comparatively small correcting forces are sufficient to hold the system near the desired position once that position has been attained. It is quite likely, therefore, that a monetary policy based on the principles of automatic regulating systems would be adequate to deal with all but the most severe disturbances to the economic system. (Phillips 1954, 314–315)

Three comments seem appropriate concerning Phillips's study: two specific, one general.

The first specific point concerns the integral policy. Phillips may be right about the virtue of an integral policy, but it is not obvious that looking back several quarters, as an integral policy does, is optimal. Thus, while Phillips seems correct in his advocacy of supplementing a proportional policy with a derivative policy, the case for also supplementing it with an integral policy seems less persuasive.

The second specific point concerns the derivative policy. It certainly seems important to supplement the most recent level of output with the most recent rate of change of output. For a given output, it surely matters whether output is rising or falling. By working in continuous rather than discrete time, Phillips knows the rate of change at each point in time t. But economic data is reported for a discrete period—for example, a quarter of a year. Suppose we receive data that the level of output in quarter t is Y_t. Ideally, the rate of change of output in quarter t is the derivative dY_t/dt at the midpoint of the quarter. But with discrete time data, our estimate of the rate of change of output would be $Y_t - Y_{t-1}$. Thus, the derivative policy, applied to discrete periods, must use data from quarter $t - 1$. Hence, a derivative policy is not as "up-to-date" as a proportional policy. This lag may turn out to be a practical argument against its use.

The more general point is that Phillips's work should be regarded as only a first step toward designing and testing the specific details of an automatic fiscal policy. Phillips tests his set of policies in a simple model in which he assigns numerical values to parameters. The model is not econometrically estimated to fit actual data. How would his specific policies do in an econometrically estimated model? Moreover, Phillips considers only one shock that disturbs output from its target: a sudden, permanent cut in demand. How would his policies do in response to other shocks that impose different patterns of demand or supply on the economy?

Nevertheless, Phillips's study is a path-breaking first step in the analysis of automatic countercyclical policy.

Pack's Empirical Study of "Formula Flexibility"

Because tax liability varies directly with income, even with fixed tax rates, a recession automatically reduces tax revenue and mitigates the decline in disposable income and consumption spending. But if tax *rates* were also cut *automatically* in a recession, the stabilizing effect should be even stronger. This automatic adjustment of tax rates has been called "formula flexibility." Pack writes:

> "Formula flexibility" is a fiscal action that activates a tax (or expenditure) change automatically when a certain pre-arranged signal of recession is observed. It differs from an automatic stabilizer in that the latter is built into the existing tax and transfer payment structure, while the former, when activated, changes the structure itself. . . . Formula flexibility can be applied to expenditures as well as to tax changes, but this paper will be concerned only with the tax side. . . . Tax rates would be reduced (or rates of transfers increased) when some economic indicator forecasts a recession. The magnitude of the tax (transfer) change as well as precise details about when the change is to be activated would be embodied in prior legislation. . . . (Pack 1968, 5–7)

Pack seeks an automatic fiscal policy that tries to limit the magnitude of any fall in real GNP below "full employment GNP." But what will trigger the fiscal policy? Pack notes that one possibility is to use a forecast of GNP by a macroeconometric model, but he says he will not consider this method in his paper. Instead, he focuses on policies that are triggered by recent actual values of GNP.

Pack chooses as his fiscal policy instrument the personal income tax rate— in particular, the first-bracket ("starting") rate. He briefly gives this reason:

> This study confines itself to the most often mentioned alternative, variation in the starting rate of the personal income tax, which also has the

advantage of being the simplest to implement [Footnote: Among the properties making the personal income tax the best fiscal instrument are the
speed with which desired changes take effect, administrative simplicity,
large yields, and a relatively small amount of uncertainty engendered by
changes in the rate]. (Pack 1968, 11)

Pack says that the magnitude of the fiscal stimulus must be adjusted to
the severity of the recession. But this still leaves open various options. He
then comments on the options, basing his discussion on Phillips's (1954)
terminology and analysis. Pack writes:

Consider the following policy as an example. A desired GNP level, Y^F, is
determined for each period; if actual GNP, Y, differs from Y^F, a policy
demand equal to $g(Y^F - Y)$ is injected into the system. This may be called
a proportional stabilization policy. [Footnote: This terminology—as well
as the terms, integral and derivative stabilizers—stems from the work of
A.W. Phillips.] (Pack 1968, 12)

Pack then gives the same arguments as Phillips for adding an "integral" component and a "derivative" component. The three components—
proportional, integral, and derivative—operate simultaneously, so the
demand injected in a given period is the sum of the three demands from
each policy.

Pack uses a small econometric model to simulate the effect of formula
flexibility. Pack's estimated consumption function implies that a $100 in-
crease in disposable income this quarter will raise consumption $42 next
quarter.

Pack gives the details of his simulation procedure:

The procedure used in the simulations is to compute GNP at the end of
every quarter (t) and to reduce tax rates immediately (at the end of t),
according to the Phillips formulae. In the next quarter $(t+1)$, disposable
income is larger by the amount of the tax cut, GNP is again computed,
and tax rates are again lowered after the end of the quarter. These steps
are repeated until the GNP gap is eliminated [Footnote: This procedure
assumes, first, that accurate preliminary estimates of GNP can be obtained; and, second, that tax rates can be adjusted immediately upon receipt of the GNP estimates. The assumption regarding the speed of the
tax cuts is probably fairly realistic, as the experience with the 1964 tax

cut indicates; the new rates went into effect within two weeks after the passage of the bill by Congress. With a two-week delay, the altered rates would be operative for five-sixths of $t+1$, and almost the full consumption impact would be felt in this period. The assumption about the speed and accuracy with which the initial GNP estimate may be obtained is less certain.] (Pack 1968, 18)

Pack assesses the impact of his automatic fiscal policy by comparing the path of real GNP predicted by his model when the policy is operating, to the path of real GNP predicted by his model when the policy is not operating (the "reference simulation"). In each policy simulation he inserts the historical value of each exogenous variable, just as he did to generate the reference simulation. The difference between real GNP under the two paths measures the impact of the automatic fiscal policy.

Pack draws these conclusions from his study:

The simulations show that substantial gains in output could be realized if formula flexibility were followed. For example, in the 1953 recession, a proportional policy . . . would have reduced the GNP loss for the cycle period as a whole by about $12 billion (in 1954 prices) at a "cost" of only a small additional deficit and very mild inflationary effects. . . .

Many of the policies analyzed in this study would have generated larger deficits than those experienced in the United States. However, continuous use of the policies would have reduced the initial gap and thus decreased the deficits substantially below those recorded by the simulations. Further, the adoption of formula flexibility would probably have improved business expectations and increased investment. Since the investment equation used in the simulations has no such expectational variable, the tax reductions necessary to achieve a given level of demand are overstated.

The suggested use of formula flexibility should not be taken as indicating a belief in the superiority of fixed rules to intelligent decision-making. It should be viewed in the context of the difficulty of achieving full employment in the late 1950's and early 1960's, and the inertia that gripped the government during that period. The tax reduction of 1964 may have ushered in a new era of more flexible tax policy. Yet it must be remembered that this legislation was enacted after several years of deliberation, and thus does not by itself provide sufficient evidence of the willingness to respond quickly to required changes in the size of the

planned deficit. Moreover, the hesitation of the Administration to propose increases in tax rates during the inflationary development in 1966
suggests that prior inertia has not been completely overcome by the 1964
experience. Clearly, formula flexibility has much to commend it over the
discretionary policy that has developed in recent years in the United States.
(Pack 1968, 37–38)

Duggal's Empirical Study of Formula Flexibility

In her study, Duggal uses a version of the Brookings macroeconometric
model to examine how the U.S. economy would have performed between
1957 and 1965 had Phillips's automatic fiscal policy (with its three components) been in place. Note that her time period overlaps with Pack's. She
writes:

> The next . . . experiments use stabilization schemes to maintain a desired
> unemployment level throughout the period. The policies automatically
> give additional stimulus to the economy whenever prestated signals war-
> rant. This is in line with the proposal of the National Planning Associa-
> tion Conference in 1949, which has come to be known as "formula flex-
> ibility." This proposal states that counter-cyclical measures be allowed to
> come into effect according to a pre-arranged schedule with specified
> changes in designated indices of inadequate demand or inflation. The
> four alternative policies differ from each other by the fiscal tool used to
> raise demand and the corresponding budget policy assumption. (Duggal
> 1975, 225)

The two policies of most interest are Duggal's policy T, in which the
instrument is taxes, and policy G, in which the instrument is government
purchases. She arrives at her numerical values for the policy parameters
after experimenting and simulating. She simulates the model with each of
these policies from 1957.1 through 1965.4, a period that covers two recessions. She then reports on the performance of policies T and G. She presents a figure for the unemployment rate that contrasts the control path with
the paths under the two policies from 1957 through 1965. Both policies
keep the unemployment rate much closer to its target of 3.5 percent than
occurs along the control path.

> Policies T and G are directly comparable, being a tax and an expenditure
> rule to achieve the goal of full employment. Both policies succeed in
> regulating the rate of unemployment, which varies in a narrow range of
> 3.5–4.6% in the tax simulation and a still narrower range of 3.5–4.4% in

the case of expenditure policy. Even the very damped cycle that still exists can be further reduced by experimenting with different combinations of values for proportional, integral, and derivative factors of correction. (Duggal 1975, 245)

She concludes:

The simulations show that an automatic stabilization scheme based on economic conditions of the recent past can be an effective way of dampening the business cycle. (Duggal 1975, 252)

My 1975 Study of Automatic Grants for Public Employment

I begin my 1975 book this way:

There is broad agreement that standard fiscal and monetary policy—the level of tax rates, government spending, and the money supply—are the appropriate instruments for eventually restoring aggregate demand and thus countering recession. Yet it is also agreed that these instruments do not operate rapidly enough to prevent an initial burst of unemployment, which lasts a significant period of time.

What is needed is a policy instrument that can engage in a *short-term holding action* until the standard tools of macroeconomic policy, as well as forces in the private economy, can come into play and ultimately overcome the recession. The need is not for a new instrument to replace standard fiscal and monetary policy, but rather for a new automatic instrument to provide the short-term holding action. That instrument is an automatic federal employment program. . . . (Seidman 1975, 3)

I explain further:

An automatic federal employment program would embody the same concept as the unemployment compensation program. In response to a rise in the national unemployment rate, federal funds would be pumped into state and local governments. The time-consuming political process would be circumvented. (Seidman 1975, 13)

I propose an Anti-Recession Program (ARP) that built on the public employment program that had been enacted in 1971:

Under the Anti-Recession Program, it is proposed that funds be automatically obligated from the federal government to state and local governments whenever the national unemployment is officially forecast to exceed the trigger level (the official forecast will be described shortly). No discretionary action by either Congress or the president will be necessary to release the funds. In this way, a major obstacle to rapid response to a rise in unemployment will be removed. (Seidman 1975, 34)

On one hand, my 1975 proposal has the disadvantage of using a lagging indicator, the unemployment rate, rather than the GDP gap (as proposed in chapters 2 and 3). On the other hand, it proposes that the grants be triggered based on an official forecast of the unemployment rate, not actual data from the last month or quarter:

> At the end of each quarter, ARP requires that an objective estimate be made of the expected unemployment rate three months hence, and of the number of public sector jobs required to achieve the trigger rate at the end of the quarter. . . . Who should have the authority to determine officially the required number of jobs and, therefore, the amount that will be automatically be obligated to state and local governments? . . Public confidence in the program can only be maintained if the number of jobs is determined in the objective manner described above, without politics influencing the result. It is therefore essential that neither the president nor Congress should be allowed to influence the quarterly estimate.
>
> Instead, it is proposed under ARP that the official estimate should be made by an independent panel of professional economic forecasters. The panel might be officially called the ARP Forecasting Unit (ARPFU). . . . The ARPFU panel would be selected on their professional competence as economic forecasters. It is probable that the panel would rely heavily on complex econometric models of the economy to arrive at the official determination of the amount of funds to be obligated to state and local governments in the following quarter. The panel should also be given the flexibility, however, to combine model forecasts with alternative techniques and professional judgment. (Seidman 1975, 37)

Note an important difference between the ARPFU and the fiscal policy advisory board that I propose in chapter 5. With my advisory board, forecasting would not be used to trigger funding. The board would recommend that Congress enact an automatic fiscal policy that triggers funding based on actual data—for example, last quarter's GDP gap—and that Congress enact the relationship between the GDP gap and the amount of the tax rebate. Thus, Congress would retain full control over fiscal policy. By contrast, with the ARPFU, Congress would in effect delegate some power over fiscal policy to the forecasting panel, because the panel would have the discretion to choose its method of forecasting, and its forecast would determine the amount of funding that is triggered. In my judgment, it is doubtful that Congress would be willing to delegate any power over fiscal policy in the near future.

Another difference between my 1975 proposal and the automatic fiscal policies of chapters 2 and 3 is that the 1975 proposal uses the instrument of federal grants to state and local governments for public employment jobs, whereas in chapter 2, I propose an automatic tax rebate, and in chapter 3, a temporary cut in a consumption tax. The proposals in chapters 2 and 3 would try to maintain the pattern of demand across sectors of the economy, thereby keeping most workers in their prerecession private sector jobs. By contrast, my 1975 proposal would involve workers being laid off from private sector jobs and obtaining new jobs in the public sector.

Concluding Remarks

These early studies represent steps in the development of automatic fiscal policies to combat recession. This kind of research virtually ceased with the coming of the new classical counterrevolution in the late 1970s. The premise of this book is that it is time to get back to the task of designing automatic countercyclical fiscal policies—a task that, as these studies show, was being pursued from the mid-1950s through the mid-1970s.

Part III

10

Early Challenges to Countercyclical Fiscal Policy

Countercyclical fiscal policy, born in the Keynesian revolution of the 1930s, has been challenged by critics of Keynesian economics for more than half a century. In this chapter I recount the early challenges mounted by Milton Friedman and James Buchanan in the 1960s and 1970s. In chapter 11, I address the challenge raised by the new classical counterrevolution, led by Robert Lucas, that began in the 1970s.

Friedman versus Lerner and Samuelson

The early debate over countercyclical fiscal policy is nicely captured by examining the early expositions of two leading Keynesians, Abba Lerner and Paul Samuelson, and the response of a leading critic, Milton Friedman.

In 1941, just five years after the publication of Keynes's *General Theory of Interest, Employment, and Money* (1936), Lerner published an article entitled "The Economic Steering Wheel," and a decade later, in his important exposition of Keynesian economics, *The Economics of Employment* (1951), he presents the article (with minor changes) as the first chapter of his book. Here is how it begins:

> Our economic system is frequently put to shame in being displayed before an imaginary visitor from a strange planet. It is time to reverse this procedure. Imagine yourself instead in a Buck Rogers interplanetary adventure, looking at a highway in a City of Tomorrow. The highway is wide and straight, and its edges are turned up so that it is almost impossible for a car to run off the road. What appears to be a runaway car is speeding along the road and veering off to one side. As it approaches the rising edge of the highway, its front wheels are turned so that it gets back onto the road and goes off at an angle, making for the other side, where the wheels are turned again. This happens many times, the car zigzagging but keeping on the highway until it is out of sight. You are wondering how long it will take for it to crash, when another car appears which behaves in the same fashion. When it comes near you it stops with a jerk.

A door is opened, and an occupant asks whether you would like a lift. You look into the car and before you can control yourself you cry out, "Why! There's no steering wheel!"

"Of course we have no steering wheel!" says one of the occupants rather crossly. "Just think how it would cramp the front seat. It is worse than an old-fashioned gear-shift lever and it is dangerous. Suppose we had a steering wheel and somebody held on to it when we reached a curb! He would prevent the automatic turning of the wheel, and the car would surely be overturned! An besides, we believe in democracy and cannot give anyone the extreme authority of life and death over all the occupants of the car. That would be dictatorship."

"Down with dictatorship!" chorus the other occupants of the car.

"If you are worried about the way the car goes from side to side," continues the first speaker, "forget it! We have wonderful brakes so that collisions are prevented nine times out of ten. On our better roads the curb is so effective that one can travel hundreds of miles without going off the road once. We have a very efficient system of carrying survivors of wrecks to nearby hospitals and for rapidly sweeping the remnants from the road to deposit them on nearby fields as a reminder to man of the inevitability."

You look around to see the piles of wrecks and burned-out automobiles as the man in the car continues. "Impressive, isn't it. But things are going to improve. See those men marking and photographing the tracks of the car that preceded us? They are going to take those pictures into their laboratories and pictures of our tracks, too, to analyze the cyclical characteristics of the curves, their degree of regularity, the average distance from turn to turn, the amplitude of the swings, and so on. When they have come to an agreement on their true nature we may know whether something can be done about it. At present they are disputing whether this cyclical movement is due to the type of road surface or to its shape or whether it is due to the length of the car or to the kind of rubber in the tires or to the weather. Some of them think that it will be impossible to avoid having cycles unless we go back to the horse and buggy, but we can't do that because we believe in Progress. Well, want a ride?"

The dilemma between saving your skin and humoring the lunatics is resolved by your awakening from the nightmare, and you feel glad that the inhabitants of your own planet are a little more reasonable. But are they as reasonable about other things as they are about the desirability of steering their automobiles? Do they not behave exactly like the men in the nightmare when it comes to operating their economic system? Do they not allow their *economic* automobile to bounce from depression to inflation in wide and uncontrolled arcs? Through their failure to steer away from unemployment and idle factories are they not just as guilty of public injury and insecurity as the mad motorists of Mars? (Lerner 1951, 3–5)

Lerner states the lesson of his parable:

> The aim of any reasonable regulation of the level of economic activity (which we may call "employment" for short) must be to arrange for the rate of spending to be neither too small (which would cause unemployment) nor too great (which would cause inflation). A satisfactory level (or range) of employment must be chosen, and the total rate of spending must be raised when employment is too low and curtailed when employment rises too high. (Lerner 1951, 7)

In an important passage from the influential first edition of his economics textbook, Samuelson also refers to the steering wheel:

> The private economy is not unlike a machine without an effective steering wheel or governor. Compensatory fiscal policy tries to introduce such a governor or thermostatic control device. As shown in the figure, compensatory policy tries to reduce the amplitude of the cycle; it does not necessarily hope to wipe out altogether every bit of fluctuation. Moreover, everyone recognizes that it is very difficult to time our public works exactly as we should want them. We can't simply throw a switch when we want more purchasing power and reverse the dial when we want less. Once under way, it would be difficult and expensive to abandon it. Because of these technical difficulties of starting and stopping public works and because we need time to discover whether we are really in a boom or a depression, our ambition must be less pretentious than that of creating 100 per cent stability of national income. (Samuelson 1948, 412)

Lerner explains why even an economy composed of intelligent, rational individuals might get into macroeconomic trouble unless the government takes action to make sure aggregate demand is at the desired level:

> *Individual understanding is not enough because individual responses are perverse.* Economic understanding is, of course, always a desirable thing. But a mere understanding of all this by members of the public at large is not of much use in the prevention and cure of inflation and deflation. Even if everybody in the economy were completely well educated in these principles and knew that the economic need of the moment was an increase or a decrease of spending, this would do no good. It might even do a great deal of harm.

This is because it is not always in the interest of individuals to do that which is good for the community as a whole. If individuals learn, for instance, that there is going to be too much spending which will lead to inflation, they may know that this is a bad thing for the economy as a whole and that the evil would be avoided if everybody reduced his spending. But each individual would nevertheless be tempted to hurry to the stores and buy immediately various things that he might be thinking of buying in the future. He will want to buy them now before the price rises. If he were sure that the inflation depended only on his own actions, he might be deterred, but he does not think that his own spending amounts to much in the total effect. His own refraining from buying will not prevent the inflation from taking place. Most people would therefore *increase* their spending if they understood that inflation was threatening, and this increase in spending would increase the inflationary pressure.

In the same way, if there is insufficient spending with heavy unemployment and falling prices, even a universal knowledge and understanding that this could be corrected by everybody's increasing his spending will not help. Most individuals will succumb to the temptation to postpone expenditures in order to benefit from the expected lower prices in the future. And quite apart from any bargain hunting, the expectation of depression and unemployment will make people reduce their spending because they will be concerned with maintaining or increasing their reserves for the difficult times ahead. The result is that spending will be less and the deflation and the unemployment worse than if the public had been ignorant.

What all this means is that the reactions of individuals are *perverse*. Instead of correcting an excess or an insufficiency in total spending, they rather tend to aggravate the situation. A knowledge and an understanding of a situation in which spending is already excessive induce individuals to *increase* their spending, while a situation in which spending is already inadequate induces individuals who know what is happening to *reduce* their spending still more.

Perversity of private action makes social action necessary. (Lerner 1951, 124–125)

So what does Friedman find objectionable in this steering (balance) wheel view of how to manage an economy? In his classic libertarian monograph, *Capitalism and Freedom*, in which he makes the case for limited government, Friedman opposes the government's undertaking countercyclical monetary or fiscal policy. For monetary policy, he calls on the Federal Reserve to keep the money supply growing at a constant rate regardless of the conditions of the economy. And in a chapter devoted entirely to fiscal policy, he argues that attempting countercyclical fiscal policy would be harmful. Before directly addressing the merits of the steering (balance) wheel argument, he argues that whatever its merit, it has led to an undesirable expansion of the size of government:

> Ever since the New Deal, a primary excuse for the expansion of governmental activity at the federal level has been the supposed necessity for government spending to eliminate unemployment. The excuse has gone through several stages. At first, government spending was needed to "prime the pump." Temporary expenditures would set the economy going and the government could then step out of the picture.
>
> When the initial expenditures failed to eliminate unemployment and were followed by a sharp economic contraction in 1937–38, the theory of "secular stagnation" developed to justify a permanently high level of government spending. Opportunities for investment had been largely exploited and no substantial new opportunities were likely to arise. Yet individuals would still want to save. Hence, it was essential for government to spend and run a perpetual deficit. The securities issued to finance the deficit would provide individuals with a way to accumulate savings while the government expenditures provided employment. This view has been thoroughly discredited by theoretical analysis and even more by actual experience, including the emergence of wholly new lines for private investment not dreamed of by the secular stagnationists. Yet it has left its heritage. The idea may be accepted by none, but the government programs undertaken in its name, like some of those intended to prime the pump, are still with us and indeed account for ever-growing government expenditures. (Friedman 1962, 75–76)

Friedman directly addresses the steering (balance) wheel argument:

> More recently, the emphasis has been on government expenditures neither to prime the pump nor to hold in check the specter of secular stagnation but as a balance wheel. When private expenditures decline for any reason, it is said, governmental expenditures should rise to keep total expenditures stable; conversely, when private expenditures rise, governmental expenditures should decline. Unfortunately, the balance wheel is unbalanced. Each recession, however minor, sends a shudder through politically sensitive legislators and administrators with their ever present fear that perhaps it is the harbinger of another 1929–33. They hasten to enact federal spending programs of one kind or another. Many of the programs do not in fact come into effect until after the recession has passed. Hence, insofar as they do affect total expenditures, on which I

shall have more to say later, they tend to exacerbate the succeeding expansion rather than to mitigate the recession. The haste with which spending programs are approved is not matched by an equal haste to repeal them or to eliminate others when the recession is passed and expansion is under way. On the contrary, it is then argued that a "healthy" expansion must not be "jeopardized" by cuts in governmental expenditures. The chief harm done by the balance-wheel theory is therefore not that it has failed to offset recessions, which it has, and not that it has introduced an inflationary bias into governmental policy, which it has done too, but that it has continuously fostered an expansion in the range of governmental activities at the federal level and prevented a reduction in the burden of federal taxes. (Friedman 1962, 76)

Friedman then advances a very different argument: he claims that the turning of the steering wheel is often in the wrong direction, thereby making the economy more, not less, unstable.

In view of the emphasis on using the federal budget as a balance wheel, it is ironic that the most unstable component of national income in the postwar period is federal expenditure, and the instability has not at all been in a direction to offset movements of the other expenditure components. Far from being a balance wheel offsetting other forces making for fluctuations, the federal budget has if anything been itself a major source of disturbance and instability.

Because its expenditures are now so large a part of the total for the economy as a whole, the federal government cannot avoid having significant effects on the economy. The first requisite is therefore that the government mend its own fences, that it adopt procedures that will lead to reasonable stability in its own flow of expenditures. If it would do that, it would make a clear contribution to reducing the adjustments required in the rest of the economy. Until it does that, it is farcical for government officials to adopt the self-righteous tones of the schoolmaster keeping unruly pupils in line. Of course, their doing so is not surprising. Passing the buck and blaming others for one's own deficiencies are not vices of which governmental officials have a monopoly. (Friedman 1962, 77)

In the appendix to this chapter, I discuss in detail three articles—Friedman (1953), Baumol (1961), and Smyth (1963)—that investigate whether it is possible for countercyclical policy to make the instability of the economy larger rather than smaller.

Friedman's shows that whether countercyclical policy does more harm, or more good, depends on how often the steering wheel is turned in the wrong, rather than the right, direction. But the automatic fiscal policies I propose in chapters 2 and 3 are likely to pass Friedman's test because they have only a one-quarter (at most, a two-quarter) lag due to automatic triggering, and because they have a threshold—say 2 percent—so that the fiscal stimulus occurs only if GDP falls at least 2 percent below its normal value. Baumol and Smyth show that countercyclical policy can cause explosive fluctuations of output in Samuelson's (1939) simple multiplier-accelerator model of the economy, but Hicks (1950) pointed out that to be realistic the multiplier-accelerator model requires a ceiling and floor for the output of the economy. Once these are imposed, I show that Baumol's and Smyth's harm from countercyclical policy vanishes.

But Friedman now makes an intriguing point, as though he were momentarily tempted to try to use the balance wheel argument to achieve his libertarian objective of small government:

> Even if one were to accept the view that the federal budget should be and can be used as a balance wheel . . . there is no necessity to use the expenditure side of the budget for this purpose. The tax side is equally available. A decline in national income automatically reduces the tax revenue of the federal government in greater proportion and thus shifts the budget in the direction of a deficit, and conversely during a boom. If it is desired to do more, taxes can be lowered during recessions and raised during expansions. Of course, politics might well enforce an asymmetry here too, making the declines politically more palatable than the rises. (Friedman 1962, 77)

Did early Keynesians ignore the tax side, emphasizing only government spending? Not at all. Indeed, both Samuelson (1948) and Lerner (1951) make the same point as Friedman. They emphasize that either side of the budget will do the trick. Samuelson writes:

> *Automatic Changes in Tax Receipts.* In addition to public-works expenditure and welfare expenditure, countercyclical compensatory fiscal policy can also rely on cyclically timed tax policies. We have already seen in the earlier chapters on pubic finance . . . that our Federal tax system has important income elements in it, so that tax collections tend to vary strongly with national income. Even without Congress or the state legislatures changing any laws, it turns out that governmental tax collections tend to rise automatically when national income rises and to fall off when national income falls off; and because of the progressive elements in our tax structure, our relative tax collections vary even more sharply than income itself.

A century ago, writers thought that stability of tax revenue was a good thing, and they would have looked with disapproval on the present-day tendency for tax receipts to rise and fall with national income. Today, most believe that the truth is just the reverse. To dampen down a boom, a budgetary surplus is needed. Now there are two ways to produce a surplus: by a reduction in government expenditure, yes; but also by an increase in tax receipts. Indeed, from the standpoint of free private enterprise, tax changes represent the more conservative policy. How lucky we are, therefore, that our present tax system to some degree has "automatic flexibility," with its collections tending to rise in inflationary times and to fall in times of depression. This is a powerful factor stabilizing the whole economy and moderating the business cycle.

Countercyclical Tax-rate Changes. Even this is not all. Congress can also change tax rates. Back before World War I (and still in a few quarters even today), people thought it obviously desirable to balance the budget in *each and every year.* Therefore, they tried to raise tax rates whenever the public was experiencing falling incomes, and to reduce tax rates when incomes were becoming inflated. Once again, the pendulum of expert opinion has swung completely around; today, all but the most conservative students of public finance are opposed to such "perverse flexibility" of tax rates. Those who believe in a countercyclical compensatory fiscal policy argue that the time to reduce tax rates is in depression, when overall purchasing power it too low; and the time to step up tax rates is during boom times.

Thus taxes as well as expenditures are important for a countercyclical compensatory policy. (Samuelson 1948, 413–414)

Lerner, like Samuelson, states his position with complete neutrality concerning the use of government spending or taxes.

The government shall maintain at all times a reasonable level of total spending in the economy. If there is not enough spending, so that there is excessive unemployment, the government shall increase total spending by lowering taxes or by increasing its own expenditures or both. If there is too much spending, so that there is inflation, the government shall reduce total spending by cutting its own expenditures or by increasing taxes or both. (Lerner 1951, 8)

But Friedman does not trust the assertions of neutrality by the Keynesians. He contends:

If the balance-wheel theory has in practice been applied on the expenditure side, it has been because of the existence of other forces making for increased governmental expenditures; in particular, the widespread acceptance by intellectuals of the belief that government should play a larger role in economic and private affairs; the triumph, that is, of the philosophy of the welfare state. This philosophy has found a useful ally in the balance-wheel theory; it has enabled governmental intervention to proceed at a faster pace than would otherwise have been possible.

How different matters might now be if the balance-wheel theory had been applied on the tax side instead of the expenditure side. Suppose each recession had seen a cut in taxes and suppose the political unpopularity of raising taxes in the succeeding expansion had led to resistance to newly proposed governmental expenditure programs and to curtailment of existing ones. We might now be in a position where federal expenditures would be absorbing a good deal less of a national income that would be larger because of the reduction in the depressing and inhibiting effects of taxes. (Friedman 1962, 77–78)

Having indulged in this dream, Friedman hastens to add that he still thinks countercyclical policy should not be attempted, even solely on the tax side, because it is likely to amplify, rather than dampen, economic fluctuations. He counters Lerner's parable this way:

What I have written elsewhere in respect of monetary policy is equally applicable to fiscal policy: "What we need is not a skillful monetary driver of the economic vehicle continuously turning the steering wheel to adjust to the unexpected irregularities of the route, but some means of keeping the monetary passenger who is in the back seat as ballast from occasionally leaning over and giving the steering wheel a jerk that threatens to send the car off the road." (Friedman 1962, 78–79)

The debate between Friedman versus Lerner and Samuelson is easy to summarize. Friedman contends that putting a steering wheel in a car runs the risk that a poor driver, or a crazy back seat passenger, will steer the car off the road, so he would rather take his chance leaving the car without a steering wheel. Lerner and Samuelson believe that without a steering wheel, the car will inevitably go off the road, so they would rather take their chance on a driver with a steering wheel.

Buchanan

In chapter 4, I proposed NUBAR (normal unemployment balanced budget rule), and recommended that when the economy is normal, surpluses should be run in Social Security and Medicare, and the rest of the budget should be balanced. Hence, I advocate keeping the budget balanced when the economy is normal (plus a surplus in Social Security and Medicare), running temporary deficits only in recession. It is important for legislators to have to weigh cost against benefit, taxes against spending. It is also important to limit the ratio of government debt to GDP so that creditors do not fear default, thereby limiting the government's ability to borrow. For James Buchanan, however, the Keynesian tolerance of even temporary deficits has been harmful.

Buchanan has written many articles and books on this subject, but perhaps his most comprehensive critique is in a book coauthored with Richard Wagner in 1977 entitled *Democracy in Deficit: The Political Legacy of Lord Keynes*. Their central point is this. A balanced budget rule forces politicians to weigh cost against benefit: If they want to raise spending to improve their popularity with some constituency, they must also raise taxes, which is inevitably unpopular. A balanced budget rule forces politicians to recognize that there is a cost to public spending. In their view, politicians took a simple message from Keynes: "It's proper to engage in deficit spending. You can raise spending without raising taxes." Whatever the macroeconomic merits of Keynes's theory, its effect was to "reduce the price" to politicians of raising spending, because they no longer had to incur the cost of raising taxes. This "price reduction" generated excessive government spending, deficits, public debt, and inflation.

After reviewing the traditional or classical view about the importance of generally maintaining a balanced budget and avoiding excessive debt, they describe the new perspective that followed the Keynesian revolution:

> The deliberate creation of budget deficits—the explicit decision to spend and not to tax—was the feature of Keynesian policy that ran most squarely in the face of traditional and time-honored norms for fiscal responsibility. But there was no alternative for the Keynesian convert. To increase aggregate demand, total spending in the economy must be increased, and this could only be guaranteed if the private-spending offsets of tax increase could be avoided or swamped. New net spending must emerge, and the creation of budget deficits offered the only apparent escape from economic stagnation.
>
> If, however, the flow of spending was to be increased in this manner, the problem of financing deficits necessarily arose. And at this point, the policy advocate encountered two separate and subsidiary norms in the previously existing "constitution." Deficits could be financed in only one of two ways, either through government borrowing (the issue of public

debt) or through the explicit creation of money (available only to central government). But public debt, in the classical theory of public finance, transfers burdens onto the shoulders of future generations. And money creation was associated, historically, with governmental corruption along with the dangers of inflation. (Buchanan and Wagner 1977, 31)

Recall that in chapter 1, I recommended a *money-financed* fiscal stimulus to combat a severe recession: spending would exceed taxation, the treasury would sell debt to the public, but the central bank would buy this debt from the public, thereby injecting money into the economy, and preventing a rise in the debt held by the public. This would be equivalent to the consolidated government (treasury plus central bank) creating money to finance spending in excess of taxation. In light of my recommendation, consider the next passage from Buchanan and Wagner:

> Retrospectively, it remains somewhat surprising that the Keynesians, or most of them, chose to challenge the debt-burden argument of classical public finance theory rather than the money-creation alternative. (By doing so, quite unnecessary intellectual confusion was introduced into an important area of economic theory, confusion that had not, even as late as 1976, been fully eliminated.) Within the strict assumptions of the Keynesian model, and in the deficient-demand setting, the opportunity cost of additional government spending is genuinely zero. From this, it follows directly that the creation of money to finance the required deficit involves no net cost; there is no danger of price inflation. In the absence of political-institutional constraints, therefore, the idealized Keynesian policy package for escape from such economic situations is the explicit creation of budget deficits along with the financing of these by pure money issue.
>
> In such a context, any resort to public debt issue, to public borrowing, is a necessary second-best. Why should the government offer any interest return at all to potential lenders of funds, to the purchasers of government debt instruments, when the alternative of printing money at negligible real cost and at zero interest is available? Regardless of the temporal location of the burden of servicing and amortizing public debt, there is no supportable argument for public borrowing in the setting of deficient demand. In trying to work out a supporting argument here, the Keynesian economists were confused, even on their own terms. (Buchanan and Wagner 1977, 32)

Buchanan and Wagner are correct on this basic point, and it is for this reason that I advocate a money-financed fiscal stimulus in chapter 1 to combat a recession. They continue:

Because they unreasonably assumed that deficits were to be financed by public borrowing rather than by money creation, the Keynesian advocates felt themselves obliged to reduce the sting of the argument concerning the temporal transfer of cost or burden. To accomplish this, they revived in sophisticated form the distinction between the norms for private, personal financial integrity and those for public, governmental financial responsibility. Budget balance did matter for an individual or family; budget balance did not matter for a government. Borrowing for an individual offered a means of postponing payment, of putting off the costs of current spending, which might or might not be desirable. For government, however, there was no such temporal transfer. It was held to be impossible to implement a transfer of cost or burden through time because government included all members of the community, and, so long as public debt was internally owned, "we owed it to ourselves." Debtors and creditors were mutually canceling; hence, in the macroeconomic context, the society could never be "in debt" in any way comparable to that situation in which a person, a family, a firm, a local government, or even a central government that had borrowed from foreigners might find itself. (Buchanan and Wagner 1977, 32–33)

They summarize their point this way:

The Keynesian economist rarely made the careful distinction between money creation and public debt issue that is required as the first step towards logical clarity. Linguistically, he often referred to what amounts to disguised money creation as "public debt," notably in his classification of government "borrowing" from the banking system. He tended to equate the whole defense of deficit financing with his defense of public debt, as a financing instrument, when, as noted above, this need not have been done at all. On his own grounds, the Keynesian economist could have made a much more effective case for deficit financing by direct money creation. Had he done so, perhaps the transmission of his message to the politicians and the public would have contained within it much stronger built-in safeguards. It is indeed interesting to speculate what might have happened in the post-Keynesian world of fiscal policy if the financing of budget deficits had been restricted to money issue, and if this means of financing had been explicitly acknowledged by all parties. (Buchanan and Wagner 1977, 34)

I agree, which is why I proposed a money-financed fiscal stimulus to combat recession. At first glance, it might seem that Buchanan and Wagner are less critical of deficits financed by money creation. But this is not so. In their view, as long as politicians are told that deficits are proper and accept-able, they face a reduced price for government spending and will therefore spend excessively. Financing by debt burdens the future, but financing by money creation generates inflation:

> The fundamental bias towards inflation will be, if anything, more severe in a regime in which budgetary unbalance is residually adjusted through changes in the money supply than one in which this is adjusted through changes in public debt. History provides perhaps the best corroboration of this hypothesis. Governments have been more severely restricted in their powers of money creation than in their abilities to borrow. Eco-nomic history abounds with evidence to the effect that, when allowed a choice, governments tend to inflate their currencies rather than impose taxation. A begrudging, and possibly subconscious recognition of this long-standing principle may have been partially responsible for the early Keynesian emphasis on debt financing rather than on the simpler and more persuasive money financing of deficits. . . . (Buchanan and Wagner 1977, 110)

But the history of the past twenty five years since their book was written should make us more optimistic about money-financed fiscal stimulus, pro-vided, as in the United States, there is an independent central bank and that the treasury is prohibited from money creation. The institutional rules in the United States require the treasury to finance a deficit by selling debt to the public. It is then up to the independent central bank to decide how much debt to buy from the public (through open market operations). Only if the central bank chooses to buy as much debt as the treasury issued is the defi-cit indirectly financed by money creation. Thus, the treasury lacks the power to choose money creation. In the early 1980s, the treasury ran large defi-cits, but the Federal Reserve, under chairman Paul Volcker, refused to buy the debt, and inflation fell rather than rose despite large budget deficits. In the 1990s, both a Democratic president and a Republican Congress scored points with the electorate by reducing budget deficits during a period when the economy was strong. The budget was balanced, and then surpluses run, even without the passage of any constitutional amendment.

Buchanan's skeptical, pessimistic theory of the behavior of politicians who accept Keynesian macroeconomics has not been supported empiri-cally in the past two decades in the United States. On one hand, the public seems to recognize that it is useful for the government to stimulate the economy when recession threatens by spending more and taxing less. This means temporarily running deficits. At the same time, the public is "classical" in its view that in normal or boom times, the government should balance its budget or even run surpluses to pay down the national debt. The institutional separation between the treasury and the central bank prevents the treasury from creating money to finance an excess of spending over taxation. It is clearly possible to use fiscal stimulus to combat recessions without abandoning the valid classical concerns emphasized by Buchanan.

Appendix to Chapter 10

Milton Friedman (1953), William Baumol (1961), and David Smyth (1963) each wrote a technical (mathematical) article contending that even automatic countercyclical policy (monetary or fiscal) might be harmful. In this appendix, I present and critique their analyses.

Friedman

In "The Effects of a Full-Employment Policy on Economic Stability: A Formal Analysis," Friedman (1953) investigates under what conditions a countercyclical policy, monetary or fiscal, will do more harm than good—destabilize, rather than stabilize, the economy. His challenge applies not only to discretionary fiscal policy, which often involves long lags, but also to the automatic fiscal policies proposed in chapters 2 and 3, because these automatic policies are subject to a one- or perhaps even two-quarter lag.

If a countercyclical policy affected demand instantaneously, and if its effect on demand could be turned on and off instantaneously, then it would certainly do good rather than harm. Specifically, let $Z(t) = X(t) + Y(t)$ where $X(t)$ is demand at time t in the absence of policy, and $Y(t)$ is the amount of demand that is added by the policy at time t. If the policy operated instantaneously, then $Z(t)$ could always be kept at its target value; any shift in $X(t)$ would be immediately offset by an equal and opposite shift in $Y(t)$. But the problem is that, due to lags, the $Y(t)$ that occurs at time t is the result of past adjustments of the policy instrument, based on earlier information, for example, of $X(t-1)$.

At the time that the policy instrument is adjusted, policy makers cannot be sure whether the proper adjustment should be up or down—that is, they cannot be sure whether, when time t arrives, they will want the effect of their policy, $Y(t)$, to move up or down. Obviously, if the policy adjustment were always perverse—raising $Y(t)$ when it should be lowered, and lowering $Y(t)$ when it should be raised—then policy would clearly makes things worse. But suppose policy is "random": suppose the policy instrument is moved half the time in the right direction, but half the time in the wrong direction. It might at first glance seem that such a policy would be "neutral," half the time improving the outcome, and half the time worsening it. But Friedman says this is not the case. He writes:

> By a well-known statistical theorem $s_z^2 = s_x^2 + s_y^2 + 2r_{xy}s_x s_y$, where s^2 is the variance of the indicated variable, Z, X, or Y and r is the correlation coefficient between X and Y. . . . Just as s_y measures one dimension of countercyclical policy—its magnitude—so r_{xy} measures another dimension—roughly speaking, its timing or "fit." If countercyclical policy were always timed and proportioned correctly, its *effects* would uniformly be in the opposite direction to the deviation of X from its mean and a fixed proportion of this deviation. In this case, Y would be perfectly negatively correlated with X, and r_{xy} would equal -1. On the other hand, if countercyclical policy were thoroughly random in its impact, its effects would be as likely to be in the same direction as the deviation of X from its mean as in the opposite direction, and r_{xy} would equal zero. . . . It is clear from the equation that a countercyclical policy for which $r_{xy} = 0$, that is, which is about as likely to have effects in the wrong as in the right direction, is not "neutral" in its impact but rather destabilizing. For if $r_{xy} = 0$, the variance of Z exceeds the variance of X by the variance of Y; that is, by the magnitude of the countercyclical action. In order, therefore, for countercyclical action to succeed in its objective, its effects must be in the right direction more often than in the wrong. (Friedman 1953, 123–124)

I can illustrate Friedman's point with a numerical example in a simple Keynesian system (Seidman 1987, chapter 8). Consider the three-equation model:

(1) $Y = C + I + G$
(2) $C = 0.8(Y - T + R)$
(3) $T = tY,$

where G is government purchases, T is taxes, and R is government transfer payments. Specifically, we assume $G = 300$ and $R = 250$, so the system becomes:

(1) $Y = C + I + 300$
(2) $C = 0.8(Y - T + 250)$
(3) $T = tY.$

Assume the target for Y is 2,200. If Y is made lower than 2,200, there is a recession, and if Y is made higher than 2,200, there is rising inflation. If investment I were known with certainty, then it would be easy to select the tax rate t that would achieve $Y = 2,200$. If we knew that $I = 380$, then a bit of algebra yields the value of the tax rate t that would make $Y = 2,200$. It turns out that $t = 25$ percent would do the trick. With that tax rate, T would be 550, C would be 1,520, so $C + I + G$ would equal 2,200.

But, of course, I is not known with certainty at the time that t must be set by policy makers. To simplify, suppose I can take on only three values, 300, 380, or 460, each with a 1/3 probability. Suppose the policy maker makes no attempt to anticipate the particular value of I but simply sets $t = 25$ percent . Then for each numerical value of I we can compute the value of Y that would result. The outcomes would be as follows:

$t = 25\%$ probability	1/3	1/3	1/3
I	300	380	460
Y	2,000	2,200	2,400

Now suppose the policy maker is more ambitious, tries to anticipate the value of I, and then adjusts t in advance. But suppose the policy maker has no skill at choosing the desired t. In other words, when the policy maker antici-pates 300, there is really only a 1/3 chance of 300, and a 1/3 chance of each of the other two; similarly when the policy maker anticipates 380 or 460. If the policy maker anticipates 300, the lowest value for I, he sets a low tax rate, 20.5 percent, to stimulate C in order to achieve $Y = 2,200$. But, of course, I may turn out to be 380 or 460, and then Y will turn out to be greater than 2,200, causing a rise in inflation. Symmetrically, if the policy maker antici-pates 460, the highest value for I, he sets a high tax rate, 29.5 percent, to restrain C in order to achieve $Y = 2,200$. But, of course, I may turn out to be 380 or 300, and then Y will turn out to be less than 2,200, causing a recession.

Note that rather than leaving the choice of t to the discretion of a policy maker, this could be implemented as an automatic fiscal policy. We have assumed that I can take on three values, 300, 380, and 460, each with a 1/3 probability, and moreover, that value of I this period is in fact independent of its value last period. Consider the automatic fiscal policy that looks at last period's value of I, and then automatically sets this period's tax rate t so that Y would hit its target if and only if I stayed constant—that is, this period's value equals last period's value. Whether the fiscal policy is automatic or not, here are the outcomes that will occur:

Probability	1/9	1/9	1/9	3/9	1/9	1/9	1/9
Y	1,835	2,000	2,018	2,200	2,400	2,418	2,637

When there is no skill in adjusting t (whether automatically or by discretion), the spread of possible outcomes for Y is wider (the variance of Y, s_y^2, is greater) if an attempt is made to adjust t in advance than if t is simply set at 25 percent. What produces 1,835, the deep recession? The policy maker thinks I will be strong, 460, so he sets a high $t = 29.5$ percent to restrain C, but then I turns out to be weak, 300. What produces 2,637, the inflationary boom? The policy maker thinks I will be weak, 300, so he sets a low $t = 20.5$ percent to stimulate C, but then I turns out to be strong, 460.

Friedman makes the useful point that if the adjustment of the policy instrument is merely "random," it will do more harm than good. To do more good than harm, on average, the policy adjustment must be right more often than it is wrong. But how much more often? This is clearly a complicated quantitative question. To clarify the issue, let us consider two extreme cases.

At one extreme, suppose fiscal stimulus is triggered if and only if real output is 6 percent less than target in the preceding quarter. Using a rough Okun's Law of 2 to 1, this implies that the unemployment rate is 3 percentage points above its target rate; for example, if the target unemployment rate is 6 percent, last quarter's unemployment rate must exceed 9 percent to trigger the fiscal stimulus. Under a rule with such a high conservative threshold, it will almost always be the case that the fiscal stimulus will still be needed by the time it hits the economy in subsequent quarters.

At the other extreme, suppose fiscal stimulus is triggered if real output is less than target in the preceding quarter. In the above example, any rise in the unemployment rate above 6 percent would trigger stimulus. Under such a "trigger-happy" rule, it will often be the case that the fiscal stimulus is no longer needed by the time it hits the economy in subsequent quarters. In chapters 2 and 3, I considered triggering the policy only after the GDP gap exceeds a threshold—for example, 2 percent—in order to reduce this problem.

Baumol and Smyth

Baumol (1961) and Smyth (1963) use a simple Keynesian multiplier-accelerator model pioneered in a famous paper by Samuelson (1939) to question whether a particular automatic fiscal policy might in fact be destabilizing. Each makes the provocative assertion that an automatic fiscal policy might cause explosive business cycles in the Samuelson model. I will show that their argument collapses once a realistic ceiling and floor is imposed on the model of the economy (Hicks 1950).

Chiang (1974) gives a clear exposition of Samuelson's analysis. Samuelson analyzes the following system:

(1) $Y_t = C_t + I_t + G_0$,

(2) $C_t = gY_{t-1}$, (note also that $C_{t-1} = gY_{t-2}$),

(3) $I_t = a(C_t - C_{t-1})$,

where G_0, g, and a are assumed to be constant. The second equation is a consumption function, with this period's consumption depending on last period's income $(0 < g < 1)$. The third equation is the investment accelerator, with this period's investment depending on the change in consumption between last period and this period $(a > 0)$. The plausible idea behind the investment function is that expected sales determines the capital stock a firm needs, and firms invest—increase their capital stock—only to the degree that their sales are increasing. In Samuelson's original formulation, consumption sales affect investment, but others have substituted Y for C in the investment function. The properties of the system are similar in either case. Combining the equations yields a second-order difference equation:

(4) $Y_t - g(1 + a)Y_{t-1} + agY_{t-2} = G_0$.

The steady-state value is obtained by setting $Y_t = Y_{t-1} = Y_{t-2}$, and solving for Y to obtain

(5) $Y^* = G_0/(1 - g)$.

If the value of Y in periods 0 and 1, Y_0, and Y_1, happen to equal Y^*, then the value of Y in period 2, Y_2, will also equal Y^*, and Y will stay constant at Y^* over time. But suppose Y_0 or Y_1 differ from Y^*: what path will Y follow over time according to (4)? Samuelson shows that a variety of outcomes are possible mathematically, depending on the magnitudes of the key parameters of the system, g and a. It is possible to have damped oscillations in which Y_t eventually converges to its steady-state value Y^*. But it is also possible to have explosive oscillations where Y_t fluctuates with ever-increasing amplitude.

This last result, explosive oscillations, while mathematically possible in this system, should give an economist pause. After all, what would happen in the actual economy if such oscillations began to occur. Clearly, a ceiling would be imposed on Y_t by the capacity of the basic stocks of capital and labor required to generate output. The Samuelson system imposes no such ceiling, so that Y_t can rise without limit. At the same time, clearly there is a floor to Y_t—zero. Although the mathematics permits Y_t to oscillate downward to negative values of enormous magnitude, in the actual economy the minimum value of Y_t is zero. Similarly, neither consumption, nor gross investment, can be negative in the actual economy. Before any practical analysis of the impact of the automatic stabilizers is conducted, realistic ceilings and floors must be imposed on the system. This is the central contribution of Hicks in his *A Contribution to the Theory of the Trade Cycle:*

> I have now come to the centre of my argument. . . . I assume that the investment and saving coefficients are such . . . that an upward displacement from the equilibrium path will tend to cause a movement away from equilibrium. . . . It may itself have a cyclic character, so that it shows itself in the form of explosive cycles; or it may take the simple (and more explosive) form of a direct movement away from equilibrium without fluctuation. This is what would happen in the absence of constraints. But I assume that there is a direct restraint upon upward expansion in the form of a scarcity of employable resources. Thus, it is impossible for output to expand without limit. There is no such direct limit on contraction. But the working of the accelerator on the downswing is different from its working on the upswing; this difference in mechanism, though it does not provide a direct check, provides an indirect check which is practically certain, sooner or later, to be effective. (Hicks 1950, 94)

However, Baumol and Smyth analyze the impact of countercyclical policies and automatic stabilizers in the system similar to Samuelson's *without* realistic ceilings or floors. Baumol begins his article, "Pitfalls in Contracyclical Policies: Some Tools and Results," as follows:

> It is not generally recognized by economists that where governmental contracyclical policies are concerned common sense is a particularly dangerous tool. Policies—automatic or not—which appear to be properly designed may very well turn out to aggravate fluctuations [Footnote: Several warnings on this problem have already appeared in the literature. See Milton Friedman, "The Effects of a Full-Employment Policy on Economic Stability: A Formal Analysis," and A.W. Phillips, "Stabilization Policy in a Closed Economy." The extent of my debt to Phillips' work should be perfectly clear. Also, as he has pointed out, engineers have long known about these dangers in automatic stabilization devices.] Miscalculations on delicate questions of timing or magnitudes can be crucial, and these matters may well be out of the range of competence of the good judgment and experience of most of the practical men who determine or advise on our monetary and fiscal policies.
>
> This article describes tools which can be used to deal with at least some simple variants of these problems. Such tools can be particularly useful in indicating the nature of the pitfalls in the area. In particular, I

will describe two rather plausible types of contracyclical fiscal policy and show that they can lead to some rather surprising results. . . .

The discussion assumes that we are living in the world of the Samuelson accelerator-multiplier model. . . .

Let us now suppose that the government determines to regulate its net outlays, G_t, in a way which reduces the severity of the cycle in income. . . . Let us consider several possibilities.

a. *A policy to offset income trends.* Suppose the government decides to offset income trends by deficit spending ($G_t > 0$) when income has just been falling [$(Y_{t-1} - Y_{t-2}) < 0$] and by collecting a budget surplus when income has been rising, and that the magnitude of this action is proportional to the size of the change in income. This policy, which is designed to offset income trends [Footnote: Phillips calls such a measure a "derivative policy," since net outlays are, in effect, based on dY/dt], is described algebraically by $G_{t,1} = -a(Y_{t-1} - Y_{t-2})$ where $a > 0$.

b. *A policy to adjust income levels.* Suppose the government determines always to compensate for the difference between effective demand, Y, and some desired (near full employment) level, E. That is, it seeks to move effective demand toward the full employment level [Footnote: Phillips has called this a "proportionate policy."] If there is no lag in government response this yields $G_{t,2} = w(E - Y_t)$; if there is a one-period delay in government reactions we have $G_{t,3} = w(E - Y_{t-1})$. (Baumol 1961, 21–22)

Baumol then mathematically analyzes how the difference-equation system would behave with each of these plausible policies. For certain magnitudes of the key parameters, these plausible policies might actually make the cycles worse.

Conclusion. The results of this discussion may reasonably be considered somewhat frightening. Plausible and reasonable contracyclical policies turn out to be capable of increasing the explosiveness and frequency of economic fluctuations. In fact, none of the possibilities examined proved to be entirely harmless in these respects, even in the highly simplified world of the multiplier-accelerator model. There would, therefore, seem to be little ground for confidence in such measures in the far more complex and unpredictable world of reality.

This, of course, is not meant to imply that good automatic stabilizers cannot be invented [Footnote: But common sense remains a dangerous ally]. The relatively crude model and blunt tools of this article can be of little help in designing such policies, but it is certainly easy to argue, in principle, that effective stabilizers can be found. What the analysis does show clearly is that the design of an automatic stabilization policy is a dangerous game which requires careful calculation and testing. Certainly it is not a game for amateurs, not even those whose mathematical skill is considerable or those whose good common sense and workaday knowledge of monetary and fiscal institutions has in so many other ways been invaluable to the community. (Baumol 1961, 24)

Note above that Baumol says explosive oscillations may occur "*even* in the highly simplified world of the multiplier-accelerator model." I have added the italics to the word *even*. I would rephrase his statement to read: Explosive oscillations may occur *especially* in the unrealistic world of a multiplier-accelerator model that imposes no ceiling or floor on output. Baumol implies that if one makes the model more realistic and complex, the automatic policies will probably perform even worse. On the contrary, taking the simple realistic step of imposing a ceiling and a floor is all that it takes to make the common sense policies work better. The best way to see this is to examine Smyth's article.

Smyth begins his article "Can 'Automatic Stabilizers' Be Destabilizing?" as follows:

It is now widely recognized that government activity aimed at stabilizing the economy may actually be destabilizing as the timing and magnitude of government intervention may be wrong [Footnote: See, for instance, the analysis of A.W. Phillips, "Stabilization Policy in a Closed Economy," and M. Friedman, "The Effects of Full Employment Policy on Economic Stability: A Formal Analysis."]. This has tended to increase support for "automatic stabilizers," such as built-in flexibility of taxation, in the belief that they, at least, cannot act perversely [Footnote: For instance, a recent study that attempts to measure the stabilizing effect of built-in flexibility of taxation is prefaced with the remark that: "In any system of taxation cyclical movements of the national income are damped by automatic compensatory fluctuations in the yields of taxes."] The object of the present paper is to cast doubt on the view that "automatic stabilizers" are necessarily stabilizing by means of a simple counter-example. Indeed in the counter-example presented the presence of built-in flexibility of taxation *necessarily* makes the system more liable to oscillations and more liable to instability. (Smyth 1963, 357)

This is indeed a provocative assertion. Countless professors of economics have taught their students that in a recession automatically tax revenue owed to the government falls, thereby mitigating the fall in consumer spending and the severity of the recession. Does Smyth show that countless professors have misled countless students? Like Baumol, the system he uses is a version of Samuelson's multiplier-accelerator system of Samuelson *without* any imposition of a realistic ceiling or floor on output. Here is his system:

(1) $Y_t = C_t + I_t + A_t$.

Consumption depends on disposable income in the two preceding periods,

(2) $C_t = c_1 (Y_{t-1} - T_{t-1}) + c_2 (Y_{t-2} - T_{t-2})$,

and investment depends on the change in output, lagged one quarter

(3) $I_t = v (Y_{t-1} - Y_{t-2})$.

If taxation were autonomous, then T_t would be independent of Y_t and consolidating the three equations yields

(4) $Y_t = (c_1 + v)Y_{t-1} - (v - c_2)Y_{t-2} - c_1 T_{t-1} - c_2 T_{t-2} + A_t$.

Built-in flexibility means that T_t varies automatically and directly with Y_t.

(5) $T_t = mY_t$.

With (5), T_t and T_{t-1} can be eliminated in (2) yielding

(6) $C_t = c_1 (1 - m)Y_{t-1} + c_2 (1 - m)Y_{t-2}$,

and combining (6) with (1) and (3) yields

(7) $Y_t = (c_1 + v - mc_1)Y_{t-1} - (v - c_2 + mc_2)Y_{t-2} + A_t$.

Note that in (4), without built-in flexibility (5), the steady-state Y^* is obtained by

setting $Y_t = Y_{t-1} = Y_{t-2} = Y^*$, yielding
(4*) $Y^* = [1/(1 - c_1 - c_2)]\{A_t - c_1 T_{t-1} - c_2 T_{t-2}\}$, so that the multiplier is
(4**) $dY^*/dA_t = [1/(1 - c_1 - c_2)]$.

Hence, beginning at an initial steady state, without built-in flexibility

(5), a small decrement in autonomous spending DA_t will eventually cause a small decline in steady-state Y^* equal to

$$[1/(1 - c_1 - c_2)]DA_t.$$

Note that in (7), with built-in flexibility (5), the steady-state Y^* is obtained by setting $Y_t = Y_{t-1} = Y_{t-2} = Y^*$, yielding

(7*) $Y^* = \{1/[1 - c_1 - c_2 + m(c_1 + c_2)]\}\{A_t\}$, so that the multiplier is
(7**) $dY^*/dA_t = \{1/[1 - c_1 - c_2 + m(c_1 + c_2)]\}$.

Hence, beginning at an initial steady state, with built-in flexibility (5), a small decrement in autonomous spending DA_t will eventually cause a small decline in steady-state Y^* equal to

$$\{1/(1 - c_1 - c_2) + m(c_1 + c_2)]\}DA_t.$$

Comparing (7**) and (4**) we see that because $m(c_1 + c_2)$ is positive, dY^*/dA_t in (7**) with built-in flexibility is smaller than dY^*/dA_t in (4**) without built-in flexibility.

> The usual way of demonstrating the stabilizing effect of built-in flexibility of taxation is to compare shifts in static equilibrium positions as a result of changes in autonomous expenditures with and without built-in flexibility of taxation. The multiplier in (4), the case without built-in flexibility, is $1/(1 - c_1 - c_2)$. The multiplier in (7), the case with built-in flexibility, is $1/[1 - c_1 - c_2 + m(c_1 + c_2)]$. As $(c_1 + c_2)$ and m are both positive and less than unity the multiplier is smaller in the case with built-in flexibility and consequently the size of shifts in equilibrium positions as a result of changes in autonomous expenditures are less with built-in flexibility than without. Also, an increase in an existing marginal tax rate is apparently stabilizing as the multiplier is reduced. (Smyth 1963, 358–359)

This is what countless professors have told countless students. But Smyth continues:

> This approach entirely neglects dynamic factors. There may be a stable static equilibrium but dynamic reactions to the disequilibrium may be such that static equilibrium is never reached—the system may be dynamically unstable. Further, the system may oscillate in its adjustment

process. Can the presence of built-in flexibility of taxation increase the likelihood of such dynamic instability and increase the likelihood of oscillation? (Smyth 1963, 359)

Like Baumol, Smyth then mathematically analyzes the system and shows that for certain parameter values explosive oscillations can occur. But he also does something more illuminating than Baumol. He presents a numerical example and a graph that plots the path of Y_t with and without the built-in stabilizer, and assets:

> The system without built-in flexibility, oscillates but damps down to a new equilibrium. On the other hand, the system with built-in flexibility, shows oscillations which get bigger and bigger so that the system never settles down to a new equilibrium. It is interesting to note that the oscillations are faster with built-in flexibility than without. The present analysis has run in terms of built-in flexibility of taxation but clearly a similar sort of analysis could be applied to other "automatic stabilizers."
>
> The policy conclusion of the analysis is this. We should beware of advocating changes that appear to increase the stability of the economic system purely on the basis of static analysis without paying attention to the dynamic structure of the system. (Smyth 1963, 362–363)

But in Smyth's figure, for the first eight periods the path of Y_t with the automatic response of taxes is much more desirable than the path without the automatic response; the tax response damps the boom and returns Y_t to its target at the same time the other boom is reaching a peak twice as high as ever reached with tax flexibility. So in this example, the economy with the automatic tax response significantly outperforms the economy without an automatic tax response for at least eight periods. In Smyth's model, as in Baumol's, a problem arises only if there is a failure to impose a realistic ceiling and floor on output.

Conclusion

The two challenges to automatic fiscal policy examined in this appendix should be distinguished. Under the first, expounded by Friedman (1953), there is a risk that the policy instrument will be moved in a direction that seems stabilizing at the time, but turns out to be destabilizing. The point is correct in theory, but its practical relevance depends on the design of the automatic fiscal policy. For example, if there is a threshold so that the fiscal stimulus is not activated until output falls X percent below target, the risk is reduced. Similarly, as long as the policy can be implemented with a short lag—a major feature of an "automatic" fiscal policy—the risk of a destabilizing result is also reduced.

Under the second, expounded by Baumol (1961) and Smyth (1963), it can be shown that in a simple Samuelson multiplier-accelerator model of the economy that has no ceiling or floor for output, the introduction of an automatic fiscal policy can cause destabilizing explosive oscillations. But as soon as a realistic ceiling and floor are imposed, as Hicks (1950) showed, this threat vanishes, and the automatic fiscal policy is indeed stabilizing.

11

The New Classical Counterrevolution

A False Path for Macroeconomics

In this chapter, I describe and critique the "new" classical counterrevolution that began in the 1970s. My critique relies especially on the analyses of three leading Keynesian economists: Robert Solow, James Tobin, and Alan Blinder. In our view, the classical counterrevolution has been a false path for macroeconomics. After a run of two decades, the new classical counterrevolution finally appears to have lost its appeal for many economists. Unfortunately, its challenge required many Keynesian economists to spend time and energy over the past two decades debating new classical economists, thereby diverting time and energy that might have been spent developing the design of fiscal and monetary policies that can improve the performance of the actual economy—an economy in which excess supply of labor (and some goods) can persist because of the downward stickiness of wages (and some prices).

Lucas and Sargent and the Launching of the New Classical Counterrevolution

To understand the spectacular fireworks generated by Robert Lucas and Thomas Sargent at the annual conference of the Federal Reserve Bank of Boston at Edgartown, Massachusetts in June 1978, one needs a bit of background. There is little doubt that their aggressive onslaught at this conference changed the direction of macroeconomics—in my view, for the worse—for many years to come.

In the mid-1960s, two leading Keynesian economists, Gardner Ackley, chairman of the council of economic advisers, and his successor, Arthur Okun, warned President Johnson that the attempt to continue Great Society programs while increasing military spending for Vietnam would generate excess aggregate demand and inflationary pressures unless offset by a stiff tax increase to damp down consumer demand. While Johnson delayed proposing a tax surcharge, the economy overheated with unemployment approaching 3 percent and inflation was indeed generated. Because the general public knew that Keynesian economists had been advising President Johnson, it was easy for critics of Keynesian economics to blame Keynesians for the inflation.

The Nixon administration and the Fed cooled the economy, generating a recession in 1970, but inflation came down slowly and stubbornly. None of this was news to Keynesian economists who had long emphasized inertia in wage and price inflation. When the Nixon administration imposed wage and price controls in 1972 so that it could expand aggregate demand without inflation in an election year, Keynesian economists predicted that once the controls were removed, inflation would resume as long as aggregate demand remained excessive. And so it did. Until the oil shock of 1973, the economic history of 1960–73 was quite consistent with Keynesian economics.

The oil shock, by contrast, was initially a problem for the Keynesian framework. Keynesian economics had focused on aggregate demand ($C + I + G$); and the Keynesian forty-five–degree cross and IS/LM, tools which were entirely demand oriented, had dominated the text books. It was only in response to the oil shock that Keynesian economists recognized that they needed the same basic tool as microeconomics—the supply/demand diagram—with the price level plotted vertically and output horizontally. Whereas all traditional Keynesian economics fed into the aggregate demand curve, the aggregate supply curve was brand new. But once the AD/AS diagram was introduced in the late 1970s in the early editions of intermediate macroeconomics textbooks of Keynesian economists like Robert Gordon, and soon made its way into the principles textbooks, it became evident that it was easily integrated with Keynesian economics. In the 1960s, the aggregate demand curve shifted right, so we got more output and more inflation—a boom. But in the mid-1970s, the OPEC oil producers raised the world price of oil, shifting up a key cost to producers in our economy, thereby shifting up the aggregate supply curve. A shift up of the supply curve simultaneously raises price and reduces output, thereby generating "stagflation," the unpleasant combination of inflation and recession. By the late 1970s, Keynesian economists were armed with a new diagram that explained the consequences of the oil price shock while at the same time preserving the demand-oriented insights of the traditional Keynesian framework (because the IS/LM apparatus was linked to the AD curve).

Unfortunately, understanding something doesn't necessarily lead to a satisfactory policy solution. The new AD/AS diagram showed clearly that an upward supply shock was inescapably bad news. It caused inflation and recession simultaneously, and there was no magic way to get rid of both together. Initially the Ford administration spent the fall of 1974 focused on inflation, and this implied measures to reduce demand in the economy which might limit the inflation but at the expense of worsening the recession. In January of 1975, the administration joined Congress in making the recession its highest priority, and in three months enacted a useful tax cut that stimulated demand and helped combat the recession (while inevitably ignoring the still high inflation). The public, however, was understandably frustrated by the inability of Keynesian economists to find a way to reduce both inflation and recession simultaneously. Keynesian economists who enjoyed high public standing in the early 1960s during the Kennedy administration's tax cut now found themselves on the defensive, forced to give the public the bad news that they had an understanding of, but no satisfactory solution for, a stagflation generated by an upward supply shock.

As the conference convened in June 1978, at a moment of high public discontent with "the results of Keynesian economic policies," Lucas and Sargent decided to strike at the very foundation of Keynesian economics and the leadership of Keynesian economists. While claiming to be launching a scholarly scientific challenge to the Keynesian framework, their tone and language revealed a more ambitious agenda. They modestly entitled their presentation "After Keynesian Macroeconomics." After briefly conceding that Keynesians somehow managed to win public relations points with the public in the early 1960s, they continued:

> We dwell on these halcyon days of Keynesian economics because, without conscious effort, they are difficult to recall today. In the present decade, the U.S. economy has undergone its first major depression since the 1930s, to the accompaniment of inflation rates in excess of 10 percent per annum. . . . These events did not arise from a reactionary reversion to outmoded, "classical" principles of tight money and balanced budgets. On the contrary, they were accompanied by massive government budget deficits and high rates of monetary expansion: policies which, although bearing an admitted risk of inflation, promised according to modern Keynesian doctrine rapid real growth and low rates of unemployment. (Lucas and Sargent 1978, 49)

Incredibly, Lucas and Sargent made *no* mention whatsoever of the oil price supply shock that simultaneously generated both "the first major depression since the 1930s" and inflation above 10 percent. I have searched their article in vain for the word "oil." In contrast to Keynesians who quickly incorporated aggregate supply into the aggregate demand of macroeconomics, thereby arriving at a satisfactory explanation and synthesis that has served well ever since, Lucas and Sargent offer *no* explanation for these mysterious economic events of the 1970s. Yet trying to understand the 1970s while ignoring the oil supply shocks is like trying to understand the play *Hamlet* while ignoring the prince's soliloquies. Keynesians, learning from the oil shocks and constructing a new AS/AD tool to handle it, would not predict rapid real growth and low unemployment in the face of a huge upward oil price shock that surprised the world including Lucas and Sargent, in late 1973 (following the surprise attack of Egypt and Syria on Israel) and 1974, and would surprise it once again following the Iranian revolution in 1979. Instead, Lucas and Sargent claimed that Keynesians predicted a decade of economic success:

> That these predictions were wildly incorrect, and that the doctrine on which they were based is fundamentally flawed, are now simple matters of fact, involving no novelties in economic theory. The task which faces contemporary students of the business cycle is that of sorting through the wreckage, determining which features of that remarkable intellectual event called the Keynesian Revolution can be salvaged and put to good use, and which others must be discarded. Though it is far from clear what the outcome of this process will be, it is already evident that it will necessarily involve the reopening of basic issues in monetary economics which have been viewed since the thirties as "closed," and the reevaluation of every aspect of the institutional framework within which monetary and fiscal policy is formulated in the advanced countries. (Lucas and Sargent 1978, 49–50)

Rather than incorporate aggregate supply and oil shocks to make sense of the 1970s, they ignore oil and instead launch a classical counterrevolution, postulating competitive markets that clear instantaneously and rational expectations for all economic agents. Whatever the merits of their approach, it has nothing to do with an attempt to understand the 1970s. What contribution does the Lucas and Sargent new classical macroeconomics make toward explaining the 1970s? Yet remarkably, they managed to exploit the poor economic performance of the 1970s to successfully launch their new classical counterrevolution.

For our purpose, what matters most is their sweeping denunciation of the use of Keynesian models to guide the design and implementation of countercyclical policy. Without caveat, they write:

> First, and most important, existing Keynesian macroeconometric models are incapable of providing reliable guidance in formulating monetary, fiscal, and other types of policy. This conclusion is based in part on the

spectacular recent failures of these models, and in part on their lack of a sound theoretical or econometric basis. Second, on the latter ground, there is no hope that minor or even major modification of these models will lead to significant improvement in their reliability. (Lucas and Sargent 1978, 69)

Yet at the very same conference, Lawrence Klein, a pioneer of Keynesian econometric models, explained how international disturbances such as oil supply shocks can be incorporated into Keynesian models, thereby providing a satisfactory explanation of the 1970s.

As the discussant for the Lucas and Sargent presentation, Benjamin Friedman tried his best to ignore their provocative language and assertions, and sought to find some common ground and some basis for praising Lucas and Sargent's paper. His effort at conciliation was met with this reply from Lucas and Sargent:

Benjamin Friedman's comments provide clear testimony to the complete failure of our efforts to engage in substantive discussion of the reliability of current macroeconomic models. (Lucas and Sargent 1978, 81)

Having observed the results of Ben Friedman's attempt at conciliation, and having no inclination to conciliate Lucas and Sargent in the first place, Robert Solow went directly after them:

What really brings us here is Steve McNees' picture of the 1960s and the 1970s. . . . The question is: what are the possible responses that economists and economics can make to those events?

One possible response is that of Professors Lucas and Sargent. They describe what happened in the 1970s in a very strong way with a polemical vocabulary reminiscent of Spiro Agnew. Let me quote some phrases that I culled from their paper: "wildly incorrect," "fundamentally flawed," "wreckage," "failure," "fatal," "of no value," "dire implications," "failure on a grand scale," "spectacular recent failure," "no hope." Now if they were doing that just to attract attention, for effect, so that people don't say, "yes dear, yes, dear," then I would really be on their side. Every orthodoxy, including my own, needs to have a kick in the pants frequently, to prevent it from getting self-indulgent, and applying very lax standards to itself. But I think that Professor Lucas and Sargent really seem to be serious in what they say, and in turn they have a proposal for constructive research that I find hard to talk about sympathetically. They call it equilibrium business cycle theory, and they say very firmly that it is based on two terribly important postulates—optimizing behavior and perpetual market clearing. . . . (Solow 1978, 81)

But, Solow asks, is this really a promising way to understand the 1970s, to return to the pre-Keynesian classical postulate of perpetual market clearing while ignoring the word "oil"? Wouldn't it be more sensible to actually look at the huge oil price shock, and try to incorporate it into the rest of the Keynesian framework that otherwise has generally worked well?

> There is still another, even less cataclysmic, line of thought that one could take about recent events. Up until very recently, for historical reasons, macroeconomics had devoted almost all of its efforts to refining its understanding of the components of aggregate demand. . . . Macroeconomics had utterly neglected to elaborate the supply side of the models. Not surprisingly, then, the sequence of supply shocks in the 1970s from the side of food, oil, nonfuel minerals, and the depreciation of the dollar caught the macroeconomics community by surprise. . . . We know now that it is possible to rebuild the supply side of macro-models so that they do tell a consistent story and can explain the 1970s. (Solow 1978, 205)

Solow says that Lawrence Klein, Ray Fair, and others have introduced supply into their Keynesian models so that an upward supply shock generates both inflation and recession, nicely explaining the 1970s. He continues:

> So fast does the economics profession move now that there are already textbooks that do the supply side quite adequately. . . . (Solow 1978, 206)

But Solow opposes Lucas and Sargent's new classical agenda not only for its failure to mention the oil shock and its consequent inability to explain the 1970s. Solow strongly rejects their central pre-Keynesian postulate of perpetual market clearing. It's pre-Keynesian because it reminds Solow of the claims during the Great Depression that the labor market was clearing nicely and any alleged "unemployment" was purely voluntary. Solow explains:

> It is as plain as the nose on my face that the labor market and many markets for produced goods do not clear in any meaningful sense. Professors Lucas and Sargent say after all there is no evidence that labor markets do not clear, just the unemployment survey. That seems to me to be evidence. Suppose an unemployed worker says to you, "Yes, I would be glad to take a job like the one I have already proved I can do because I had it six months ago or three or four months ago. And I will be glad to work at exactly the same wage that is being paid to those exactly like myself who used to be working at that job and happen to be lucky enough still to be working at it." Then I'm inclined to label that a case of excess

supply of labor and I'm not inclined to make up an elaborate story of search or misinformation or anything of the sort. By the way I find the misinformation story another gross implausibility. I would like to see direct evidence that the unemployed are more misinformed than the employed, as I presume would have to be the case if everybody is on his or her supply curve of employment. Similarly, if the Chrysler Motor Corporation tells me that it would be happy to make and sell 1000 more automobiles this week at the going price if only it could find buyers for them, I am inclined to believe they are telling me that price exceeds marginal cost, or even that marginal revenue exceeds marginal cost, and regard this as a case of excess supply of automobiles. Now you could ask, why do not prices and wages erode and crumble under those circumstances? Why doesn't the unemployed worker who told me, "Yes, I would like to work, at the going wage, at the old job that my brother-in-law or my brother-in-law's brother-in-law is still holding," why doesn't that person offer to work at that job for less? Indeed why doesn't the employer try to encourage wage reduction? That doesn't happen either. Why does the Chrysler Corporation not cut the price? Those are questions that I think an adult person might spend a lifetime studying. They are important and serious questions, but the notion that excess supply is not there strikes me as utterly implausible. (Solow 1978, 208)

Solow makes one final comment in response to Lucas and Sargent's assertion that they will do macroeconomics using the assumption that all markets are always in competitive equilibrium:

Deep down I really wish I could believe that Lucas and Sargent are right, because the one thing I know how to do well is equilibrium economics. The trouble is I feel so embarrassed at saying things that I know are not true. (Solow 1978, 206–207)

Two years later, at a conference on rational expectations, James Tobin emphasized that the most crucial assumption of the new classical economics is that there is continuous clearing of a competitive labor market.

Rationality of expectations is one essential component of the new classical approach. . . . By itself, however, it does not lead to the strong propositions that excite the consumers, not just the producers, of economic theory. There are several other ingredients in the models that generate the dramatic conclusions. I want to remind you of two of these at the outset. . . . The two are the assumptions of continuous market-clearing equilibrium and the specification of imperfections and asymmetries in the information on which economic agents act and form expectations. . . .

> The market-clearing assumption is just that, an assumption. It is not
> justified by any new direct evidence. . . . In one of his seminal articles,
> Robert Lucas introduces the assumption quite casually, saying "The
> issue of whether to treat observed prices and quantities as market clear-
> ing arouses more controversy than it deserves. I prefer thinking of mar-
> kets as cleared partly because of logical difficulties with the leading
> alternative view. . . ."
> In short, the long-time controversy about the degree of price inflex-
> ibility in the economy and its consequences is resolved by assuming, in
> formerly customary jargon, perfect price flexibility. . . . Without the con-
> tinuous market-clearing assumption, the postulate of rational expecta-
> tions would not justify the characteristic strong proposition that anticipated
> policies of demand management have no real effects. Indeed, the main
> practical controversy of the day is to what extent, if any, the ongoing
> inflation is inertial—as well as expectational. Such inertia is a phenom-
> enon of disequilibrium; markets are not always clearing at these wages
> and prices; therefore demand management policies, even though
> unsurprising, may be able to increase or decrease both quantities de-
> manded and quantities supplied. This is the Keyensian message. . . .
> (Tobin 1980, 788–789)

Despite the critiques by Solow, Tobin, and other Keynesians, the next
decade witnessed the Lucas and Sargent agenda absorbing the time and
energies of a large share of young macroeconomists. A decade later, in the
introduction to a collection of his own article, Keynesian Alan Blinder writes:

> Then came 1986, the fiftieth anniversary of the publication of Keynes's
> *General Theory*. The number of symposia, conferences, and other schol-
> arly events marking the occasion must have exceeded the number of pro-
> fessed Keynesians under the age of 50. So those of us who fit the descrip-
> tion were besieged with invitations to go here or there to reflect on the
> rough treatment Lord Keynes's ideas had been receiving of late and/or on
> where Keynesian economics might be headed. I accepted a few of these
> invitations, and Chapters 7 and 8 are two of the results. (Blinder 1989, x)

Blinder's chapter 7, "Keynes After Lucas," begins this way:

> I come here neither to praise Keynes nor to bury him, but to ruminate
> about where Keynesian economics is going in view of what it has been
> through. The last 10–15 years have been a period of intellectual ferment
> in macroeconomics. Old beliefs have been questioned, old models dis-
> carded. Many creative and imaginative—some might say fanciful—new

ideas have come to the fore. Many clever people have toiled long hours in the macro vineyards seeking to develop new, more critique-resistant strains of theory and econometrics. Many new techniques have been added to our toolkit. To be the very model of a modern macroeconomist today, your technical baggage must be much heavier than was true a decade or two ago. Yet do we know much more today than we did then about how the macroeconomy really works? I am not convinced. (Blinder 1989, 101)

After reviewing in detail the research generated by the Lucas and Sargent agenda, Blinder draws this conclusion:

The Forgotten Agenda. Despite some important new ideas, the New Classical Economics (NCE) counterrevolution does not seem to me to mark a major step forward from the Keynesian tradition it supplanted. The attempted revival of market clearing was quixotic, in the worst sense of the word. The attack on the Phillips curve was scurrilous and without empirical foundation. Although the basic idea that expectations are not purely mechanical is certainly important, the wholesale adoption of rational expectations was dubious, even though the hypothesis is doubtless of considerable use in some places (such as financial markets). The renewed search for microfoundations was welcome, but the insistence on neoclassical purity probably did macroeconomics little good. Finally, the Lucas critique, while conceptually correct, is of unproven empirical significance.

To my mind, that does not add up to a major improvement over the macroeconomics of 1972. Does that mean we had it all right in 1972? Hardly. It may mean, instead, that the RE/NCE revolution concentrated its fire in the wrong directions, that our macroeconomic research resources have been misallocated. I want to close this paper by suggesting that that was indeed the case—that the most serious flaws in 1972 Keynesianism were not prominent on the NCE hit list.

I begin with a brief mention of an obvious flaw. Vintage 1972 macroeconomics—whether it was Keynesian or monetarist—was all about demand fluctuations, a term then thought to be synonomous with economic fluctuations. The 1970s and 1980s destroyed this narrow-minded focus forever. We now know that Marshall's celebrated scissors also comes in a giant economy size. Economic fluctuations can, and sometimes do, emanate from the supply side—from oil shocks, food shocks, and the like. Much theoretical and empirical work has been done on supply shocks in the last dozen years; there was no misallocation here. This work will have a lasting and salutary effect on macroeconomics. But it is basically orthogonal to the debate between Keynesians and new classicals.

My main point, however, is different. It is that macroeconomics might be in better shape today if, instead of arguing interminably about clearing markets, the rationality of expectations, the Phillips curve, and the Lucas critique, economists had devoted more time to improving the theoretical and empirical foundations of IS/LM. . . .

In conclusion, by the early 1950s, the Keynesian revolution was consolidated. The next 20 years or so were a productive time in which Keynesian ideas were developed further, modified in places, and given empirical content. New features like the Phillips curve were grafted on; and the entire apparatus was built into giant "realistic" models of the economy. Much, but not all, of that development stopped in the 1970s as macroeconomics turned introspective and nihilistic.

Some of the fundamental questions raised were good ones (why should expectations be adaptive), others were not (does the labor market really clear every period). But they did stop a constructive research agenda dead in its tracks. Some will say that was necessary, for the 1972 consensus was leading us astray. I am less convinced. I cannot help thinking that macroeconomics would be better off today if Lucas's valid questions about how expectations were handled in theoretical and empirical models had redirected the Keynesian research agenda rather than derailed it. It may now be time to get the train back on the tracks. (Blinder 1989, 108–111)

Empirical Evidence Against the New Classical Counterrevolution: The 1982 Recession

At the end of the 1970s, a sharp practical difference crystallized between Keynesians and new classicals concerning a specific prediction. Keynesians predicted that if the Federal Reserve applied a tight money policy to the economy, it would throw the economy into recession, and that the recession would eventually reduce inflation. Keynesians emphasized that tight money could not reduce inflation without generating a recession. The reason was inertia in setting wage and price increases. Having gotten used to large wage and price increases (following the oil price shocks of the 1970s), workers and managers would continue to set large increases unless a recession compelled them to moderate the increases. Only when workers feared layoffs would they agree to smaller wage increases; only when employers experienced falling demand and profits would they have the backbone to insist on smaller wage increases. Smaller cost increases would then permit smaller price increases.

By contrast, new classicals contended that the Federal Reserve could reduce inflation without generating a recession. The reason was their assumption that workers and employers possessed forward looking rational expectations about wage and price increases. If the Fed clearly signaled its intent to reduce inflation through a firm tight money policy, rational workers and employers would immediately expect lower inflation, and hence would immediately agree to smaller wage and price increases. Thus, disinflation would occur without the economy going through a recession.

Then the experiment was run. At the beginning of the 1980s, in the United States, Britain, and most other economically advanced countries, the head of the central bank publicly pledged to reduce inflation and applied a tight money policy, evidenced by a very sharp rise in interest rates. In every case, the economy was thrown into a recession. In no case did inflation subside without recession.

The outcome of the experiment should have been devastating to the classical counterrevolution. But the new classicals were skillful debaters. They argued that the central banks had surprised workers and employers by actually applying a tight money policy. Having seen central banks tolerate the rise in inflation during the 1970s, workers and employers simply did not believe that central bankers were now serious about applying a tight money policy. If only central bankers had been more "credible," the tight money policy would have reduced inflation without recession.

There was one little problem with this new classical argument. How is it that supposedly "rational," "forward-looking," intelligent workers and employers were so mistaken about what their central bank would actually do? The new classicals replied that the central bankers had lost credibility with the public after a decade of tolerating rising inflation. Somehow, this argument succeeded with many young economists eager to get on with mathematically exploring new classical models. But, of course, this argument was a complete surrender to the Keynesian view that inertia shapes expectations. The public continued to believe that the central bank would tolerate high inflation until it actually saw a decline in inflation. So workers and employers continued to set high wage and price increases.

The Lucas Critique

One particular article of Lucas's has special relevance to this study. In several places I have made reference to econometric estimates from Keynesian macroeconometric models. It obviously did not take an article from Lucas to point out that all quantitative estimates of the impact of fiscal or monetary policy from such models involve some degree of error. But Lucas's article, "Econometric Policy Evaluation: A Critique," went much further. It asserted that such quantitative estimates of responses to policy were completely worthless and should never be used. Needless to say, such a prohibition, if heeded, would make it impossible to design and implement a sensible automatic fiscal policy, or even to conduct countercyclical monetary policy. Should the Lucas prohibition really be heeded? Surprisingly, many economists (including a few who have never read the article) frequently assert that Lucas's article is a devastating critique that renders all policy formulation based on traditional Keynesian macroeconometric models erroneous. Specifically, if we want to simulate the likely impact of our automatic fiscal policy with a particular numerical parameter (that translates the output gap into an automatic transfer of a particular magnitude) using a standard Keynesian macroeconometric model, as we (Seidman and Lewis 2002) did in the study described in detail in chapter 2, is the exercise really worthless? Or is a proper interpretation of the Lucas critique far less dramatic, namely, that he has added to the list of possible sources of error an additional one, thereby providing one more reason to treat macroeconometric estimates of responses to policy with caution?

Early in his article, Lucas asserts:

> I shall argue that the features which lead to success in short-term forecasting are unrelated to quantitative policy evaluation, that the major econometric models are (well) designed to perform the former task only, and that simulations using these models can, in principle, provide *no* useful information as to the actual consequences of alternative economic policies. (Lucas 1976, 105)

What is the basis of Lucas's extreme claim that *no* useful information can be derived? He begins with several pages of theoretical argument that boils down to this: *If* ordinary people—"economic agents" in Lucas terminology—are generally rational, forward-looking economists with a coherent, correct model of the economy, they will look beyond the current period change in the monetary or fiscal policy instrument; project the likely subsequent future shifts in the instrument; and formulate an optimal multiperiod plan of spending, saving, and labor supply to this future path of the policy instruments, correctly incorporating any future reactions the policy authorities are likely to have to agents' rational behavior. Clearly, *if* people behave this way, then it will be difficult to estimate the response of the economy to current period changes in monetary or fiscal policy instruments. The question that should obviously be asked of Lucas, of course, is whether there is much accuracy, and therefore, much practical importance in the actual economy to his *hypothesis* about how ordinary people behave. It is a question Lucas completely ignores here and, to my knowledge, in all his voluminous writings.

Lucas then presents three examples: consumption, investment, and the Phillips curve. I will concentrate on consumption which is central to my purpose.

On consumption, he asserts that Friedman's permanent income hypothesis "has both a sound theoretical rationale and an unusually high degree of empirical success." The recent literature, theoretical and empirical, that I reviewed in chapter 2, is far less enthusiastic than Lucas. According to the hypothesis, consumption this period varies with permanent, not current income. Surprisingly, despite all his rhetoric about the sophisticated forecasting abilities of ordinary people, Lucas accepts Friedman's assumption that the ordinary person uses a weighted average of *past* incomes to forecast his future income and hence estimate his permanent income. A time series regression is run of current period consumption against a distributed lag of past disposable incomes. The estimated coefficient of current disposable income indicates the average response, over the historical period, of current consumption to a change in current disposable income. Economists who utilize macroeconometric models with such a consumption function to estimate response to policy changes are fully aware that current disposable income has changed for many reasons over their historical sample, and the equation only estimates the average response. The gross income of the economy may have risen with a boom or fallen with a recession. Congress may have enacted a household tax change to which it gave the term "permanent," "temporary," or no term at all. The term "permanent" may have been given but Congress reversed the tax change the very next year. The term "temporary" may have been given, but the tax change lasted several years. Understandably, ordinary people may often be confused about the source of changes in their current disposable income, and their likely permanence. As Dolde explains:

> Factors which cause current income to change may also cause changes in expected future income. The higher the *permanence presumption ratio* (PPR) about an income change, the greater is consumer response. Obviously lower PPRs are more associated with temporary than with permanent tax changes. It is less obvious that PPRs for temporary tax changes are lower than those for most income fluctuations. Tax legislation is much discussed in the media and on the street. Consumers learn about it very rapidly. Consumers learn about and infer the permanence of many other income fluctuations only over time, as in the framework discussed by John Muth. This argument applies to temporary tax changes lasting a few quarters, but not, of course, to rebates.
>
> The credibility of the government in consumers' eyes also affects

the PPR associated with temporary tax changes. The cynical observer may doubt that tax increases announced as temporary will actually be so. Indeed the 1968 surcharge was extended beyond the termination date announced at its inception. Symmetry suggests that the PPR associated with temporary tax cuts might thus be moderated. In fact, the 1975 tax cut was subsequently extended. The need to offset fiscal drag in a growing economy is one factor that would cause temporary tax cuts to be extended.

Finally, it is worth noting that many "permanent" tax changes have not lasted much longer than those announced as temporary. There were eleven major federal tax change acts between 1945 and 1975. . . . The year 1977 brought a twelfth, and Congress is considering a thirteenth at present. (Dolde 1979, 81–82)

All of this is well known to practitioners of macroeconometric models. But Lucas seems to believe he is making a novel point when he writes:

Now let us imagine a consumer of this type, with a current income generated by an "experimenter" according to the pattern described by Muth (so that the premises of the theory of economic policy are correct for a single equation consumption function). An econometrician observing this consumer over many periods will have good success describing him by (6) [Friedman's equation, relating current consumption to a distributed lag of past disposable incomes] whether he arrives at this equation by the Friedman-Muth reasoning, or simply hits on it by trial and error. Next, consider *policies* taking the form of a sequence of supplements $\{x_t\}$ to this consumer's income from time T on. Whether $\{x_t\}$ is specified deterministically or by some stochastic law, whether it is announced in advance to the consumer or not, the theory of economic policy prescribes the *same* method for evaluating its consequences: add x_t to the forecasts of y_t for each $t > T$, insert into [the Friedman equation], and obtain the new forecasts of c_t.

If the consumer knows of the policy change in advance, it is clear that this standard method gives incorrect forecasts. For example, suppose the policy consists of a constant increase $x_t = x$, in income over the entire period. From (4) [by raising permanent income by x] this leads to an increase in consumption of kx. The forecast based on (6) [Friedman's fitted equation] is of an effect in period t. (Lucas 1976, 113)

In other words, the equation predicts an impact on current consumption due solely to an increment in the current period's disposable income, because the equation contains a distributed lag of past values that are unaffected, instead of the future values that policy makers *assert* that they intend to affect.

But given Dolde's observation about the frequent reversals of policy, it is not obvious that sensible consumers will believe the assertion of the policy makers that all future incomes will in fact increase by x. It seems quite possible that they will respond as they have, on average, to past changes in current disposable income, which is captured in the estimated equation. It is Lucas who is asserting, without evidence, that ordinary people will both know and believe the assertion of policy makers. In response to the announced policy, Lucas may raise his own consumption more than the ordinary person, whose response may be better predicted by Friedman's fitted equation.

Lucas continues:

> More interesting divergences between forecasts and reality emerge when the policy is stochastic, but with characteristics known in advance. (Lucas 1976, 114)

But "known in advance" by whom? The ordinary consumer? Or the Keynesian economist? Or the "new classical" economist?

Finally, Lucas makes a concession. He admits:

> For certain policy changes we can, with some confidence, guess at the permanent income recalculations consumers will go through and hope to predict their consumption responses with some accuracy. (Lucas 1976, 115)

In chapter 6, I discussed in detail how economists, in recent studies, attempt to provide rough estimates of the response of consumers to particular temporary tax changes. Nothing in Lucas section on consumption undermines the methods these economists have used for estimating how ordinary people responded to the particular tax change.

Two brief comments can be made on Lucas's two other examples. First, on investment, it certainly should matter to the ordinary business manager whether an investment tax credit is announced to be temporary (with an expiration date one year's hence), or is instead announced to be a permanent subsidy for investment with no expiration date. Second, on the Phillips curve, by the time of Lucas's paper, most Keynesian economists (for example, Robert Gordon, Otto Eckstein, Lawrence Klein) were estimating Phillips curves that implied a nonaccelerating inflation rate of unemployment (NAIRU), and an inability to achieve a higher stable inflation rate by running a permanently low unemployment rate. Instead, their equations predicted that if the unemployment rate were held below the NAIRU, inflation would keep rising gradually without limit.

Writing nearly a decade after Lucas's article, Blinder puts the "Lucas critique" into perspective. In his 1989 book, *Macroeconomics Under Debate,* Blinder writes:

> *Lucas critique.* Similarly, the Lucas critique, which at first was misinterpreted as a directive to throw the baby out with the bath water, has been put into perspective. While Lucas's conceptual point is valuable and indubitably correct, so are the well-known points that heteroskedastic or serially correlated disturbances lead to inefficient estimates and that simultaneity leads to inconsistent estimates. But we also understand that small amounts of serial correlation lead to small inefficiencies and that minor simultaneity leads to only minor inconsistencies; so suspected violations of the Gauss-Markov theorem do not stop applied econometrics in its tracks. In the same spirit, the realization is now dawning that the Lucas critique need not be a show stopper. Indeed, evidence that it is typically important in applied work is lacking. (Blinder 1989, 107)

In that same volume, Blinder devotes a chapter to the subject, "A Skeptical Note on the New Econometrics." He begins this way:

> In an important paper published in 1976, Robert E. Lucas offered an insightful and stunning critique of what were then standard econometric practices. The critique took the profession by storm, and econometricians —or at least macro-econometricians—have been struggling with the problem of how to reconstruct econometrics ever since. In this brief paper, I argue that one of the major approaches that has been developed for dealing with the Lucas critique may introduce errors of its own into econometric estimates—errors that may well be more serious in practice than those pointed out by Lucas.
>
> *The Old Econometrics and the Lucas Critique.* I begin with an example that characterizes the way in which econometrics worked before Lucas, and illustrates why Lucas (correctly) claimed that this way might lead to error. Consider the problem of estimating a supply curve and a demand curve for a single market. . . .
>
> Why, apart from the general quest for knowledge, would we want to estimate such parameters? There are many possible reasons. One which seems germane to the issue raised by Lucas is that the government might be considering regulating the supply of the commodity, and would like to estimate the changes in price and quantity that would result. The standard

procedure of the "old econometrics" would be to estimate the parameters of the demand curve (say, by two-stage least squares) and then use these estimates to predict behavior into the future.

Enter the Lucas critique. Lucas argued, quite correctly, that the supply and/or demand curves observed in the past might change if there were a change in the economic environment (e.g., in government policy). (Blinder 1989, 128)

Blinder then gives a specific example showing that indeed this could lead to an incorrect estimate of the impact of the new policy. But Blinder is skeptical of a solution proposed by Sargent and others: to try to estimate taste and technology parameters. He says that while interesting in principle, in practice the new approach "may err systematically—and by gross amounts," because the data we observe may often be generated by disequilibria. He gives a specific example demonstrating the error that may be generated by the new approach. Here is his conclusion:

This short paper should not be misinterpreted as a brief against rational expectations. The criticisms of the old econometrics made by Lucas, Sargent and others are not wrong. . . .

The paper *is*, however, a brief against the view that there is any one "right way" to do econometrics. In statistical work with dirty data, there is no room for purity and no such thing as a free lunch. The applied econometrician who single-mindedly devotes his energies to coping with the Lucas critique is likely to be blind-sided by another problem.

Saying this in no way denies the validity of the Lucas critique, but merely points out that it may not always be of great empirical importance. In my view, the critique should take its place as one among many serious problems that confront the applied econometrician—on a par, perhaps, with violations of the assumptions of the Gauss-Markov theorem. The realization, for example, that least squares bias can always be present has not stopped applied econometrics in its tracks (though it has given cause for humility). Perhaps the Lucas critique should be treated the same way.

The broader perspective dictates that we follow a more pragmatic, case-by-case approach in which we recognize that other problems may be more important than the Lucas critique in particular cases. Certainly, there is no *a priori* reason to suppose that the best econometric estimates are those that are most immune to the Lucas critique if the procedures employed to deal with the critique introduce errors of their own.

Specifically, the example in this paper suggests that the new econometrics—which views the world as composed of concave consumers and concave firms that compute mathematical expectations and meet atomistically in blissful equilibrium along separating hyperplanes—is potentialy fraught with error. Using these techniques to go "beyond supply and demand curves" to the taste and technology parameters that presumably underlie them may be a high-risk strategy. And in many cases we may conclude that, the Lucas critique notwithstanding, extrapolating supply and demand curves based on past behavior is the best technique we have for predicting the future. (Blinder 1989, 137)

Fair explains how and why, despite the Lucas critique, he continues updating and refining his Keynesian macroeconometric model of the U.S. economy using what he calls the "Cowles Commission approach." It is Fair's model that Lewis and I used in our simulation of the automatic fiscal policy described in detail in chapter 2. Fair writes:

The logic of the Lucas critique is certainly correct, but the key question for empirical work is the quantitative importance of this critique. Even the best econometric model is only an approximation of how the economy works. Another potential source of coefficient change is the use of aggregate data. As the age and income distributions of the populations change, the coefficients in aggregate equations are likely to change, and this is a source of error in the estimated equations. This problem may be quantitatively much more important than the problem raised by Lucas. Put another way, the representative agent model that is used so much in macroeconomics has serious problems of its own, and these problems may swamp the problem of coefficients changing when policy rules change. (Fair 1994, 13)

Barro's Unrealistic Hypothesis

In 1974 Robert Barro propounded an unrealistic hypothesis which has come to be known as "Ricardian equivalence" because the famous nineteenth-century British economist David Ricardo, originator of the theory of comparative advantage in international trade, considered the argument before rejecting it as unrealistic. Because Ricardo does not deserve to have his name attached to this unrealistic hypothesis, I will therefore call it "Barro equivalence."

Barro contends that people would entirely save any income tax cut or cash transfer because they would actually engage in the following reasoning: "If the government leaves me with more cash today by either cutting my tax or sending me a cash transfer, it will have to borrow more today and will therefore have to tax me more tomorrow to pay back its debt; so I better set aside all of the cash today to get ready to pay the tax tomorrow." Clearly, if people reasoned this way, temporary changes in taxes and transfers would have no effect on current consumption.

It cannot be overemphasized that Barro has never provided any empirical evidence whatsoever that ordinary people think this way. Even worse, he and other economists who accepted the truth of his hypothesis have felt no need to discover whether ordinary people actually reason this way. But this didn't prevent his hypothesis from being taken seriously by many economists, even though the majority ended up unpersuaded.

In his macroeconomics textbook, Mankiw describes how a consumer must think to make Barro's hypothesis empirically correct:

> The government is cutting taxes without any plans to reduce government spending. Does this policy alter my set of opportunities? Am I richer because of this tax cut? Should I consume more? Maybe not. The government is financing the tax cut by running a budget deficit. At some point in the future, the government will have to raise taxes to pay off the debt and the accumulated interest. So the policy really represents a tax cut today coupled with a tax hike in the future. The tax cut merely gives me transitory income that eventually will be taken back. I am not any better off, so I will leave my consumption unchanged. (Mankiw 2000b, 419)

Mankiw cites two practical objections to the realism of Barro equivalence: myopia and borrowing constraints:

> *Myopia.* One possible argument for the traditional view of tax cuts is that people are shortsighted, perhaps because they do not fully comprehend the implications of government budget deficits. It is possible that some people follow simple and not fully rational rules of thumb when choosing how much to save. Suppose, for example, that a person acts on the assumption that future taxes will be the same as current taxes. This person will fail to take account of future changes in taxes required by current government policies. A debt-financed tax cut will lead this person to believe that his lifetime income has increased, even if it hasn't. The tax cut will therefore lead to higher consumption and lower national saving.
> *Borrowing constraints.* The Ricardian view of government debt assumes that consumers base their spending not only on current income but on their lifetime income, which includes both current and expected fu-

ture income. Advocates of the traditional view of government debt argue that current income is more important than lifetime income for those consumers who face binding borrowing constraints. A borrowing constraint is a limit on how much an individual can borrow from banks or other financial institutions. A person who would like to consume more than his current income—perhaps because he expects higher income in the future—has to do so by borrowing. If he cannot borrow to finance current consumption, or can borrow only a limited amount, his current income determines his spending, regardless of what his lifetime income might be. In this case, a debt-financed tax cut raises current income and thus consumption, even though future income is lower. In essence, when the government cuts current taxes and raises future taxes, it is giving taxpayers a loan. For a person who wanted to obtain a loan but was unable to, the tax cut expands his opportunities and stimulates consumption. (Mankiw 2000b, 420–421)

According to Mankiw, Ricardo considered the argument but rejected it as unrealistic. Mankiw writes:

Although Ricardo viewed these alternative methods of government finance as equivalent, he did not think other people would view them as such:

"The people who pay taxes . . . do not manage their private affairs accordingly. We are apt to think that the war is burdensome only in proportion to what we are at the moment called to pay for it in taxes, without reflecting on the probable duration of such taxes."

Thus, Ricardo doubted that people were rational and farsighted enough to look ahead fully to their future tax liabilities. . . . It is one of the great ironies in the history of economic thought that Ricardo rejected the theory that now bears his name! (Mankiw 2000b, 424)

Buchanan and Wagner make the same point:

In his discussion of the practical political comparison of the tax and debt alternatives, Ricardo did not, himself, adhere to the equivalence theorem. (Buchanan and Wagner 1977, 135)

In his macroeconomics textbook, Blanchard makes these comments on Barro's hypothesis:

Ricardian Equivalence. How does taking into account the government budget constraint affect the way we should think of the effects of deficits on output? One extreme view is that once this constraint is taken into account, neither deficits nor debt has an effect on economic activity! This argument is known as the Ricardian equivalence proposition. David Ricardo, a nineteenth-century English economist, was the first to articulate its logic. His argument was further developed and given prominence in the 1970s by Robert Barro, then at Chicago, now at Harvard University. For this reason, the argument is also known as the Ricardo-Barro proposition. . . .

What will be the effect of the initial tax cut on consumption? A plausible answer is that it will have no effect at all. Why? Because consumers realize that the tax cut is not much of a gift: Lower taxes this year are exactly offset, in present value, by higher taxes next year. . . . To say that consumers do not change consumption in response to the tax cut is the same as saying that private saving increases one for one with the deficit. . . .

How seriously should you take the Ricardian equivalence proposition? Most economists would answer, "Seriously, but not seriously enough to think that deficits and debt are irrelevant."

A major theme of this book has been that expectations matter. . . . But insofar as future tax increases appear more distant and their timing more uncertain, consumers are more likely to ignore them. This may be the case because they expect to retire before taxes go up, or more likely, because they just do not think that far into the future. In either case, Ricardian equivalence is likely to fail. So it is safe to conclude that budget deficits have an important effect on activity. In the short run, larger deficits are likely to lead to higher demand and higher output. (Blanchard 2000, 525)

In my view, Mankiw and Blanchard are too polite in their discussion of Barro's hypothesis. Barro and others who accept his hypothesis have never presented a shred of empirical evidence that people actually think this way in response to a tax cut. Without such evidence, the Barro hypothesis does not deserve to be taken seriously as an empirical proposition about the actual economy. I suppose it might be interesting to examine the hypothesis on an island economy populated only by Barro and other economists who say they accept his hypothesis. I suspect that, even on this Barron island, a tax cut might not be entirely saved.

Prescott and Real Business Cycles

No one disputes the statement that technology shocks affect output. Like oil price shocks, technology shocks must be incorporated into a Keynesian macroeconomic model in order to fully explain fluctuations in output. For example, in the 1990s, a "good" technology shock from the rapid introduction of information technology reduced production costs, shifted down the aggregate supply curve, and caused a simultaneous increase in output and reduction in inflation—the opposite of the "bad" oil price shock of the 1970s.

Real business cycle theory, however, is not simply a claim that technology shocks matter. It is a branch of new classical economics because it assumes all markets are competitive and "clear" instantaneously so that all fluctuations in output and employment are the consequence of voluntary choice of labor supply in response to technology shocks, and are therefore socially optimal.

Perhaps the leading pioneer of real business cycle theory is Edward Prescott. When Prescott uses the phrase "economic theory," he means the particular (Walrasian) microeconomic theory of continuous competitive equilibrium in all markets. Following is his summary of his article in the *Quarterly Review* of the Federal Reserve Bank of Minneapolis with the intriguing title, "Theory Ahead of Business Cycle Measurement":

> Economic theory implies that, given the nature of shocks to technology and people's willingness and ability to intertemporary and intratemporally substitute, the economy will display fluctuations like those the U.S. economy displays. . . . In other words, theory predicts what is observed. . . .
> The policy implication of this research is that costly efforts at stabilization are likely to be counterproductive. Economic fluctuations are optimal responses to uncertainty in the rate of technological change. (Prescott 1986, 21)

In the same issue of the *Quarterly Review,* Lawrence Summers critiques real business cycle theory:

> The increasing ascendancy of real business cycle theories of various stripes, with their common view that the economy is best modeled as a floating Walrasian equilibrium, buffeted by productivity shocks, is indicative of the depths of the divisions separating academic macroeconomists. These theories deny propositions thought self-evident by many academic macroeconomists and all of those involved in forecasting and controlling the economy on a day- to-day basis. They assert that monetary and fiscal policies have no effect on real activity, that fiscal policies influence the economy only through their incentive effects, and that economic fluctuations are caused entirely by supply rather than demand shocks. . . . (Summers 1986, 23)

Summers notes that if real business cycle theorists are correct, then the Keynesian revolution was a false path for macroeconomics:

> Let me follow Prescott in being blunt. My view is that real business cycle models of the type urged on us by Prescott have nothing to do with the business cycle phenomena observed in the United States or other capitalist economies. . . . (Summers 1986, 24)

Summers raises several objections. First, real business cycle theory postulates that all fluctuations in employment are voluntary in the sense that workers are always on their labor supply curve, and that workers voluntarily reduce labor supply in response to a temporary cut in wages and increase labor supply in response to a temporary increase in wages. Moreover, this intertemporal elasticity of substitution is large enough in magnitude to account for the large fluctuations in employment witnessed in several postwar recessions and even in the Great Depression.

> A more fundamental problem lies in Prescott's assumption about the intertemporal elasticity of subsitution in labor supply. He cites no direct microeconomic evidence on this parameter, which is central to his model of cyclical fluctuations. Nor does he refer to any aggregate evidence on it. . . . My own reading is that essentially all the available evidence suggests only a minimal response of labor supply to transitory wage changes. Many studies . . . suggest that the intertemporal substitution model cannot account at either the micro or the macro level for fluctuations in labor supply. (Summers 1986, 24)

Second, Summers challenges real business cycle theorists to identify the source of each alleged negative technology shock that supposedly caused each recession:

> My second fundamental objection to Prescott's model is the absence of any independent corroborating evidence for the existence of what he calls *technological shocks*. This point is obviously crucial since Prescott treats technological shocks as the only driving force behind cyclical fluctuations. . . . Prescott assumes that technological changes are irregular, but is unable to suggest any specific technological shocks which presage the downturns that have actually taken place. A reasonable challenge to his model is to ask how it accounts for the 1982 recession, the most serious downturn of the postwar period. (Summers 1986, 25)

Summers then refers to the Great Depression:

> It seems clear that a central aspect of depressions, and probably economic fluctuations more generally, is a breakdown of the exchange mechanism. Read any account of life during the Great Depression in the United States. Firms had output they wanted to sell. Workers wanted to exchange their labor for it. But the exchanges did not take place. To say the situation was constrained Pareto optimal given the technological decline that took place between 1929 and 1933 is simply absurd. . . . (Summers 1986, 26)

As for postwar recessions, Summers says there is a much more plausible explanation than Prescott's negative technology shocks and voluntary withdrawal of labor supply:

> While it is hard to account for postwar business cycle history by pointing to technological shocks, the account offered by, for example, Otto Eckstein and Allen Sinai of how each of the major recessions was caused by a credit crunch in an effort to control inflation seems compelling to me. (Summers 1986, 26)

Summers draws this conclusion:

> Improvement in the track record of macroeconomics will require the development of theories that can explain why exchange sometimes works well and other times breaks down. Nothing could be more counterproductive in this regard than a lengthy professional detour into the analysis of stochastic Robinson Crusoes. (Summers 1986, 26)

The New Classical Counterrevolution and the Role of Mathematics in Economics

In light of the fact that the crucial assumptions of the new classical counterrevolution were not merely empirically false, but *obviously* empirically false, how could the new classical counterrevolution happen? Two elements characterized the counterrevolution: (1) mathematics that was challenging, and (2) crucial assumptions that were empirically false. Of course, challenging mathematics is not unique to new classical economists. Most of the leading Keynesian economists—for example, Samuelson, Solow, Tobin, Klein, Fair, and Blinder—pioneered the use of mathematics in macroeconomics. Their use of mathematics was a great step forward in bringing clarity and precision to Keynesian intuitions. I agree fully with virtually all economists that there was too little use of mathematics in economics up through the 1930s. As Keynesian economists introduced mathematics into macroeconomics, however, they never lost sight of the crucial importance of choosing empirically realistic assumptions. It was taken for granted that a high-quality economist required not only mathematical skill, but also a realistic grasp of institutions, psychology, and behavior, and a strong dose of common sense.

By the time of the launching of the new classical counterrevolution, however, mathematical skill became the sole criterion for an economics Ph.D. As long as an undergraduate demonstrated high mathematical skill, he was deemed eminently qualified to pursue an economics Ph.D.; and as long as the Ph.D. thesis demonstrated high mathematical skill, the candidate was deemed eminently qualified to become an economics professor. Graduate programs in economics often sought undergraduates who majored in mathematics or physics. The undergraduate with an outstanding grasp of institutions, psychology, and behavior, who demonstrated merely a good but not an exceptional grasp of mathematics, was often rejected from Ph.D. programs. New classical economists may have been better than Keynes in mathematics, but they lacked his ability to understand why excess supply often persists in labor markets where actual human beings are workers and employers. But with mathematical skill now the sole criterion for entering the economics profession, a poor grasp of institutions, psychology, and behavior was no longer a barrier to entry. With the denigration of these other skills, the stage was set for the new classical counterrevolution.

Consider this passage from Keynes's biographical sketch of his teacher, Alfred Marshall, in which Keynes explains the multidimensional skills required of a high quality economist:

> The study of economics does not seem to require any specialised gifts of an unusually high order. Is it not, intellectually regarded, a very easy subject compared with the higher branches of philosophy and pure science? Yet good, or even competent, economists are the rarest of birds. An easy subject, at which very few excel! The paradox finds its explanation, perhaps, in that the master-economist must possess a rare *combination* of gifts. He must reach a high standard in several different directions and must combine talents not often found together. He must be mathematician, historian, statesman, philosopher. . . . No part of man's nature or his institutions must lie entirely outside his regard. (Keynes 1924, 140–141)

Here is an example from Keynes's *General Theory* of his skill at observing actual behavior:

Now ordinary experience tells us, beyond doubt, that a situation where labour stipulates (within limits) for a money-wage rather than a real wage, so far from being a mere possibility, is the normal case. Whilst workers will usually resist a reduction of money-wages, it is not their practice to withdraw their labor whenever there is a rise in the price of wage-goods. It is sometimes said that it would be illogical for labour to resist a reduction of money-wages but not to resist a reduction of real wages. For reasons given below, this might not be so illogical as it appears at first; and, as we shall see later, fortunately so. But whether logical or illogical, experience shows that this is how labour in fact behaves. (Keynes 1936, 9)

It is impossible to imagine a new classical economist saying, "But whether rational or irrational, experience shows that this is how labor in fact behaves." As the economics profession has come to give virtually all weight to mathematics and virtually none to "experience," many entered the profession who would never think of making a statement similar to Keynes's. Keynes then explains why it is sensible for workers to behave the way they do:

Any individual or group of individuals who consent to a reduction of money-wages relatively to others, will suffer a *relative* reduction in real wages, which is a sufficient justification for them to resist it. On the other hand, it would be impracticable to resist every reduction of real wages, due to a change in the purchasing-power of money which affects all workers alike. (Keynes 1936, 14)

Keynes then explains why the key assumption of classical macroeconomics—that real wages fall promptly to "clear" the labor market to immediately eliminate involuntary unemloyment—is usually false:

Thus it is fortunate that the workers, though unconsciously, are instinctively more reasonable economists than the classical school, inasmuch as they resist reductions of money-wages, which are seldom or never of an all-around character, even though the existing real equivalent of these wages exceeds the marginal disutility of the existing employment; whereas they do not resist reductions of real wages, which are associated with increases in aggregate employment and leave relative money-wages unchanged, unless the reduction proceeds so far as to threaten a reduction of the real wage below the marginal disutility of the existing volume of employment. Every trade union will put up some resistance to a cut in money-wages, however small. But since no trade union would dream of striking on every occasion of a rise in the cost of living, they do not raise the obstacle to any increase in aggregate employment which is attributed to them by the classical school. (Keynes 1936, 14–15)

The new classical substitution of mathematics for empirical realism is illuminated by contrasting the new classical approach to the labor market with the brilliant empirical work of Yale economist Truman Bewley in his book *Why Wages Don't Fall During a Recession* (2000). Earlier in his career Bewley made his mark as a mathematical economist. But after years of doing mathematical modeling, Bewley concluded that the only way to make progress with understanding why wages don't fall during a recession is to do extensive interviewing of participants in the labor market. Here is how Bewley's work is described in the February 26, 2000 "Economic Focus" column of the *Economist* magazine:

> Economists dislike talking to people. They prefer a more "scientific" approach to research, such as number-crunching or abstract theorising. But that can be a weakness, as a new book by Truman Bewley, an economist at Yale University, makes clear. In "Why Wages Don't Fall During a Recession," published by Harvard University Press, he tackles one of the oldest, and most controversial, puzzles in economics: why nominal wages rarely fall (and real wages do not fall enough) when unemployment is high. But he does so in a novel way, through interviews with over 300 businessmen, union leaders, job recruiters and unemployment counsellors in the northeastern United States during the early 1990s recession. . . .
>
> Why, then, are wages sticky? Mr. Bewley concludes that employers resist pay cuts largely because the savings from lower wages are usually outweighed by the cost of denting workers' morale: pay cuts hit workers' standard of living and lower their self-esteem. Falling morale raises staff turnover and reduces productivity. Cheerier workers are more productive workers, not only because they work better, but also because they identify more closely with the company's interests. This last point is crucial. Mr. Bewley argues that monitoring workers' performance is usually so tricky that firms rarely rely on coercion and financial carrots alone as motivators. In particular, high morale fosters teamwork and information-sharing, which otherwise are difficult to encourage.
>
> Firms typically prefer layoffs to pay cuts because they harm morale less, says Mr. Bewley. Pay cuts hurt everybody and can cause festering resentment; layoffs hit morale only for a while, since the aggrieved have, after all, left. And whereas a generalised pay cut might make the best workers leave, and a selective one damage morale because it is seen as unfair, firms can often lay off their least competent staff. (*Economist* 2000, 90)

It is impossible to imagine new classical economists even thinking of interviewing labor market participants. Instead, they simply postulate that wages always fall immediately to clear the labor market, and then enjoy playing with mathematical models built on that unrealistic postulate.

Now a question naturally arises to any economist: If new classical macroeconomics was really a defective product, how could it prevail in the market place? The answer is that it did *not* prevail. Customers in government and the business community never "bought" it. The Federal Reserve Board has remained thoroughly Keynesian throughout the entire two decades of the classical counterrevolution, continuously practicing countercyclical monetary policy to combat both inflation and recession. The business community takes it for granted that the Fed will practice such countercyclical policy, and there would be general alarm if new classical economists ever took over the Fed. The undergraduate macroeconomics textbooks—both principle and intermediate—that dominate the market continue to use a Keynesian framework based on the assumption of sticky wages and prices, and give a sympathetic treatment of countercyclical monetary policy and automatic fiscal stabilizers. When recession hit the United States in 2001, the public expected the Fed to cut interest rates, and even expected Congress and the president to provide fiscal stimulus (like the $600 rebate). The fact is that new classical economics failed in the marketplace.

The only place that the classical counterrevolution succeeded was in academia. In academia, many "impractical," "unrealistic" subjects thrive, as they should, because the consumers of academia do not always seek "realism." They often seek intellectual games and gymnastics, flights of the imagination, and the enjoyment of a subject as an end in itself, whatever its realism. In academia, new classical economics was right at home with many other subjects. A literature professor might ask students to imagine a world with emotionless people. A new classical economics professor might ask students to imagine an economy with emotionless workers where wages are cut promptly to clear the labor market without harming worker morale and productivity, and everyone in the economy carries a new classical model of the economy in his head. Undergraduates (and their tuition-paying parents) tolerated new classical economics professors just as they tolerated literature professors. So in academia new classical economics for a time thrived, and even now survives. Such is the tolerance of academia.

The driving force behind new classical economics in academia was the new set of mathematical models that it provided for new Ph.D. candidates and assistant professors. Instead of refining the Keynesian framework, which had been worked on continuously for several decades, the classical counterrevolution gave young economists of the late 1970s and 1980s new mathematical macroeconomic models to explore and extend. It was intellectually stimulating for mathematically skilled young economists to work with models in which all "economic agents" were assumed to have rational expectations or even perfect foresight, and all markets, including the labor

market, were assumed to be perfectly competitive and to "clear" instantaneously. Such classical assumptions had been rejected by Keynesians because they were so obviously unrealistic; rejecting these unrealistic
assumptions was the essence of the Keynesian revolution against classical
economics. Just as Keynesians had spent several exciting decades using
mathematics to develop the implications of Keynesian assumptions, now
new classical economists had the opportunity to use mathematics to develop the implications of classical assumptions. Just as Keynesian economics in the decades after Keynes's *General Theory* beckoned like a newly
discovered continent to be explored, so new classical economics was the
new continent of the last quarter of the twentieth century.

But now this continent has been explored mathematically for a quarter
of a century. The novelty has worn off, and new classical models have been
worked over. Today, young economists are confronted with two mathematically well-explored continents: one Keynesian, the other new classical. There
is still exploration to be done in each continent. But new classical economics no longer has the advantage of novelty and vast unexplored territory. It
will no doubt survive indefinitely in academia. But young economists interested in influencing actual policy have begun to notice that new classical
economics never succeeded in influencing policy makers for a simple reason: its crucial assumptions are empirically unrealistic. Young economists
interested in influencing the design of actual monetary and fiscal policy are
unlikely to enlist in the classical counterrevolution.

Conclusion

In conclusion, I want to return to the provocative quote from Lucas and
Sargent's launching of the new classical counterrevolution at the 1978 conference. Within academia, the late 1970s and early 1980s were the halcyon
days of new classical economics, as many young economists were drawn to
its research agenda and its rejection of the basic tenet of Keynesian economics—the failure of the labor market to promptly eliminate excess supply. From today's vantage point, I offer a revision of their quote (Lucas and
Sargent 1978, 49–50), substituting new classical counterrevolution for
Keynesian revolution; substitutions into the original quote are indicated by
brackets below:

> [I] dwell on these halcyon days of [new classical] economics because,
> without conscious effort, they are difficult to recall today. . . . [At the end
> of the 1970s, new classical economists predicted that the Federal Re-
> serve, and other central banks, would be able to engineer disinflation

without recession because economic agents were rational and labor and product markets were perfectly competitive and cleared instantaneously]. That these predictions were wildly incorrect, and that the doctrine on which they were based is fundamentally flawed, are now simple matters of fact, involving no novelties in economic theory. The task which faces contemporary students of the business cycle is that of sorting through the wreckage, determining which features of that remarkable intellectual event called the [new classical counterrevolution] can be salvaged and put to good use, and which others must be discarded.

12

Fiscal Policy and the Ending of the Great Depression

Throughout this book, "fiscal stimulus" has usually meant transfers and tax cuts rather than government purchases of goods and services. Transfers and tax cuts have the advantage of evenly stimulating all sectors of the economy. In the emergency of a depression, however, government direct purchases of goods and services—G in the textbook $C + I + G$—should complement transfers and tax cuts. The huge increase in government purchases for war preparation in 1940 and 1941 and war execution in 1942 played a crucial role in finally ending the Great Depression of the 1930s. The much smaller G from New Deal public works projects during the 1930s certainly provided some stimulus to the economy, but was on far too small a scale to cope with the depression. If the G from public works spending had been made *much* larger, and had been money-financed (as explained in chapter 1), it would have had a powerful impact comparable to the huge G from military-related spending in 1940, 1941, and 1942. Although this massive increase in peacetime G should therefore have been undertaken, it was not. It was the impending war that made it politically feasible to raise G enough to end the depression. Thus, it is essential that government be prepared to use G aggressively even in peacetime should a depression threaten.

This role of G in the ending of the Great Depression, however, has recently been challenged. In this chapter, I review this challenge and conclude that it is unpersuasive. The conventional view of the key role of G withstands this challenge, so that it remains essential to be prepared to use G aggressively in response to a depression.

Romer and the Ending of the Great Depression

The role of government military purchases in ending the Great Depression of the 1930s in the United States has been challenged by Christina Romer. She concludes her article this way:

> Monetary developments were a crucial source of the recovery of the U.S. economy from the Great Depression. Fiscal policy, in contrast, contributed almost nothing to the recovery before 1942. (Romer 1992, 781)

She contends that a rapid growth of the money supply resulting from a large inflow of gold beginning in 1933 was the key to the recovery. She does not regard this as monetary "policy" adopted with an intent to stimulate the economy, but rather as the fortunate (for the United States) consequence of the devaluation of the dollar and the political instability in Europe resulting in a flight of capital to the United States. She says the consequent monetary stimulus to the U.S. economy was large, and was the key to the recovery from the depression:

> That monetary developments were very important, whereas fiscal policy was of little consequence even as late as 1942, suggests an interesting twist on the usual view that World War II caused, or at least accelerated, the recovery from the Great Depression. Since the economy was essentially back to its trend level before the fiscal stimulus started in earnest, it would be difficult to argue that the changes in government spending caused by the war were a major factor in the recovery. (Romer 1992, 782)

Romer's view conflicts with the conventional view of the role of fiscal stimulus in ending the depression. According to this view, given the huge magnitude of the collapse in output during the depression in the United States in the 1930s, it would have taken an enormous fiscal stimulus to successfully counter the depression. The public works spending of President Franklin Roosevelt's administration was a step in the right direction, but its modest magnitude was simply no match for the depression. The U.S. economy finally did begin to recover from its disastrous trough of 1933 when the unemployment rate reached 25 percent. The recovery, however, was interrupted in the latter part of the decade, so that in 1939, the unemployment rate was 17 percent (Gordon 1988, 276), and the ratio of actual output to "natural output" was 83 percent (compared with 67 percent in 1933, and a normal value of 100 percent) according to Gordon (2000). Germany's conquest of France in mid-1940, and her attack on Britain, stimulated military spending in the United States in order to sell military hardware to Britain, and to prepare the United States itself for war. The Japanese attack on Pearl Harbor on December 7, 1941, brought the United States into the war both in the Pacific and in Europe, and resulted in a tremendous fiscal stimulus from military spending. The huge fiscal stimulus from the preparation for, and actual fighting of World War II, played a key role in finally ending the Great Depression. As Gordon writes:

Table 12.1

Unemployment and Output in the Great Depression

Year	Percent unemployment rate	Actual GDP	Natural GDP	Actual GDP/ Natural GDP
1929	3.2	951.7	901.8	1.06
1930	8.9	862.1	925.0	0.93
1931	16.3	788.8	948.7	0.83
1932	24.1	682.9	973.1	0.70
1933	25.2	668.6	998.1	0.67
1934	22.0	719.8	1,023.8	0.70
1935	20.3	778.2	1,050.1	0.74
1936	17.0	888.2	1,077.0	0.82
1937	14.3	932.5	1,104.7	0.84
1938	19.1	890.8	1,133.1	0.79
1939	17.2	961.1	1,162.2	0.83
1940	14.6	1,036.6	1,192.0	0.87
1941	9.9	1,219.7	1,222.7	1.00
1942	4.7	1,448.9	1,254.1	1.16

Source: Data from Robert J. Gordon, *Macroeconomics*, 8th ed. (Reading, MA: Addison-Wesley), p. A2.

This fiscal stimulus occurred in the United States in 1940–41 as military expenditures increased. Also, the IS curve was pushed rightward in 1940–41, even before Pearl Harbor in December 1941, by a boom in exports to war-ravaged Britain and a boom in investment by many firms providing military goods and other supplies to the British and to the U.S. government. . . . (Gordon 2000, 137)

Is it really true, as Romer claims, that the U.S. economy was "back to its trend level before the fiscal stimulus started in earnest?" Gordon (2000) presents data for 1929–1942, shown in Table 12.1. Prior to the Great Depression in 1929, the unemployment rate was 3.2 percent. Recovery began in 1933 and continued into 1937, reducing the unemployment rate to 14.3 percent, but then another recession occurred, raising the unemployment rate to 19.1 percent in 1938, and 17.2 percent in 1939. Although Christina Romer and others have emphasized the fluctuations in the unemployment rate between 1933 and 1939, it is crucial not to forget that during this entire period the unemployment rate was staggering by the norm of the 1920s, and the norm since the 1940s—an unemployment rate norm of roughly 5 percent. Gordon (2000) constructs a series for "natural" (trend) real GDP from 1875 to the present. Table 12.1 shows series for actual real GDP, natural real GDP, and the ratio of actual to natural real GDP from 1929 through 1942. As late as 1939, the ratio was only 0.83, compared to a norm of 1.00.

In May 1940, Hitler conquered France and the U.S. military build-up began. In their recent book on the Great Depression, Hall and Ferguson report the following:

> The major event of 1940 occurred in May when Germany invaded France. Western Europe's two major military powers were at war and, to almost everyone's shock, within just a few weeks France had surrendered and their British allies were forced into a humiliating retreat. These events had a significant impact on the U.S. economy for two reasons. First, Britain and her allies began placing large orders for war material from the United States and paid for it with gold. This set off a stimulus to U.S. demand from abroad, as well as the gold inflow that raised the U.S. monetary base. Second, there was great concern that the United States would be drawn into the war to support her close ally Great Britain. In preparation for that event the United States initiated a defense buildup. Federal defense expenditures, which had been $2.2 billion during 1940, rose to $13.7 billion during 1941. From 1940 to 1941 GDP rose by about $25 billion, so the increase in defense spending accounts for 46 percent of the increase in output. (Hall and Ferguson 1998, 155)

Thus, in 1939, the unemployment rate was 17.2 percent, and the ratio of actual GDP to natural GDP was 0.83. Then three years of huge fiscal stimulus from military spending took place, and in 1942 the unemployment rate was 4.7 percent, and the ratio of actual GDP to natural GDP, 1.16. In light of these facts, it is hard to understand how Romer can claim that fiscal stimulus "contributed almost nothing to the recovery before 1942."

But what about her claim that monetary stimulus was strong during the 1930s, and played a key role in ending the depression? Hall and Ferguson, who in contrast to Romer recognize the importance of military spending in ending the depression, agree with her that monetary stimulus was also important.

> Therefore, the Great Depression was ended by an enormous stimulus to aggregate demand caused by a combination of rapid monetary growth beginning in 1938 and, later, the U.S. defense buildup and increased orders for war material from Great Britain. (Hall and Ferguson 1998, 155–156)

There is no question that there were periods of rapid monetary growth during the 1930s. From 1929 to 1933, the money supply declined drastically in the face of widespread bank failures. With the stabilizing of the banking system and the introduction of federal deposit insurance, the

Table 12.2

Interest Rates in the Great Depression

Year	Percent prime interest rate	Percent 90-day commercial paper rate
1929	5.85	5.03
1930	3.59	2.48
1931	2.64	1.57
1932	2.73	1.28
1933	1.73	0.63
1934	1.02	0.25
1935	0.75	0.13
1936	0.75	0.15
1937	0.94	0.43
1938	0.81	0.44
1939	0.59	0.44
1940	0.56	0.44
1941	0.53	0.44

Source: Data from Jonathan Hughes, *American Economic History,* 2d ed. (Glenview, IL: Scott Foresman/Little Brown, 1990), p. 483.

money supply began to recover from its trough. Apparently, there were also periods of substantial gold inflows from abroad due to the U.S. devaluation of the dollar, and a flight of capital from politically unstable Europe. The question is not whether the money supply began to recover after 1933—it did—but whether its recovery played the key role in ending the depression.

An extremely serious problem for the claim that monetary stimulus was decisive is that during the 1930s as the money supply recovered, *nominal interest rates remained constant near zero*. Hughes (1990, 483) presents the series shown in Table 12.2 on the prime interest rate, and the ninety-day commercial paper rate.

Romer admits that this presents a problem:

The argument that monetary developments were the source of the recovery can be made more plausible by identifying the transmission mechanism. It is generally assumed that the usual way an increase in the money supply stimulates the economy is through a decline in interest rates. . . .

For the interest-rate transmission mechanism to have been operating in the mid- and late 1930s, it would also have to have been the case that the rapid money growth rates generated expectations of inflation. By 1933 nominal interest rates were already so low that there was little scope for a monetary expansion to lower nominal rates further. Therefore, the main way that the monetary expansion could stimulate the economy was by generating expectations of inflation and thus causing a reduction in real interest rates. (Romer 1992, 775)

Recall from chapter 1 that this is precisely the mechanism Krugman proposes today for Japan. Although the *nominal* interest rate was stuck at its floor of zero and couldn't be reduced, Romer claims that a monetary expansion generated inflation, and this reduction in the *real* interest rate (defined as the nominal interest rate minus the inflation rate) in turn stimulated spending.

Krugman makes this sympathetic comment on Romer's thesis:

It seems to be part of the folk wisdom in macroeconomics that this is in fact how the Great Depression came to an end: the massive one-time fiscal jolt from the war pushed the economy into a more favorable equilibrium. However, Christina Romer contends that most of the output gap created during 1929–33 had been eliminated before there was any significant fiscal stimulus. She argues that the main explanation of that expansion was a sharp decline in real interest rates, which she attributes to monetary policy (although most of the decline in her estimate of the real interest rate is actually due to changes in the inflation rate rather than the nominal interest rate). Indeed, Romer estimates that for most of the recovery period ex ante real rates were sharply negative, ranging between –5 and –10 percent [Footnote: Indeed, seen through the lens of the analysis in the present paper, Romer's evidence seems to suggest a somewhat different interpretation of events. One might think of her findings as showing that the real expansion of the economy—and the associated rise in prices—was the result of a rise in inflation expectations, which reduced real interest rates when nominal rates were already at the floor. Without this expected inflation, the expansion of monetary base that Romer emphasizes would have been ineffectual]. My point is that the end of the Depression, which is the usual, indeed perhaps the sole, motivating example for the view that a one-time fiscal stimulus can produce sustained recovery, does not actually appear to fit the story line too well. Much, though by no means all, of the recovery from that particular liquidity trap seems to have depended on inflation expectations that made real interest rates substantially negative. (Krugman 1998, 159–160)

But how much inflation occurred after 1933? Table 12.3 presents data on inflation and deflation from 1930 through 1941. Hughes (1990, 469) presents data for wholesale prices and for consumer prices, citing as his source,

Table 12.3

Prices and Inflation in the Great Depression

Year	Wholesale prices	Inflation rate %	Consumer prices	Inflation rate %	GDP prices	Inflation rate %
1929	61.9		73.3		11.4	
1930	56.1	−9.4	71.4	−2.6	11.0	−3.5
1931	47.4	−15.5	65.0	−9.0	10.1	−8.2
1932	42.1	−11.2	58.4	−10.2	8.9	−11.9
1933	42.8	+1.7	55.3	−5.3	8.7	−2.2
1934	48.7	+13.8	57.2	+3.4	9.5	+9.2
1935	52.0	+6.8	58.7	+2.6	9.7	+2.1
1936	52.5	+1.0	59.3	+1.0	9.7	0.0
1937	56.1	+6.8	61.4	+3.5	10.2	+5.2
1938	51.1	−8.9	60.3	−2.1	10.0	−2.0
1939	50.1	−2.0	59.4	−1.5	9.9	−1.0
1940	51.1	+2.0	59.9	+0.8	10.1	+2.0
1941	56.8	+11.2	62.9	+5.0	10.7	+5.9

Source: Data from Jonathan Hughes, *American Economic History*, 2d ed. (Glenview, IL: Scott, Forseman/Little Brown, 1990), p. 469, and Robert J. Gordon, *Macroeconomics*, 8th ed. (Reading, MA: Addison-Wesley, 2000), p. A2.

Historical Statistics, 1960, series X 267; E 25, 113, p. 11: these two series are shown in the left and middle columns of Table 12.3. Gordon (2000) presents data for the GDP deflator, citing as his source the U.S. Department of Commerce; this series is shown in the right column of Table 12.3.

As the table shows, it is useful to divide 1929 through 1940 into three periods. From 1929 through 1933 there was significant deflation. From 1934 through 1937 there was significant inflation. *But in the crucial period from 1938 to 1940, prices were stable: the value of each price index was roughly the same in 1940 as it was in 1938.* Thus, from 1938 to 1940, the real interest rate (defined as the nominal interest rate minus the inflation rate)—was roughly equal to the nominal interest rate; hence, the real interest rate stayed roughly constant at a value near zero. It is therefore hard to see how money growth played the key role in launching the huge push at the end of the decade that finally ended the depression: it did not reduce the nominal interest rate, and it did not generate the inflation needed to reduce the real interest rate.

It is true, of course, that the money supply, which had contracted catastrophically with waves of bank failures at the beginning of the 1930s, began to be restored after 1933 with the stabilization of the banking system through the introduction of deposit insurance, and later increased due to gold inflows. At the same time the economy did climb out of its disastrous trough so that the unemployment rate fell from 25.2 percent in 1933 to 17.2 percent in 1939. Beginning in 1934, the restoration of the money supply and the stabilization of the banking system surely helped restore the confidence of consumers and business managers, thereby inducing them to raise their demand for goods and services, which raised both output and prices and helped the economy climb out of its trough. So, for that matter, did the fiscal stimulus from New Deal employment programs. And so did a simple accelerator mechanism for investment, so that after several years of deterioration of the capital stock between 1929 and 1933, investment spending was bound to revive. But the fact remains that after ten long years (1930–39), the unemployment rate was still a catastrophic 17.2 percent. What happened to change the unemployment rate from 17.2 percent in 1939 to 4.7 percent in 1942? The best answer remains the conventional one: an enormous fiscal stimulus from military spending in preparation for World War II.

In the first edition of his influential textbook, Paul Samuelson (1948) draws these conclusions about monetary policy from the experience of the 1930s and 1940s:

The Inadequacies of Monetary Control of the Business Cycle
Today few economists regard Federal Reserve as a panacea for controlling the business cycle. Purely monetary factors are considered to be as much symptoms as causes, albeit often symptoms with aggravating effects that should not be completely neglected.

By increasing the volume of their government securities and loans and by lowering Member Bank legal reserve requirements, the Reserve Banks can encourage an increase in the supply of money and bank deposits. They can encourage but, without taking drastic action, they cannot compel. For in the middle of a deep depression just when we most want Reserve policy to be effective, the Member Banks are likely to be timid about buying new investments or making loans. If the Reserve authorities buy government bonds in the open market and thereby swell bank reserves, the banks will not put these funds to work but will simply hold reserves. Result: no 5 for 1, "no nothing," simply a substitution on the bank's balance sheet of idle cash for old government bonds. If banks and the public are quite indifferent between gilt-edged bonds—whose yields are already very low—and idle cash, then the Reserve authorities may not even succeed in bidding up the price of old government bonds; or what is the same thing, in bidding down the interest rate.

Even if the authorities should succeed in forcing down short-term interest rates, they may find it impossible to convince investors that long-term rates will stay low. If by superhuman efforts, they do get interest rates down on high-grade gilt-edged government and private securities, the interest rates charged on more risky new investments financed by mortgage or commercial loans or stock-market flotations may remain sticky. In other word, *an expansionary monetary policy may not lower effective interest rates very much but may simply spend itself in making everybody more liquid.*

What if interest rates are finally lowered? A number of questionnaire studies of businessmen's behavior suggest that the level of the interest rate is not an important factor in their investment decisions. Particularly in deep depression when there is widespread excess capacity, *investment is likely to be inelastic with respect to the interest rate.* The same is even more true about people's decisions on how much of their incomes to spend on consumption.

In terms of the quantity theory of money, we may say that the velocity of circulation of money does not remain constant. "You can lead a horse to water, but you can't make him drink." You can force money on the system in exchange for government bonds, its close money substitute; but you can't make the money circulate against new goods and new jobs. You can get some interest rates down, but not all to the same degree. You can tempt businessmen with cheap rates of borrowing, but you can't make them borrow and spend on new investment goods [Footnote: The banking authorities—unlike the fiscal authorities—deal only in secondhand assets, in transfer items. They are powerless to act directly on people's incomes and on production!]. (Samuelson 1948, 353–354)

Writing three decades later, Robert J. Gordon describes the lessons most economists learned from the depression and the war:

The central paradigm of macroeconomics as it emerged from the Second World War was the Keynesian multiplier theory and its endorsement of an activist fiscal policy to overcome the inherent stability of private investment. Monetary theory lurked in the shadows, ignored by most economists except in academic exercises based on the simplified Hicksian IS-LM apparatus that allowed an instructor to demonstrate how a low interest elasticity of investment or a high interest elasticity of the demand for money could render monetary policy impotent to cope with a depression.

The major event that had discredited monetary policy was the juxtaposition between early 1938 and late 1940 of a weak economic recovery, explosive monetary growth, complete price rigidity, and a short-term interest rate that had dropped close to zero. Despite a monetary growth rate that was rapid and constant between early 1938 and late 1941, the economy's recovery floundered until defense spending began in earnest in late 1940, after which real GNP suddenly jumped by almost 20 percent in a single year, a chronology that ingrained the deep-seated belief in the potency of fiscal policy and the 'pushing on a string' analogy for monetary policy. (Gordon 1980, 111)

In fact, in his textbook, Samuelson makes this memorable comment about the potency of fiscal policy:

The war years have shown fiscal policy to be a very powerful weapon. Indeed, some would argue that it is like the atomic bomb, too powerful a weapon to let men and governments play with; that it would be better if fiscal policy were never used. However, it is absolutely certain that, just as no nation will sit idly by and let smallpox decimate the population, so too in every country fiscal policy always comes into play whenever depressions gain headway. There is no choice then but to attempt to lead fiscal policy along economically sound rather than destructive channels. Every government always has a fiscal policy whether it realizes it or not. The real issue is whether this shall be a constructive one or an unconscious, bumbling one. (Samuelson 1948, 410)

References

Auerbach, Alan J., and Daniel Feenberg. 2000. "The Significance of Federal Taxes as Automatic Stabilizers." *Journal of Economic Perspectives* 14(3), Summer: 37–56.

Baily, Martin N. 1978. "Stabilization Policy and Private Economic Behavior." *Brookings Papers on Economic Activity* 1: 11–59.

Barro, Robert J. 1974. "Are Government Bonds Net Wealth." *Journal of Political Economy* 82, November/December: 1095–1117.

Baumol, William J. 1961. "Pitfalls in Contra-Cyclical Policies: Some Tools and Results. *Review of Economics and Statistics,* vol. 43, 21–26.

Bernanke, Ben S. 2000. "Japanese Monetary Policy: A Case of Self-Induced Paralysis?" In *Japan's Financial Crisis and Its Parallels to U.S. Experience*, eds. Ryoichi Mikitani and Adam S. Posen. Washington, DC: Institute for International Economics.

Bewley, Truman. 2000. *Why Wages Don't Fall During a Recession.* Cambridge, MA: Harvard University Press.

Blanchard, Olivier. 2000. *Macroeconomics* (2d ed.). Englewood Cliffs, NJ: Prentice-Hall.

Blinder, Alan S. 1979. *Economic Policy and the Great Stagflation.* New York: Academic Press.

———. 1981. "Temporary Income Taxes and Consumer Spending." *Journal of Political Economy* 89(1), February: 26–53.

———. 1989. "Keynes after Lucas." In *Macroeconomics Under Debate*, by Alan S. Blinder. Ann Arbor: University of Michigan Press.

———. 1997. "Is Government Too Political?" *Foreign Affairs* 76 (6), November/December: 115–126.

———. 2001. "The Economic Stimulus We Need." Editorial, *New York Times*, September 28.

Branson, William H. 1973. "The Use of Variable Tax Rates for Stabilization Purposes." In *Broad-Based Taxes: New Options and Sources*, ed. Richard A. Musgrave. Baltimore: Johns Hopkins University Press.

Browning, Martin, and M. Dolores Collado. 2001. "The Response of Expenditures to Anticipated Income Changes: Panel Data Estimates." *American Economic Review* 91(3), June: 681–692.

Buchanan, James M., and Richard E. Wagner. 1977. *Democracy in Deficit: The Political Legacy of Lord Keynes.* New York: Academic Press.

Campbell, John Y., and N. Gregory Mankiw. 1989. "Consumption, Income, and Interest Rates: Reinterpreting the Times Series Evidence." In *NBER Macroeconomics Annual: 1989*, eds. Olivier J. Blanchard and Stanley Fischer. Cambridge, MA: MIT Press.

Carroll, Christopher D. 1997. "Buffer-Stock Saving and the Life Cycle/Permanent Income Hypothesis." *Quarterly Journal of Economics* 112(1), February: 1–55.

Chiang, Alpha C. 1974. *Fundamental Methods of Mathematic Economics* (2d ed.). New York: McGraw Hill.

Cohen, Darrel, and Glenn Follette. 2000. "The Automatic Fiscal Stabilizers: Quietly Doing Their Thing." *Economic Policy Review* (Federal Reserve Bank of New York) 6(1), April: 35–67.

Dolde, Walter. 1979. "Temporary Taxes as Macro-Economic Stabilizers." *American Economic Review Papers and Proceedings*, 69(2), May: 81–85.

Duggal, Vijaya G. 1975. "Fiscal Policy and Economic Stabilization." In *The Brookings Model: Perspective and Recent Developments*, eds. Gary Fromm and Lawrence R. Klein. Amsterdam: North-Holland.

"Economic Focus: Could Finance Ministers Learn a Few Tricks from Central Bankers?" 1999. *Economist*, November 27: 80.

"Economic Focus: Why Wages Do Not Fall in Recessions." 2000. *Economist*, February 26: 90.

"Economic Focus: Remember Fiscal Policy?" 2002. *Economist*, January 19: 64.

Eckstein, Otto. 1978. *The Great Recession*. Amsterdam: North-Holland.

Fair, Ray C. 1994. *Testing Macroeconometric Models*. Cambridge, MA: Harvard University Press.

———. 1999. "A Fiscal Policy Rule for Stabilization." Unpublished working paper, Cowles Foundation, February.

———. 2000a. "Fed Policy and the Effects of a Stock Market Crash on the Economy." *Business Economics* 35(2): 7–14.

Feldstein, Martin. 1976. "Taxing Consumption." *The New Republic*, February 28, 14–17.

———. 2001. "Japan Needs to Stimulate Spending." Editorial, *Wall Street Journal*, July 16.

Fisher, Irving, and Herbert Fisher. 1942. *Constructive Income Taxation*. New York: Harper and Brothers.

Friedman, Milton. 1953. "The Effects of a Full-Employment Policy on Economic Stability. A Formal Analysis." In *Essays in Positive Economics*, a collection of his essays. Chicago: University of Chicago Press.

———. 1962. *Capitalism and Freedom*. Chicago: University of Chicago Press.

———. 1969. *The Optimum Quantity of Money and Other Essays*. Chicago: Aldine.

Gordon, Robert J. 1980. "Postwar Macroeconomics: The Evolution of Events and Ideas." In *The American Economy in Transition*, ed. Martin Feldstein, 101–162. Chicago: University of Chicago Press.

———. 1988. "Back to the Future: European Unemployment Today Viewed from America." *Brookings Papers on Economic Activity* 1: 271–304.

———. 2000. *Macroeconomics* (8th ed.). Reading, MA: Addison-Wesley.

Hall, Thomas E., and J. David Ferguson. 1998. *The Great Depression*. Ann Arbor: University of Michigan Press.

Hicks, John R. 1950. *A Contribution to the Theory of the Trade Cycle*. Oxford, UK: Clarendon Press.

Hoffman, Saul, and Laurence Seidman. 2003. *Helping Working Families: The Earned Income Tax Credit*. Kalamazoo, MI: The Upjohn Institute.

Hsieh, Chang-Tai. 1999. "Do Consumers React to Anticipated Income Shocks? Evidence from the Alaska Permanent Fund." Mimeo, Princeton University.

Hughes, Jonathan. 1990. *American Economic History* (3d ed.). Glenview, IL: Scott, Foresman/Little Brown.

Johnson, Nicholas, and Iris Lav. 2001. "A Federally Financed Sales Tax Holiday: A Bad Idea." *Tax Notes*, November 26, 1218–1221.

Juster, F. Thomas. 1977. "Comment on the Modigliani-Steindel Paper." *Brookings Papers on Economic Activity* 1: 206–208.

Kaldor, Nicholas. 1955. *An Expenditure Tax.* London: George Allen and Unwin.

Keynes, John Maynard. 1924. "Alfred Marshall." Reprinted in J.M. Keynes, *Essays in Biography.* New York: Norton 1963, 125–217.

Keynes, John Maynard. 1936. *The General Theory of Employment, Interest, and Money.* New York: Harcourt, Brace and World.

Klein, Lawrence R., ed. 1991. *Comparative Performance of U.S. Econometric Models.* New York: Oxford University Press.

Klein, Lawrence R., and F. Gerard Adams. 1991. "Performance of Quarterly Econometric Models of the United States: A New Round of Model Comparisons." In *Comparative Performance of U.S. Econometric Models*, ed. Lawrence R. Klein. New York: Oxford University Press.

Krugman, Paul R. 1998. "It's Baaack: Japan's Slump and the Return of the Liquidity Trap." *Brookings Papers on Economic Activity* 2: 137–205.

Kuttner, Kenneth N., and Adam S. Posen. 2001a. "The Great Recession: Lessons for Macroeconomic Policy from Japan." *Brookings Papers on Economic Activity* 2: 93–160.

———. 2001b. "Passive Savers and Fiscal Policy Effectiveness in Japan." Prepared for CEPR-CIRJE-NBER Conference on Issues in Fiscal Adjustment, December 2001, Tokyo, Japan.

Lewis, Kenneth, and Laurence Seidman. 2003. "Combating Recessions With New Automatic Fiscal Policies." University of Delaware, working paper, January.

Lerner, Abba. 1951. *Economics of Employment.* New York: McGraw-Hill.

Lucas, Robert E. 1976. "Econometric Policy Evaluation: A Critique." Reprinted in Robert E. Lucas, *Studies in Business-Cycle Theory*, Cambridge, MA: MIT Press, 1981: 104–130.

Lucas, Robert E. and Thomas J. Sargent. 1978. "After Keynesian Macroeconomics." In *After the Phillips Curve: Persistence of High Inflation and High Unemployment.* Proceedings of a Conference Held at Edgartown, Massachusetts, June, The Federal Reserve Bank of Boston.

Mankiw, N. Gregory. 2000a. "The Savers-Spenders Theory of Fiscal Policy." *American Economic Review Papers and Proceedings* 90(2), May: 120–125.

———. 2000b. *Macroeconomics* (4th ed.). New York: Worth Publishers.

Modigliani, Franco, and Charles Steindel. 1977. "Is a Tax Rebate an Effective Tool for Stabilization Policy." *Brookings Papers on Economic Activity* 1: 175–203.

Musgrave, Richard A. 1959. *The Theory of Public Finance.* New York: McGraw-Hill.

Okun, Arthur M. 1970. *The Political Economy of Prosperity.* New York: W.W. Norton & Company.

Pack, Howard. 1968. "Formula Flexibility: A Quantitative Appraisal." In *Studies in Economic Stabilization*, eds. Albert Ando, E. Cary Brown, and Ann F. Friedlaender, 5–40. Washington, DC: Brookings Institution.

Parker, Jonathan. 1999. "The Response of Household Consumption to Predictable Changes in Social Security Taxes." *American Economic Review* 89(4), September: 959–973.

Phillips, A.W. 1954. "Stabilization Policy in a Closed Economy." *Economic Journal* 64 (June): 290–323.

Posen, Adam S. 1998. *Restoring Japan's Economic Growth.* Washington, DC: Institute for International Economics.

Poterba, James M. 1988. "Are Consumers Forward Looking? Evidence from Fiscal Experiments." *American Economic Review Papers and Proceedings* 78(2) May: 413–418.

Romer, Christina D. 1992. "What Ended the Great Depression?" *Journal of Economic History* 52, December: 757–784.

Romer, David. 2001. *Advanced Macroeconomics* (2d ed.). Boston: McGraw-Hill.

Prescott, Edward C. 1986. "Theory Ahead of Business Cycle Measurement." *Quarterly Review of the Federal Reserve Bank of Minneapolis*, Fall: 9–22, vol. 10, no. 3.

Samuelson, Paul A. 1939. "Interactions between the Multiplier Analysis and the Principles of Acceleration." *Review of Economics and Statistics*, vol. 21 May: 75–78.

———. 1948 *Economics: An Introductory Analysis*. New York: McGraw Hill.

Seidman, Laurence S. 1975. *The Design of Federal Employment Programs*. Lexington, MA: D.C. Heath and Company

———. 1987. *Macroeconomics*. San Diego, CA: Harcourt Brace Jovanovich.

———. 1990. *Saving for America's Economic Future*. Armonk, NY: M.E. Sharpe.

———. 1997. *The USA Tax: A Progressive Consumption Tax*. Cambridge, MA: MIT Press.

———. 1998. *Economic Parables and Policies*. Armonk, NY: M.E. Sharpe.

———. 1999. *Funding Social Security: A Strategic Alternative*. Cambridge, UK: Cambridge University Press.

———. 2000. "Prefunding Medicare Without Individual Accounts." *Health Affairs* 19(5), September/October: 72–83.

———. 2001. "Reviving Fiscal Policy." *Challenge* 44(3): 17–42.

Seidman, Laurence, and Kenneth Lewis. 2002. "A New Design for Automatic Fiscal Policy." *International Finance* 5(2) Special Summer Issue: 251–284.

Shapiro, Matthew D., and Joel Slemrod. 1995. "Consumer Response to the Timing of Income: Evidence from the Change in Tax Withholding." *American Economic Review* 85(1) March: 274–283.

———. 2002. "Consumer Response to Tax Rebates." University of Michigan and NBER working paper, June 25.

Smyth, David J. 1963. "Can 'Automatic Stabilizers' Be Destabilizing?" *Public Finance/Finances Publiques* 18(3–4): 357–363.

Solow, Robert M. 1978. "Summary and Evaluation." In *After the Phillips Curve: Persistence of High Inflation and High Unemployment*. Proceedings of a Conference Held at Edgartown, Massachusetts, June, The Federal Reserve Bank of Boston.

Souleles, Nicholas S. 1999. "The Response of Household Consumption to Income Tax Refunds." *American Economic Review* 89(4), September: 947–958.

———. 2001. "Consumer Response to the Reagan Tax Cuts." Finance Department University of Pennsylvania, working paper (March), *Journal of Public Economics* (forthcoming).

Summers, Lawrence H. 1986. "Some Skeptical Observations on Real Business Cycle Theory." *Quarterly Review of the Federal Reserve Bank of Minneapolis*, vol. 10, no. 3 Fall: 23–27.

Taylor, John B. 1993. "Discretion Versus Policy Rules in Practice." *Carnegie-Rochester Conference Series on Public Policy* 39: 195–214.

———. 2000. "Reassessing Discretionary Fiscal Policy." *Journal of Economic Perspectives* 14(3), Summer: 21–36.

Tobin, James. 1980. "Are New Classical Models Plausible Enough to Guide Policy?" *Journal of Money, Credit, and Banking* 12(4) Part 2, November: 788–799.

Tversky, Amos, and Daniel Kahneman. 1973. "Availability: a Heuristic for Judging Frequency and Probability." *Cognitive Psychology* 5(2), September: 207–232.

U.S. Treasury. 1977. *Blueprints for Basic Tax Reform*. Washington, DC: *U.S. Treasury*.

Wolff, Edward N. 1998. "Recent Trends in the Size Distribution of Household Wealth." *Journal of Economic Perspectives* 12(3), Summer: 131–150.

Index

1975 recession
stagflation *(continued)*
new classical counterrevolution, 180,
181
recession priority, 98, 99, 100–01
Republican Party, 98–99, 100, 101
supply and demand, 97
supply-side economics, 99, 100
tax rate increase, 98–99, 100
tax rate reduction, 98–99, 100, 101, 102–4
tax rebate design
coverage, 25–26, 96, 101–4
limitations, 26
triggering formula, 26, 96, 101–2
tax rebate implementation
Congressional fiscal stimulus, vii, x, 26,
96, 98–99, 100–3
Congressional preenactment, x, 26, 96
Democratic Party, x, 96, 99, 100, 101,
102, 103
partisanship, 96, 98–101
political cooperation, 99, 101–3
rebate enactment (March), x, xii, 26, 96,
98, 103
rebate mailings (April–June), x, 26, 96,
98
Republican Party, x, 96, 98–99, 100,
101, 103
time constraints, 26, 96
Tax Reduction Act (1975), 103–4
1982 recession
Congressional fiscal stimulus, 96
inflation, 25
interest rate, 25
policy simulation, 37–38
unemployment rate, 97
1991 recession
Congressional fiscal stimulus, 57
federal budget deficit, 57
GDP/debt ratio, 17, 57
policy simulation, 37–38
Nixon, R., 99, 180–81
Normal economy
fiscal policy advisory board
fiscal discipline, 60–61
GDP/debt ratio, 60, 61
money-financed fiscal stimulus, 9, 11
federal budget deficit, 17–18
federal debt, 17–19
fiscal discipline, 17–19
GDP/debt ratio, 17–19
Normal unemployment balanced budget rule
(NUBAR)
characteristics, xv, 18, 53–55, 60–61
Congressional Budget Office (CBO), 54
countercyclical fiscal policy, 57, 161–62
discretionary fiscal policy, 56–57, 61

Normal unemployment balanced budget rule
(NUBAR) *(continued)*
federal budget balance, xv, 18, 54, 55–57,
60–61
full employment assumption, 53, 56–57
federal budget deficit, 18, 53, 55–57, 60
federal budget surplus, xv, 53, 54, 55–57,
60–61
fiscal discipline, xv–xvi, xvii, 18–19, 54,
61
fiscal policy advisory board, xvii, 60–61
forecast utilization, 54, 55, 61
GDP/debt ratio, 18–19, 53, 57, 61
long-run objectives, xv–xvi, 54, 60
Medicare
baby-boomer preparation, 18, 53, 54, 60
federal budget separation, xv, 18, 53,
54, 60
surplus maintenance, xv, xvi, 18–19, 53,
54, 57, 60, 61
monetary policy, 56–57
overview, xv–xvi, xvii
policy limitations
consumer demand, 54–55
consumer spending, 54–56
depression, 55, 57
economic impact, 54–56
forecast utilization, 55
government goods/service purchase,
54–55
response to, 55–56
severity impact, 54–56
tax rate, 55, 56, 57
severe recession, 18–19, 56–57
short-run objectives, xv–xvi
Social Security
baby-boomer preparation, 18, 53, 54,
60
federal budget separation, xv, 18, 53,
54, 60
surplus maintenance, xv, xvi, 18–19, 53,
54, 57, 60, 61
unemployment
benefit level, xv–xvi, 18
full employment assumption, 53, 56–57

Office of Management and Budget, 43
Oil industry, 22–23, 25, 97, 98, 180–83, 184,
188, 200
Okun, A., 94, 179–81

Pack, H., 143–46
Parker, J., 82–84, 85, 86
Partisanship. *See* Congress
Permanent income theory. *See* Counter-
cyclical fiscal policy studies; 1975
recession

About the Author

Laurence Seidman is Chaplin Tyler Professor of Economics at the University of Delaware. He is the author of *Funding Social Security: A Strategic Alternative* (1999), *Economic Parables and Policies* (1998), *The USA Tax: A Progressive Consumption Tax* (1997), and of the article "Reviving Fiscal Policy" (2001). He is coauthor (with Saul Hoffman) of *Helping Working Families: The Earned Income Tax Credit* (2003), and (with Kenneth Lewis) of the article, "A New Design for Automatic Fiscal Policy" (2002).